Rugby's Greatest Rivalry

Paul Dobson

Rugby's Greatest Rivalry
South Africa vs New Zealand
1921-1995

Paul Dobson [signature]

HR&R

HUMAN & ROUSSEAU

Cape Town Pretoria Johannesburg

To Douglas de Jager of Lenco
who made writing this book possible

Copyright © 1996 by Paul Dobson
First edition in 1996 by Human & Rousseau (Pty) Ltd
State House, 3-9 Rose Street, Cape Town
Cover design and typography by Annelize van Rooyen
Typeset in 11 on 12.5 pt New Baskerville
by Human & Rousseau
Printed and bound by National Book Printers, Drukkery Street,
Goodwood, Western Cape

ISBN 0 7981 3620 0

Contents

Thanks

INEVITABLY THERE ARE many people who helped in many ways. Amongst them I should like to thank my wife, Margaret, my son, John, and my daughter, Clare, John Gardener, Duncan Cruickshank who saw to the photographs, Bob Howitt of *Rugby News* and Jen, Sue Stamper, Geoff Blake, Gerry Burdzick, Geoff Miller of Hamilton in New Zealand, Tony Rubin, South Africa's Ian Kirkpatrick, Piet van der Schyff, Leonard Kaplan, Jonathan Goslett, Sylvia Ross, Ben Erwee, Tionette Swart, Keith Clayton, Andrew Lourens and John Rubython of *Sport for Africa*, David Shead of the Loft in Auckland, Johan Oosthuysen, John Quinn, Neil Hayward, Nicholas Durrant, Zoë Neame, Robert Denton, Phil Recordan, Peter Berthold, Ric Salizzo, Robin Binckes, the staff of the South African Library, especially Petri le Roux, the staff of the State Archives in Cape Town, Louis Luyt, Owen Doyle, Lawton Fourie, Eddie Tonks, Neil Gray and wonderful friends far away who looked after me when I was far away – Bruce Currie, John Sinclair, Colin Hawke and Glenys, Lindsay McLachlin, Lindsay Knight, Steve Walsh and Dave Bishop.

CHAPTER 1

At War

"WHEN SOUTH AFRICA plays New Zealand, consider your country at war."

Those words were spoken by Boy Louw in the Springbok dressing room before the start of the first test in 1949. It was the first test after the War. In that war he had been Bombardier M M Louw. He knew what war was.

Before the war Boy Louw had been one of the greats of South African rugby, a massive forward who played for his country with a matchless passion. He knew about the All Blacks. He had done battle with them in 1928 in South Africa and again in 1937 in New Zealand. They had fought together and played against each other in the Western Desert and up the leg of Italy and further into Europe.

There was between the two countries that special bond which makes sparks fly higher and brighter when they meet.

The truth is that matches between South Africa and New Zealand, whatever anybody else may say or believe, are the real tests of rugby nerve, sinew and skill.

And real contact between those two separated lands started in wartime and on the rugby field.

A game like rugby was, perhaps, first played in South Africa in 1861, brought to the country by the British and it spread with them. Eventually the people of Dutch descent caught on as well, and now the game is played mostly by people who speak Afrikaans.

A game like rugby was, perhaps, first played in New Zealand in 1862, brought to the country by the British and it spread with them, more rapidly in that small and more homogeneous country. Soon the Maoris caught on, and now the top players in New Zealand are mostly those with Polynesian blood. Way back in 1884 the first New Zealand team went on tour to New South Wales and two of the players were Maoris – John Taiaroa, a half, and Joe Warbrick, a three-quarter who was only 15 when he first played for Auckland.

9

Whereas New Zealand was, Maoris and Pakehas notwithstanding, really homogeneous, South Africa was heterogeneous, with its many tribes and languages, its bloody clashes. New Zealand had wars, soon resolved them, and got on with the business of getting closer to each other. In South Africa the clashes were long and bloody and tended to drive people into compartments.

It may just be that this was so because of the numbers of people and the size of the country and, perhaps the most telling, the split amongst the settlers. This split became a horrible war when British greed met Boer obstinacy in the Orange Free State and the Transvaal. This was the war that destroyed mankind's hope that a golden age was at hand with the advent of the new century, for in this war women and children suffered most, and at the hands of people who preached fair play. Farmers fought an empire and knocked it about.

There was a strong feeling of Empire at the time. To fight for Queen and Empire was a noble duty, and the Empire's headquarters sent out messages requiring the support of its vassals. The "slender thread" that held the Empire together drew some 25 000 troops from Australia, Canada and New Zealand to South Africa. They sank their differences with the Mother Country in the wave of jingoism which swept the Empire – or at least part of the Empire. India had first offered troops, an offer declined. It was a war for whites only.

In the first war that they would fight abroad, New Zealanders went to South Africa, taking their rugby skills with them.

One of the most fertile grounds for the growth of rugby football has been wherever there has been a conglomeration of physically active men – public schools, universities, mining camps and the army. There is a lot of idle time in an army. Sport is a good way to fill that time. Rugby is the best way of all for men who are inclined to physical activity, as soldiers often are.

The New Zealanders played. Amongst those who played was the great Dave Gallaher. Bud Abbott also played, and both of those would be amongst the first All Blacks of 1905-06. In fact Abbott first learned to play rugby football in South Africa during the Anglo-Boer War. W J Hardham played in South Africa. Farrier-Sergeant-Major Hardham of the 4th New Zealand Contingent was awarded a Victoria Cross for his bravery at Naauwpoort on 28 January 1901. At the time it was a vital railway junction and the hunt was on for General De Wet. Hardham played 53 times for Wellington between 1897 and 1910.

An NZRFU minute of 1902 reads:

"Many have gained special distinction, and two – Lieutenant Hardham and Captain Coutts – have attained the summit of a soldier's ambition, the former having been awarded the Victoria Cross and the latter one of the Queen's Scarves for gallantry on the field. All footballers will be proud of the fact that the only New Zealanders to gain these distinctions were of their number."

The scarves were apparently knitted by Queen Victoria herself.

During the Anglo-Boer War three rugby internationals were awarded Victoria Crosses – Tommy Crean of Ireland at Tygerskloof in 1901, and Robert Johnson of Ireland and a South African, Charles Mullins, who had toured in 1896 with the British Isles, both at Elandslaagte in 1899.

During the war there was almost a truce for a match. The Boers and the British actually agreed to a ceasefire on 29 April 1902 near Okiep, but there was a skirmish on the night of 28 April and the match did not happen, which is a grievous pity.

But that year Corporal Dave Gallaher of the 6th New Zealand Contingent led a team of New Zealand soldiers against a South African team in Johannesburg, and the New Zealand soldiers won. That was the first real match between a team representing New Zealand and a team representing South Africa, however partial the representation might have been.

At the end of that war there was all the business of sorting out peace and demobilisation. Unlike rugby players in modern times, they could not simply leap on a plane the next day and sleep off the celebrations. Three clubs of New Zealanders were established – one in Pretoria, one in Ladysmith and one in Durban. The one in Durban was highly successful, winning the Moor Cup three years in a row, 1904-06, and being instrumental in the foundation of the Durban Rugby Sub-Union.

Not only the fighting men waiting for a ship home were involved. Leonard Harris, businessman and New Zealand cricket international, moved from New Zealand to Durban and set up a business which is still thriving, and got involved in rugby football. The New Zealand RFC became Durban's second rugby club. And they played New Zealand rugby – five-eighths and all. In fact they went back to the old days of three three-quarters.

In Durban, as elsewhere, the New Zealanders wore black jerseys with a silver fern on the breast. Their patron was R J (Richard John) Seddon, the Prime Minister of New Zealand, who actually went on a tour of New Zealand units during the Anglo-Boer War.

They had a dummy run in 1902 and then entered the league, winning it three times in successive years. Thereupon, in 1907, after Seddon's death, they closed their doors as their numbers had waned. Bob Goldstone of Waimate stayed on to play an important part in education in Natal, especially at Maritzburg College.

Up in Newcastle, in the area where the Boers caused the British so many headaches, New Zealand troops got involved in the game – the 7th New Zealand Regiment above all.

When Mark Morrison's British toured in 1903, they whacked Pretoria 15-3. Six of the Pretoria team were New Zealanders – F Hazeldene, J Bonar, Fitzherbert, Mangles who scored Pretoria's lone try, Taplin and Kerr.

Just after the Anglo-Boer War attempts were made to get rugby contacts between South Africa and New Zealand going. The first move came from South Africa, as the minutes of the SARFB of 14 October 1904 confirm:

> Mr Smuts, on behalf of the Western Province Union, moved that it be an instruction to the Hon. Secretary to place himself in communication with the New Zealand Union with a view to inducing them to play a series of matches in South Africa.
> Seconded by Mr Orpen and agreed to.

L B Smuts was a great president of the Western Province RFU. Gerald Orpen was the mainspring behind the proposal that the springbok become South Africa's rugby symbol.

The South African Board had heard that New Zealand were sending a team to Great Britain for the 1905-06 season. They asked New Zealand to play matches on their way to England. In June 1905, eight months after the invitation was issued, the Hon. Secretary reported that New Zealand had replied saying that "arrangements would not permit their team about to tour Great Britain touching at South Africa". The All Blacks that year sailed round Cape Horn, not round the Cape of Good Hope and came home via New York, where they played an exhibition match at a baseball stadium in Brooklyn, Niagara Falls, the Grand Canyon and San Francisco, where they played two exhibition matches against a team called British Columbia, Honolulu and Pago Pago.

The South Africans toured Britain in 1906-07 and they made some money out of the tour, some of which was to be kept in reserve for possible visits by teams from Great Britain or New Zealand.

By the next March the SA Board had received an invitation from the New Zealand RFU, dated 31 January 1907 and signed by Edgar Wylie, the Hon. Secretary:

"I am directed to convey to you the very hearty congratulations of my Union upon the very triumphant tour just concluded by your representative team. The tour of the Springboks will, I am sure, remain a record for all time, of which your Union may feel justly proud. I am at the same time directed to extend to your team a very hearty invitation to visit these shores, and try conclusions with our players. I trust to hear from you by early mail if your Union will accept the invitation, and that you will submit proposals and terms for a tour of, say, six weeks in this colony, and from 10 to 12 matches during the tour. I am sure your players would enjoy the stay in New Zealand, and if the tour should eventuate they would have an opportunity of seeing that colony from north to south and to visit the principal scenic resorts for which the colony is much noted."

The Board did not think such a tour would be possible for some time but the eager men of Griqualand West suggested that all the unions receive a copy of Wylie's letter so that they could discuss the matter. Eventually the Board declined the invitation with thanks, as it did to an invitation from the New South Wales RFU which arrived at the same time.

Late in 1911, the NZRFU sent an invitation, written by J D Avery, inviting the SA Board to send its team in 1912. The SA Board regarded the invitation as a compliment but it would take too long to organise finances and the tour would interfere with the planned Currie Cup tournament for 1912. So the Board turned down the invitation.

Undeterred, the NZRFU again invited the Board in August 1913 for 1914, but again the Board regretted being unable to accept the invitation for the same reasons as in 1912, adding that there was a danger of overdoing tours, which would be seen as bizarre reasoning in 1996! It had concern at the time about the financial arrangements of a tour after some acrimonious correspondence with the RFU before the RFU paid certain unpaid expenses on the 1912-13 Springbok tour of Britain.

So it came about that the next contact after the Anglo-Boer War was again in wartime, the First World War – a horrible war. Several South African rugby internationals paid the greatest price in that war – Gerald Thompson, Jackie Morkel, Sep Heyns, Adam Burdett and Toby Moll who played for South Africa, Beak Steyn and Mike Dickson who had played for Scotland, and Reggie Hands who had played for England. Several New Zealanders also gave their lives for King and Empire – Jimmy Baird, R S Black, who was killed at the Battle of the Somme, Norkey Dewar, who

13

was one of the many ANZACs to fall at Gallipoli, Ernest Dodd, Doolan Downing, another Gallipoli casualty, Eric Harper, James McNeece, George Sellars and Reg Taylor, a trio who were killed in action at Messines, Frank Wilson and the great Dave Gallaher, who had survived the Anglo-Boer War and captained the first All Blacks to tour Britain only to die in the merciless Battle of Passchendaele.

As soon as the War was over, rugby broke out again. An Inter-Services tournament took place in England in March 1919. At stake was the King's Cup, presented by King George V, the first Rugby World Cup, if you like. Taking part were Mother Country, Royal Air Force, Australian Imperial Forces, Canadian Expeditionary Force, New Zealand Services and South African Forces.

New Zealand were the strongest side, beating the South Africans 14-5 at Twickenham. Australia and Mother Country also beat the South Africans, while the Kiwis lost only to Australia who were beaten by the RAF, who had ten South Africans in their side, and Mother Country. There was a decider between Mother Country and New Zealand, which New Zealand won 9-3, thus taking the King's Cup.

Putting the chance of a rugby tour above a speedy return, the New Zealanders went on an Odyssey through South Africa. They did two other things in preparation for the tour. They lifted all the ranks of the "other ranks" so that there were no privates in their team. They also sent Ranji Wilson home.

This last decision was a ghastly one. It happened quietly enough then, but later would be a massive and contentious issue.

Sgt Nathaniel Arthur Wilson, whose nickname was Ranji, went straight home to New Zealand, a star player, an All Black in ten tests, later a national selector, the son of an Englishman, but his mother was a West Indian.

The Anglo-Boer War had been a white man's war. Rugby football would be a white man's game. In those times nobody objected and it would be a long time before real objections occurred.

Ironically, the captain of the team, Charlie Brown, had in 1913 played for the Maoris. Later, when the Imperial Services were due to travel to South Africa, it was said, belatedly, that he had played for the Maoris as a guest player. Winston McCarthy believed that he was a Maori.

The idea of the tour originated from the Transvaal RU. The Annual General Meeting of the SARFB on 28 March 1919 recorded: "It is thought by many here, interested in our game, that there is a good opportunity to endeavour to secure a visit from a military team, when the forces are returning to Australia and New Zealand, and I am directed to bring the matter before your Board for their consideration. It is suggested that your Board invite the co-operation of the English Union to arrange for a visit by an Australian or a New Zealand Team or visits by both, separately or jointly."

The Board wanted the tour to revive the game after the war and wanted the New Zealand team as it would save money on fares, because the team would be on its way home from England to New Zealand. Furthermore the New Zealanders would not require the same guarantees which the English would and which the Board could not afford.

The Transvaal suggestion was accepted "by a large majority".

By May arrangements were provisionally completed. The budget for the tour was £2 500. It was resolved that they would not play a representative South African team.

In June they received a cable from the Hon. W P Schreiner, the former president of the Board and then the South African High Commissioner in London: "New Zealand team leaving on the *Cap Polonio* due sailing 7th June should arrive Cape Town about 28th."

The *Cap Polonio* was a Union-Castle liner, taking troops to Cape Town, amongst them the New Zealanders. It was the three-funnelled ship's only voyage for Union-Castle and a notorious one. The ship was completed in Germany in 1914 but first went to sea only at the end of World War I when the British sailed it to England amongst several ships surrendered in terms of the Treaty of Versailles. It was then passed on for management to Union-Castle who found the ship so difficult that they were glad to be relieved of it after its single voyage. The Germans, it would seem, had cunningly made the running of the ship as difficult as possible, making its only voyage an exasperating one.

It was fitting that Union-Castle should be the carrier as they had brought out previous teams to South Africa and had given South African rugby the cup named after its owner Sir Donald Currie – the Currie Cup, the Holy Grail of South African rugby.

At the time that decisions were being made about the tour, the Board discussed "the question of procedure in view of the fact that the New Zealand team was believed to contain one or more Maoris".

After much discussion Mr McIntyre proposed and Mr Schreiner seconded and the proposal was adopted by eight fatal votes to six that the following cable be sent to the High Commissioner in London:

> "Confidential. If visitors include Maoris tour would be wrecked and immense harm politically and otherwise would follow. Please explain the position fully and try arrange exclusion."

15

The matter of financing the tour was then discussed at greater length.

The "Army All Blacks" broke their Odyssey in South Africa with a diversion of fifteen matches in 54 days, ending in Durban where they embarked for their beautiful Ithaca. Of those fifteen matches – fourteen actually and an unofficial match, whatever that means, against Natal to fill in the time before their ship sailed – the New Zealanders won 11, losing to Griqualand West, Western Province Universities and Western Province. They drew with Cape Town Clubs.

Percy Day, a discerning rugby gentleman, said of them: "I have been manager to many Rugby football teams that have either toured South Africa or participated in Currie Cup tournaments, but I assert confidently that I have never been associated with a more gentlemanly, sportsmanlike body of footballers than those Service men of New Zealand whom it was a pleasure to manage during their tour of the Union." And on the score of their rugby ability he said: "In my considered opinion the best fifteen of the Services' team was superior to the best fifteen the 1928 All Blacks in this country could field. Being all ex-soldiers, their team-work and team spirit were alike admirable, and they blended into a most workmanlike side."

The great Bill Schreiner, who selected Springbok teams from 1912 to 1952, said of them: "There can be no two opinions as to the benefit derived by South Africa from the visit of this team. It gave a much needed impetus and fillip to the game, and everywhere large crowds attended the games, and the greatest enthusiasm prevailed. The New Zealand team was deservedly most popular, consisting, as it did, of keen, unassuming players, playing football of a high order."

The various unions had to put up guarantees of £150 to host the tourists. And in Kimberley each of the players was told he would be presented with a gold medal inset with diamonds. Each union was required to contribute £30 to pay for the medals. The medals reached New Zealand early in 1920.

The tour was such a success that the Board was able to declare that it had now £1 000 in the bank, but remember this was a time when the South West Africa RFU withdrew from the Board because it could not afford the affiliation fee of three guineas.

Oh innocent days before inflation! Oh lucrative amateur days! Actually the visitors battled to pay their way, and were saved when an ex-New Zealander, making his living in South Africa as a jockey, gave them useful tips for the races.

Seventeen of them had played or were to play for New Zealand, including their captain, Staff-Sgt Chas Brown, a halfback who played for New

Zealand on either side of World War I. In 1921 some of them would play real tests against South Africans – Percy Storey and Moke Belliss, who scored two of the three All Blacks' tries at Carisbrook, Jim Moffit, Dick Fogarty, who was 88 when he died, tough Alf West, and Bill Fea. And Dick Roberts was there to give the Springboks a tough old time when they played Taranaki. Jack Stohr did not play against the Springboks for he migrated to South Africa and became a chemist in Springs, dying in Johannesburg in 1973 at the age of 84.

The stage was set in 1919 for the real tests. By that time South Africa and New Zealand were clearly the top rugby nations in the world. South Africa had won series against the British Isles in 1903 and 1910. The Springboks had gone to Europe in 1912-13 and beaten England, Ireland, Scotland, Wales and France. New Zealand had demolished Australia several times and the mighty All Blacks had lost only one match on their 1905 tour of Britain, and to this day the New Zealanders believe the Welshmen cheated them of a try which would have produced at least a draw.

War was over. It was time to play. One of sport's biggest rivalries was set to begin.

TOUR STATISTICS

P	W	D	L	Pf	Pa	Tf	Ta
14	10	1	3	159	64	33	13

The New Zealand Imperial Services Team in South Africa in 1919:
Sgt-Major J G O'Brien (Auckland), Sgt W L Henry (South Canterbury), Sgt L B Stohr (Taranaki), Sgt E Ryan (Wellington), Sgt W A Ford (Canterbury), S-Sgt P W Storey (South Canterbury), Lieut E W King (Wellington), Sgt R W Roberts (Taranaki), Sgt W R Fea (Otago), Lieut G J McNaught (Wanganui), Sgt-Major J Ryan (Wellington), Staff-Sgt C Brown (Taranaki) (c), Sgt D McK Sandman (Canterbury), Sgt A A Lucas (Auckland), Sgt A P Singe (Auckland), Sgt M Cain (Taranaki), Staff-Sgt H G Whittington (Taranaki), Sgt S J Standen (Wellington), Staff-Sgt E W Hasell (Canterbury), Lieut J E Moffitt (Wellington), Sgt J A Bruce (Wellington), Sgt J Kissick (Taranaki), Sgt A H West (Taranaki), Sgt E A Belliss (Wanganui), Sgt A Gilchrist (Wellington), Staff-Sgt R Fogarty (Otago), Staff-Sgt E J Naylor (Otago), Staff-Sgt E L J Cockroft (Southland)

TOUR RESULTS

DATE	VENUE	OPPONENTS	SCORE
24 July	Newlands	Western Province Country Clubs	8-6
26 July	Newlands	Western Province Town Clubs	3-3
29 July	Oudtshoorn	South Western Districts	23-0
2 August	Port Elizabeth	Eastern Province	15-0
6 August	Bloemfontein	Orange Free State	16-5
9 August	Kimberley	Griqualand West	3-8
13 August	Johannesburg	Witwatersrand	6-0
16 August	Johannesburg	Mines	24-3
20 August	Pretoria	Pretoria	5-4
23 August	Johannesburg	Transvaal	5-3
27 August	Durban	Natal	17-3
4 September	Newlands	Western Province Universities	8-9
6 September	Newlands	Western Province	6-17
12 September	Newlands	Western Province XV	20-3

The tour made a profit for the South African Board of £584-8-6.

CHAPTER 2

The Saga Begins

AT THE END of it all the toast was: Till we meet again. It has, bumpiness notwithstanding, remained rugby's most solemn toast. And the bumpiness began way back then, right at the start.

Just before Christmas in 1919, the South African Rugby Football Board received an invitation from the New Zealand Rugby Football Union to send a team to New Zealand that year, a tour to include Australia. Amongst others Bennie Osler's father, the delegate for North Eastern Districts, thought it was too soon, and the invitation was accepted to tour in 1921.

The New South Wales RU also asked the team to play in Australia as they drifted around the bottom of Australia on their way to Sydney and a change of ship to the *Mararoa*, bound for the Land of the Long White Cloud, a voyage of five days.

They played five times in Australia without getting involved in a test match, though they limped away with eight serious injuries. New Zealand was the serious venue for Theo Pienaar and his 28 players, 23 of whom had seen service in World War I.

Injuries were a problem throughout the tour. Jack Siedle, the smallest forward ever to play for South Africa at 168 lbs (76,4 kg), did not even get beyond the Australian leg. But when the team asked for replacements, the request was refused by the SARFB. It may have been difficult to get replacements there but there was time enough to do so.

Tours were long affairs in those days. The team left Cape Town early in May on the *Aeneas*, a ship of the Blue Funnel line. The *Ulysses* got them back to Cape Town on 1 November. They were obviously classic voyages!

When the tour eventually came to an end in New Zealand, the New Zealand Prime Minister, William Massey, said: "The South Africans are the finest body of sportsmen that have ever visited the shores of New Zealand."

Theo Pienaar was a successful captain. He was chosen for his good sense, diplomacy and his ability to keep young rugby players both in place and happy. After all, H C Bennett was the manager but he had no other assistant and certainly nobody who could be described as a coach. But there were two veterans, the Morkels, Boy and Gerhard, both older than Pienaar.

They were not the only Morkels in the team. In all there were five of them, and Boy, aged 35, would be South Africa's forceful captain in the tests.

Frank Mellish was a remarkable member of the side. He had stayed on in Britain after the war and had played for England. In 1921 he came hot-footing it back to South Africa and was chosen as a strong forward. He is the only serious international to have played rugby for two countries in the same year. Later he became chairman of the national selectors and the great manager of the lovable 1951-52 Springboks.

Mighty Phil Mostert was there and so was little Billy Sendin, still the lightest (60 kg) player ever to play for South Africa. On the wing was Attie van Heerden, an Olympic sprinter at the Antwerp Games, who later went off to rugby league in Britain, as did Tank van Rooyen.

Their forwards were regarded as a pack of big men, though their average height was only 5 ft 7 ins (1,70 m), their average weight 187 lbs (85 kg), despite having two huge men in Royal Morkel who was 6 ft 2 ins (1,87 m) and weighed 230 lbs (104,5 kg), and Baby Michau who was 6 ft 4 ins (1,94 m) and weighed 245 lbs (111 kg), the heaviest Springbok forward until 1968.

No tour of New Zealand is easy. The rugby in that country is intense. After all, rugby is the most noteworthy thing that happens. The 1921 Springboks were remarkably successful. In the nine matches before the first test they lost one, drew one and won seven.

The first match between teams of the NZRFU and the SARFB took place in Wanganui, a small coastal town in the middle of that open mouth where the North Island gasps in horror at the South Island.

They had little time to get their land legs. They reached a huge welcoming crowd at Auckland on the Tuesday morning for a mayoral reception, and a run at Victoria Park, took the train down to Wanganui where they arrived at about eleven on the Wednesday morning and played that afternoon against a strong Wanganui side.

They kicked off in windy Wanganui in grand style. Tank van Rooyen led the charge on the Wanganui line. Mannetjies Michau passed from the rapid ruck to Sas de Kock who sent big Attie van Heerden over in the corner as he was tackled. I B de Villiers missed the conversion, and the Springboks led 3-0. Even though Sas de Kock broke an ankle and, understandably, went off, the big forwards kept getting possession and Wanganui continued to defend. Then Royal Morkel came bursting away with the ball and fed Theuns Krüger who burst over in the tackle to score. This time De Villiers converted and the Springboks led 8-0 at half-time.

Now it was Wanganui's turn to attack. Jackson kicked a penalty goal and O'Connell scored a try and the Springboks led 8-6. Back came the Springboks and I B de Villiers kicked a long penalty goal to make the final score 11-6. The Springboks soon found that rugby in New Zealand was, in New Zealand parlance, "hard yakker", tough work for tough men.

The train stopped for a long time at each station so that people could greet the "Africans", who caused surprise by being white, on their journey to New Plymouth on the west coast of North Island, under the snow-capped cone of Mt Egmont. Taranaki, a proud and powerful team captained by Dick Roberts, showed the guts that is a hallmark of New Zealand rugby and the match ended scoreless.

The Springboks had an easy time against the Wairarapa-Bush combination in Masterton and then won a famous victory in windy Wellington against, reputedly, the strongest side in New Zealand. That night, in a gale, they left on the *Maori* for the South Island, whose inhabitants call it the Mainland.

The voyage was eventful as the captain struggled to keep the ship pointed in the right direction in the storm, and when day broke they were still within sight of Wellington! There was a great deal of seasickness and big Royal Morkel's desperate cries earned him the nickname Mama. A queasy team reached Lyttelton and then went on to Christchurch from where they went over Arthur's Pass, first by train, then by "horse-bus" and again by train to Greymouth over the majestic Southern Alps. It had taken them from Saturday night to Tuesday morning to get to Greymouth.

Back they went over the mountain after Bill Zeller's hat trick of tries in an easy victory over the weakest rugby area in New Zealand and down the Alps and over the Canterbury plain to the very English city of Christchurch.

On a wet and slippery afternoon Canterbury beat the Springboks who did not cope with the conditions at all well. It was the first time that the Springboks had lost to a New Zealand team, not the last time, not even the last time they were to lose to Canterbury in their red and black jerseys, nor were they the only people to find them tough opposition.

The traditional Christchurch question is: Can Canty? The answer, this time and often, was: Canty Can.

The Springboks then moved right down to the very south, playing in friendly, sunny Timaru before their hard-earned victory over Southland, the Ranfurly Shield holders, in the clinging mud at Invercargill, the world's most southerly city, famed for the Bluff oysters. The Springboks won 12-0, four tries to none, and regarded it as a great victory. While in Invercargill, the Springboks experienced their first snowstorm.

Up they came to the cold, cold city of Dunedin with all its Scottish ancestry, and its passion for rugby football, the home of rucking. The win over Otago was a good one and then came the first-ever test between the two countries, played at Carisbrook, known internationally as the House of Pain. It's a cold place with vociferous support.

On that cold, still day in August, the vociferous support was all on the side of New Zealand – all 25 000 of them in the ground and another 10 000 perched on the hills around about, called a Scots Stand in most of New Zealand, but poshly the Caledonian Grandstand in Dunedin, for the view from there is free. That does not sound a big crowd by today's stand-ards, but even today Dunedin has a population of only some 110 000. As a percentage of the population it was a huge crowd in 1921, for there was vast interest in the match throughout New Zealand.

The Springboks surprised by leaving out Tank van Rooyen. The All Blacks surprised by including Ned Hughes, still the oldest player to have played international rugby – as far as the records go. He was 40 years 123 days old.

Theo Pienaar stood down and burly Boy Morkel captained the Spring-boks. George Aitken, who was playing his debut test and was not the cap-tain of Wellington, was New Zealand's surprise choice as captain.

The teams ran out. The crowd roared. Both teams did a war cry and Ted McKenzie blew the whistle. McKenzie was a great rugby personality – a good player, the secretary of his union for 18 years, president of the NZRFU and the sole selector who chose the All Blacks to tour South Africa in 1940, a tour cancelled because of Adolf Hitler.

The All Blacks did not wear numbers on their jerseys. Instead they wore letters – to confuse pirate programme sellers!

South Africa won the first-ever toss, and, playing into the sun, New Zealand kicked off to start rugby's greatest contest. Gerhard Morkel caught the ball and kicked it out near the halfway line.

The first-ever try in the first-ever test between South Africa and New Zealand was scored by Attie van Heerden, the Springbok wing. And pow-erful Gerhard Morkel converted from far out. The Springboks smelt vic-tory and, probably already suffering the effects of overconfidence, South African rugby's besetting sin, they did not score again. The All Blacks did with three tries for a well-deserved 13-5 victory.

22

The startling try of the afternoon came with the scores level and South Africa on the attack. Jack Steel caught a diagonal kick from Ces Badeley, beat Henry Morkel and raced more than half the field for perhaps the greatest try in matches between the two countries. That sounds simple. What Steel actually did was to trap the ball on his back and then set off running with it while still clasping it to his back. He beat Meyer and the great Gerhard Morkel and only just before the line he managed to get the ball to his front, a more difficult operation in those days when the slightest of fumbles was called a knock-on. Steel scored behind the posts.

They had awards even then in New Zealand. The gold medal for the best back went to Ginger Nicholls of New Zealand. The medal for the best forward went to Baby Michau. Both of them were dropped from their teams for the second test!

Chastened, the Springboks went back to North Island and success against Manawatu-Horowhenua, disjointed Auckland-North Auckland, and Bay of Plenty. Back they went from volcanic Rotorua and its Maori traditions for the second test, and more success, at Eden Park in Auckland, South Africa's first victory over New Zealand in a test match, the first-ever test at Eden Park, one of rugby football's most famous grounds.

There had been a suggestion that the second test be postponed. The suggestion came from a little girl in Auckland who, early in the tour, wrote to the Springboks asking them to put off the match as it was her birthday that day and her dad had promised her a party, which might just not happen if there was a test match that day. The match was not postponed but when the Springboks got to Auckland they clubbed together, bought the girl a beautiful wrist watch, went to a tea party for the girl and gave her the present.

Despite the little girl's birthday party, the crowds gathered from all over New Zealand. This time the Springboks, with six changes to their team, were not overconfident, and this time they won, deservedly.

Tank van Rooyen got a game in this match and burst away from the loose to release the ball to the backs and eventually little Billy Sendin scampered over for a try which Gerhard Morkel converted. New Zealand equalised with a disputed try which Mark Nicholls, who was 19 at the time, converted. There were fewer than 20 minutes left when Steel hoofed the ball downfield. Gerhard Morkel, whose positional play was immaculate, gathered the ball near the touchline. He strode infield and let fly with a dropped goal. It won the match 9-5. It levelled the series.

An astonished spectator ran onto the field and offered Morkel a bottle of beer. The great fullback took the bottle, toasted the crowd and took a swig. "I did it more to swill my mouth out with it," he said afterwards.

It was not the only crowd intrusion. Bill Zeller got a run down the wing. When he found himself amongst spectators he stopped in the erroneous belief that he was in touch and handed the ball to an All Black who took off with it! The medal for the best forward went to Moke Belliss, for the best back to Gerhard Morkel.

That left everything to play for in the third and final test. In the land of Mooloo the Springboks beat Waikato and in Napier, where they were made welcome at a Maori marae, they beat Hawke's Bay-Poverty Bay. They stayed on for another four days in kindly Napier for the fateful match with the Maoris. The Springboks lost three players but won the match, and then they lost many, many friends. It was, really, a sad day and not too much of it had a lot to do with the players. A nonplayer sent racial slights back to South Africa, thus troubling the relationships between New Zealand and South Africa, as we shall see.

From Napier they went south again and beat a combination of Nelson, Marlborough, Golden Bay and Motueka in the north of South Island before going back to Wellington's Athletic Park for the deciding test. The trip to Nelson was bizarre.

The Maori match was on Thursday. On the Friday afternoon the *Mapourika* left Wellington, arriving in Nelson at seven on Saturday morning. The NZRFU had cancelled the hotel rooms, and there was nowhere for the Springboks to rest. That afternoon they played at Trafalgar Park and after the match went back to the boat for the uncomfortable trip back to Wellington. The only advantage was that it left the Springboks a clear week to recover and to prepare for the final test.

After the match in Nelson, H C Bennett, who was not noted for his diplomacy, complained about the arrangements, the poor facilities on the boat and the fact that the Springboks had to leave immediately after the match, without even a chance to shower. The New Zealanders agreed with him.

Wellington's notorious weather did its worst. Athletic Park in Wellington, a ground elevated amongst the hills to ensure that it gets the worst of the city's torturous weather, was awash as the teams took the field for the third test, "a lake, with an occasional patch of mud showing here and there like raisins in a poor man's Christmas pudding", according to one of the Springboks.

There were opportunities to score. The Springboks, with the wind, were better in the first half, the All Blacks in the second. Gerhard Morkel failed to score when a penalty hit the upright and Tank van Rooyen came close to scoring a try for South Africa. Keith Siddells for New Zealand went to his

24

grave believing that he had scored a try when he dived on the ball in the Springbok goal area and referee Neilson ruled that he had not got his hands to the ball. And a New Zealander said: "Who said the Springboks could not play in the wet? They can play in the Pacific." But neither side scored.

Tokkie Scholtz wrote afterwards: "The final whistle sounded no score, and South Africa and New Zealand are still joint champions of the football world." Even then they thought of the contests between the two countries as the fight for the World Crown.

Tank van Rooyen received the medal for the best forward and Jack Steel the medal for the best back. The good people of Timaru also gave Steel a medal to commemorate his try in the first test and a Sheffield firm gave him a cup as the outstanding New Zealand player of the series.

For the Springboks, the hero was again Gerhard Morkel. Phil Mostert recalled: "It was raining so heavily that we could hardly see one another. Gerhard was like a ghostly shadow somewhere at the back of us and he saved us from defeat, that's for sure."

The test series was tied. The toast was: Till we meet again.

Not that people in South Africa were all that satisfied. Theo Pienaar had to defend his team's record. He said: "True, we may not have done much that was sensational, but let me stress this point – there is neither time nor place for the sensational in New Zealand football. Go out there yourselves and fight a New Zealand team on its own soil, a team that is filled with consciousness of its own prowess and flushed with great achievements of the past. And if you do not eat humble pie on your return, well – I shall."

That all sounds simple – a drawn series, a respectable record, uninformed criticism, a happy host. But there was the memory of that match in Napier to take into account. Relations between the two countries were headed for trouble caused by South Africans' racial attitudes.

TOUR STATISTICS (NEW ZEALAND ONLY)

P	W	D	L	Pf	Pa	Tf	Ta
19	15	2	2	244	81	54	13

TESTS

3	1	1	1	14	18	2	4

25

The South African Touring Team of 1921:
I B de Villiers (Transvaal), P G (Gerhard) Morkel (Western Province), W A Clarkson (Natal), C du P Meyer (Western Province), H W (Henry) Morkel (Western Province), W D Sendin (Griqualand West), S S F Strauss (Griqualand West), A J van Heerden (Transvaal), J S Weepner (Western Province), W C Zeller (Natal), J S de Kock (Western Province), J P Michau (Western Province), J C Tindall (Western Province), W H Townsend (Natal), M C Ellis (Transvaal), T L Krüger (Transvaal), F W Mellish (Western Province), J M Michau (Transvaal), H J (Harry) Morkel (Western Province), J A (Royal) Morkel (Western Province), W H (Boy) Morkel (Transvaal), P J Mostert (Transvaal), J S Olivier (Western Province), N J du Plessis (Western Province), T B Pienaar (Western Province (c), L B Siedle (Natal), H H Scholtz (Western Province), G W van Rooyen (Transvaal), A P Walker (Natal)

TOUR RESULTS

Date	Venue	Opponents	Score
13 July	Wanganui	Wanganui	11-6
16 July	New Plymouth	Taranaki	0-0
20 July	Masterton	Wairarapa-Bush	18-3
23 July	Wellington	Wellington	8-3
27 July	Greymouth	West Coast-Buller	33-3
30 July	Christchurch	Canterbury	4-6
3 August	Timaru	South Canterbury	34-3
6 August	Invercargill	Southland	12-0
10 August	Dunedin	Otago	11-3
13 August	Dunedin	New Zealand	5-13

Date	Venue	Opponents	Score
17 August	Palmerston North	Manawatu-Horowhenua	3-0
20 August	Auckland	Auckland-North Auckland	24-8
24 August	Rotorua	Bay of Plenty	17-9
27 August	Auckland	New Zealand	9-5
31 August	Hamilton	Waikato	6-0
3 September	Napier	Hawke's Bay-Poverty Bay	14-8
7 September	Napier	New Zealand Maoris	9-8
10 September	Nelson	Nelson-Marlborough-Golden Bay-Motueka	26-3
17 September	Wellington	New Zealand	0-0

CHAPTER 3

The Trouble Begins

MARK DOWN SOME names. First of all mark down Ranji Wilson. Then mark down Charles Blackett. Wilson was a victim, Blackett was a villain. Mark him down before you mark down Verwoerd, even if you think him merely naïve.

Between the second and third tests in 1921 the Springboks played the Maoris in Napier, where they had a marvellous reception from the Maoris, especially the wealthy Mrs Perry whose father had been a Maori leader.

What happened on the field was one thing. What happened off the field was another thing. What happened during the match could be handled. What happened after the match was the start of a runaway train.

Off the field there was fun, till after the match. On the field there was a tough tussle with some untoward incidents that would not have been regarded as unusual in any other match on the tour.

The Springboks won, 9-8, and were not convincing. Tokkie Scholtz, the Springbok tourist who played in the front row that day, wrote later for South African consumption: "The Maori is a good sportsman, plays very hard but with good spirit, and as long as it's anybody's game, is a hard man to beat."

Blackett's version was different and almost fatal.

The Springboks lost three players through injury, all ruled out of the third test. That's tough. The Maoris were on the attack and Jack Blake claimed a mark in a kickable position but the referee, J F Peake of Canterbury, did not allow the mark and Blake was buried by Springboks. Taffy Townsend slipped the ball to Bill Zeller who scored.

The crowd were incensed. They believed Blake should have been given the mark and they believed that Zeller had stepped into touch. The result was victory to South Africa by a point. There would be another dispute after the same match sixty years later, but an amiable one, thanks to Billy Bush, the losing Maori captain.

All of that sounds like the normal ups and downs of rugby football, nothing new.

Enter Charles Blackett.

From the post office in Napier he sent a cable back to the newspapers in South Africa. The *Cape Times* reported him as saying: "The Maoris showed little science and were frequently off-side . . . The match was witnessed by the most excited crowd of the tour."

That's all pretty harmless.

The report in *The Cape Argus*, perhaps more fully reported or perhaps a different report after he had had time to measure his words, read: "It is perhaps unfortunate that today's match was played. In fact it was only as a result of great pressure being brought to bear that it was played. Unfortunately the crowd was the most unsportsmanlike experienced during the tour, especially the European section, and when they were not engaged in 'booing' the referee, they indulged in sarcastic remarks at his expense . . . There is no suggestion that the Maoris were unnecessarily rough; they merely threw their weight around without proper regard for the niceties of the game . . . The Maoris showed little science."

The cable itself was even worse than the report: "Most unfortunate match ever played . . . Bad enough having play team officially designated NZ Natives, but spectacle thousands Europeans frantically cheering on band of coloured men to defeat members of own race was too much for Springboks who were frankly disgusted . . . Their faithful coloured allies proved loyal to New Zealand for in addition to serious injury to Krüger's leg, Van Heerden had to stay off the field for 15 minutes. Other limping badly. Maoris flung their weight about regardless of niceties of the game."

It's no use complaining that the cable was read in the post office in Napier and its sentiments communicated to the whole of Napier and then to the whole of New Zealand through the *Daily Telegraph* and eventually to history.

The Hawke's Bay RFU immediately sent Harold Bennett a telegram asking him to disassociate himself from the "expressions contained therein derogatory to New Zealand Maori team". He did so. The Union's telegram went on to say: "Whoever was responsible for telegram does not know or understand how highly the Maori race is regarded by his Pakeha fellow citizens."

Apart from disassociating himself Bennett also said that the correspondent regretted his action, done in the heat of the moment. But Blackett was "astonished that Mr Bennett thought fit so abjectly to apologise". The South Africans believed, astonishingly, that they were in the right. There is no accounting for national madness whether it be the militarism of the Spartans, the fervour of the Crusaders, Napoleonism, the jingoism of the Empire, Hitlerism, the suicidal ardour of the Samurai, apartheid, or the racial cleansing of Bosnian Serbs.

The telegraphist in Napier in 1921 was dismissed from the post office for betraying confidence.

There was lots of Maori anger. Dr Peter Buck, the eminent Maori, said: "To everyone with Maori blood in his veins the so-called grievance of the Springboks against playing a Maori team is an unmitigated insult. If a team of reputed sports will not make honourable amends and still persist in the curious attitude of drawing a colour line in sport in this country, then the New Zealand Rugby Union should, by not extending future invitation in South Africa, protect its Maori supporters and their friends from further gratuitous insult."

The Maoris would present a problem to rugby relations between South Africa in New Zealand, not for any fault of theirs. In fact if they committed any fault it was being too passive too long. But then those were different days.

It is a grave error to imagine that racism was an invention of Verwoerd and his friends. It is wrong even to believe that it was essentially a South African phenomenon.

In those days the negroes accepted it in the USA that they were not allowed to play big-time baseball or football. In Britain and New Zealand there was no such restriction upon people of colour. Darky Peters played fly half for England from 1906 to 1908. And from the start New Zealanders let Maoris play at whatever level they chose.

The first New Zealand team to tour did so in 1884 and there were two Maoris in their number. That astonishing New Zealand "Native" team that toured all over the place, playing 107 matches in 14 months in an effort to pay their way, had four Pakehas (whites) in their team. The first official New Zealand team to tour abroad, in 1893, had four Maoris. The New Zealand team at the Rugby World Cup in 1995 had four players who did not have Polynesian blood. Being a Maori did not stop Billy Stead from being the vice-captain of the first All Blacks, in 1905, nor did it ensure that he would be the vice-captain of the All Blacks. For the New Zealanders his race was simply not an issue.

The Maoris as a rugby problem were made so by South Africa. It started with Ranji in 1919. It continued with Charles Blackett in 1921.

The Maoris, as an official entity in New Zealand rugby, dated back to 1910 when a Maori team toured New Zealand and Australia. By the time

30

they played the Springboks the Maoris had played 32 matches. They were a fixture within New Zealand rugby.

There were no Maoris in the All Black side that toured South Africa in 1928, though even then there was upset in New Zealand that this should be so. The most obvious omission was the great George Nepia. Jimmy Mill the halfback did not make it either, nor did Jake Blake, Albert Falwasser, Bill Rika and Watty Wilson. As a sop the NZRFU organised a 12-match tour of New Zealand by the Maoris in 1927. For more than three decades the NZRFU sacrificed the Maoris to continuing rugby relations with South Africa.

Why?

There are several possible reasons. Most All Blacks then were not Maoris and playing the Springboks was the ultimate challenge for the New Zealander whose greatest achievement in the world was rugby football.

They lived in different times, when conquered races in the Americas, Africa, Asia and Australasia accepted a second-class status.

Thirdly, the New Zealander is a compliant man, except on the rugby field where he will never accept defeat. There is great tolerance of other people's views amongst New Zealanders, a culture of tolerance. That presumably included tolerance of the South African racial outlook.

Fourthly, New Zealanders probably did not know how bad the colour bar/apartheid really was. As South Africans tended to believe what they were fed about the demonstrators, so the New Zealanders tended to believe what they were fed about "separate development".

Mostly, it was probably just the weight of the times. The past is a foreign country, as Scott Fitzgerald said. Understanding it is difficult. Judging it is therefore impossible.

But in 1937 there was no match between the Springboks and the Maoris. In September 1936 the SARB debated whether it should allow its Springboks to play Maoris. They decided in favour, but not before some extraordinary views had been expressed. J D de Villiers was later a president of the Western Province RFU, a man who resigned and was never welcome back at Newlands, for in his time the Grand Stand was being built and there were suggestions of financial improprieties. In the minutes in 1936 he opposed allowing the Springboks to play against Maoris and desired that "the Board take steps to ensure the prohibition of Maoris taking part in matches. He was of the opinion that if players were asked to play against Maoris, they would refuse to go at all costs. Players would definitely not play against coloured people. Parents would not allow their sons to do so." Somebody chided him for lacking a "dignified and Christian spirit".

At the end of it all, the Springboks did not play the Maoris. The man who found it most embarrassing was Dr Craven, the vice-captain of the 1937 Springboks. He described how, on arrival in Auckland, a Maori greeted him with outstretched hand, saying: "I'm a Maori. Will you shake my hand?" Craven took his hand and said: "I am very glad to meet you."

Dr Craven, the social anthropologist, got on well with the Maoris, especially with Rangitiaria Dennan, the legendary Guide Rangi, whom he would meet on every trip he made to New Zealand until she died. Craven and Rangi got on well from the start when the Springboks went to Rotorua on their way from Gisborne to Auckland to prepare for the final test of the series, and she organised a party of Maoris to go to the third test in Auckland – to support the Springboks.

There were no Maoris in 1949 either. Players like Peter and Johnny Smith, Vince Bevan, who was missed most of all as the team struggled for a halfback, Ben Couch, who was regarded as the best first five-eighth in New Zealand at the time, Brownie Cherrington, Kiwi Blake and Ron Bryers did not make the side and they were all All Blacks.

Then the world had changed. World War II had seen to that. Men had fought and suffered together, and there was a new spirit of equality abroad. It changed baseball and football in the USA and blacks were admitted.

In South Africa support amongst the coloured and black people changed. No longer did they idolise and support the Springboks. No, now they supported their opponents and rejoiced when they defeated those who excluded them and treated them as second-class citizens. After all, the election of 1948, with the Nationalist victory, had decided that. No longer was colour bar a matter of custom. Now it was a matter of "law", which, of course, greatly debased the concept of law in the country and made the outbreak of lawlessness in the Nineties all the more comprehensible.

The following appears in the Minutes of the EPRFU after the match between Eastern Province and the All Blacks at the Crusader ground in June 1949: "The coloured riots were not the first we have experienced. For all too long we have been providing accommodation for those who should not have been there; these people drink and urinate behind the covered ramp. I have examined the latrines behind the ramp, on one occasion found two drinking and three card parties there; this must be stopped. The Police are not in a position to assist us. The position must be put on a proper footing. I would suggest we appoint a sub-committee to interview a non-European deputation and place the onus on the non-Europeans as to whom we can issue tickets . . . We must issue no more tickets than we can accommodate . . . The Police were not where I asked, but we have to take the rap . . . The outside fence was broken in several places." This was the president Robert St L Searle speaking, not a nasty Nationalist! Dr R A Moore-Dyke, also not a naughty Nat, did not agree with his president: "Do not ask them. We shall get nowhere. Tell them what you are going to do and do it." Mr Swart added his bit: "We must dictate to the non-Europeans and raise the prices of admission." J P de Reuch said: "We have been too lenient with them. Raise the prices." Monty Levin said: "They are hooligans. They even climbed to the top of the stairs . . . The better class of non-European is disgusted."

This support for the visiting teams would become more vigorous and evoke ugly acts of aggression from white spectators. It happened in a nasty affair in Port Elizabeth when the 1963 Wallabies, in with a chance of winning the series, lost there. It happened again in 1970, worst at Kimberley.

At the end of the match that year several coloured spectators, happy at the All Black victory, ran onto the field from the north stand, especially to make a fuss of Bryan Williams. A "drunken White" hit one and fighting started. The whites outnumbered the coloureds and drove them back. Bricks, bottles and pieces of wood flew. Old men and a child were amongst those injured. Afterwards the Acting Divisional Commissioner of Police in Kimberley, Colonel C R Kieck, blamed a group of drunken White spectators. Peter Devlin of New Zealand called them buffaloes and said: " That hard core of White spectators destroyed two weeks of wonderful welcomes in this oh-so-pleasant land."

In 1956 the Springboks played the Maoris. It was not a successful tour but the Springboks smashed the Maoris 37-0 at Eden Park in Auckland. But in 1960 there were still no Maoris. The great Pat Walsh, Waka Nathan and Mac Herewini all stayed at home, and they are amongst the greatest All Blacks. They say that there were actually four Maoris in the 1960 team. In fact certain people made it known and tried to use the fact to get the tour stopped, but Cuth Hogg squashed that and no questions were asked from South Africa. After all the definition of a Maori was vague and not obvious by appearance, which made the farce even more horrific. But then the definition of a white man in South Africa was also dubious, very dubious.

In June 1959, eight churches in New Zealand declared that Maoris

33

should be available for selection for the 1960 All Blacks. The churches were: Catholic, Presbyterian, Congregational, Methodist, Associated Churches of Christ, Baptist Union, Greek Orthodox and the Society of Friends. The rugby clubs would continue to support the union, except for the Marist Clubs.

A week later the NZRFU council was discussing tours. Present was the Maori representative, Ralph Love. Love was afraid that the Maoris would lose out because people felt that seeing them as a separate group was an act of racism and that the Maoris would lose a great deal, tours and special matches amongst them, if their special position was removed. Love said: "My presence here shows that we are in favour of racial discrimination." He was in favour of this form of racial discrimination which preserved Maori rugby privilege. At the same meeting the Council decided to accept the tour to South Africa without Maoris, at a time when Maori rugby was not strong.

The Council's decision caused a furore, as did Love's statement.

Early on the 1956 tour Craven won the hearts of the Maoris. The Springboks arrived in Auckland and that same night were entertained to an official reception in the City Hall. There was a programme of entertainment. At the end of it Craven identified two of the Maori songs that were sung, memories of 1937. He was received with enthusiasm.

By this time there was a lot of protest in New Zealand. In 1959 there were protests in favour of the inclusion of Maoris in the 1960 All Blacks. Danie Craven and his SARFB vice-president Gert Potgieter went to New Zealand during the Lions' tour and were apparently successful in keeping the 1960 tour on course. The Citizens' All Black Tour Association, founded in Wellington by a surgeon Rolland O'Regan and developed throughout New Zealand, held a mass protest in Wellington. Churches, trade unions, students and Maori leaders got involved and presented a petition of a quarter of a million signatures to parliament, asking for the tour to be cancelled, but the last all-white All Blacks came to South Africa, captained by Wilson Whineray, which makes his later protests, after his playing days, all the more questionable. He was not alone in this as Chris Laidlaw was even more questionable because of his greater exposure to anti-apartheid reasoning. Certainly the pair of them lacked the credibility of men like Ken Gray and Graham Mourie who actually made a sacrifice by withdrawing from All Black teams when playing for New Zealand was their greatest ambition. But nobody should be surprised at the strong feelings in New Zealand 21 years later when the Springboks came to tour. Even in 1960 there were marches and demonstrations, and slogans were painted. While the trials were being played demonstrators arrived at Athletic Park in Wellington. Police removed those who invaded the field.

What made the decision all the clearer in 1960 was Sharpeville, the massacre of 67 pass protestors in a township on 26 March 1960, followed by a shudder of horror throughout the world. But the NZRFU had decided two years earlier that there would be no Maoris in 1960 and it did not change its mind. In July 1958 the Maori Advisory Council in fact suggested to the NZRFU that, in the interests of rugby football, no Maoris be included. The NZRFU did ask the SARFB if it would be possible to include Maoris. At that stage there was no hope for such tolerance at all, not at a time when H F Verwoerd banned the film *Othello* with Laurence Olivier in the leading rôle. In June 1959 the Maori Advisory Council again unanimously advised the NZRFU not to include Maoris.

Die Burger, a newspaper closely connected to the Nationalist Party, took a vote amongst Springboks and the vote was in favour of inclusion of Maoris in the All Blacks team. But still an all-white All Black team came to South Africa, the last to do so.

By now it had become a vogue for nonwhite spectators to support the visiting team, which was quite understandable as the visitors were people who would include them whereas more and more they were being excluded in their own country. Newlands continued where it left off in 1949 and the South Stand delighted in the All Blacks victory in the second test in 1960.

That ground would again support a home team against a touring team only in 1975 when they roared their approval of John Noble's try for the racially mixed SA President's XV against France. The people at the south end of the ground, at that time still the preserve of nonwhites, could associate with Johnny Noble of Stellenbosch.

At the end of the 1960 tour Cuth Hogg of New Zealand gathered his commonsense and courage and told the SARFB that never again would New Zealand agree to discriminate against its own people.

From then on it was a case of No Maoris, No Tour. New Zealand would reserve the right to choose its own team, which seemed a reasonable demand.

Then came 1965, and the Loskop Dam fiasco, and a small inland resort on the Olifants River north of Middelburg in the Transvaal became notorious.

By this stage Craven believed that Senator Jan de Klerk, the Minister of the Interior and the father of F W de Klerk, had smoothed the way for the inclusion of Maoris in the 1967 All Black team. By this time the NZRFU

35

had actually made a stand on the issue: No Maoris, No Tour.

On 4th September, the day of a magnificent Springbok victory in New Zealand but reported after the test had happened because of the time difference, H F Verwoerd, Prime Minister of the Republic of South Africa, addressed the National Party's Jeugbond at Loskop Dam. Verwoerd made it abundantly clear that no Maoris would be allowed in South Africa, and his faithful bayed approval.

Down came the curtain on the 1967 tour.

There were people who believed that that would signify the end of rugby relations between South Africa and New Zealand because the National Party would last forever and would not yield from its granite stand. They were wrong, of course, for three years later the All Blacks arrived in South Africa with players who were declared to be Samoan and Maori. That concession was gained from B J Vorster, Verwoerd's successor and the man who had stopped Basil D'Oliveira from playing cricket in South Africa because he was coloured. From now on the focus of opposition to sporting apartheid would change. Instead of targeting teams coming to South Africa it would target teams leaving South Africa and through them sporting apartheid and beyond that the whole intricate web of apartheid itself.

The "Maori problem" was solved in 1970, more than half a century after Ranji Wilson was barred from playing rugby in South Africa.

In 1981 when the Maori issue was dead and the people of the world were at war with apartheid, Johan Claassen, manager of the Springbok team, apologised to all the past Maoris who had not been allowed to tour South Africa, amongst them great men like George Nepia and Johnny Smith. And he issued a formal invitation to the Maoris to send their team to South Africa. He assured them that Maoris would always be welcome in South Africa. This he did at the reception after the match between the Maoris and the Springboks in 1981.

The Maoris did come, but only when apartheid had been killed. They came in 1994 to take part in the M-Net Nite Series. They played two matches in the series and two other matches. They beat Vaal Triangle (119-3), drew with Orange Free State and lost to Griqualand West in Kimberley and Eastern Province at Ellis Park. In their number they had Wayne Warlow, Carlos Spencer, Stu Forster, Phil Coffin, Arran Pene and the great Zinzan Brooke.

And nobody in South Africa batted an eyelid.

The 1994 Springboks did not play the Maoris on their tour to New Zealand. The reason is not altogether clear, though Ebrahim Patel, the executive president when the tour was being organised, expressed disapproval of playing the Maoris because they were a racial selection! That may just have been flying in the face of tradition and good sense!

The Maoris were not put out. The 1994 Springboks arrived in Auckland on Tuesday 21 June 1994 and bounced straight on to Taupo where a great welcome awaited them with Maoris singing and dancing to welcome the new South Africans. The next night the Springboks went to a marae where Sir Hepi Hoani te Huehue welcomed them as the ambassadors of the New South Africa. Later Sir Hepi had a diabetic attack and Dr Brendan Venter, the Springbok centre, attended to him before he went home.

The Maoris were forgiving, friendly and welcoming – off the field of play.

CHAPTER 4

Meeting Again

In 1928 the Springbok and the All Black were again fighting for the crown, this time all over Southern Africa.

No sooner were the 1921 Springboks back than South Africa started to pepper New Zealand with invitations, and this time it was the Kiwis' turn to act coy, partly because they hoped that France would tour New Zealand in 1922. South Africa tried to get the French to call in on the way. It was all more than three decades premature.

Interestingly enough, when the Board in 1922 invited the NZRFU to send their team in 1923, it got much the same response as it had given New Zealand a decade earlier. In addition the New Zealand letter of regret added wryly: "Perhaps Mr Bennett's little homilies on our habit of making Rugby football our chief object in life have got home but, whether or no, our Annual Meeting decided that it was to the advantage of the game in New Zealand to go in more for club football for a season or so and their decision has to be carried out." The letter was signed by H E Combs, the secretary of the NZRFU. Bennett had been the Springboks' manager in 1921.

In 1926 the New Zealand Rugby Football Union were pleased to accept an invitation from the South African Rugby Football Board to send its team, sanitised of Maoris, to South Africa for a tour of 22 matches in 1928.

The NZRFU wanted fewer matches because it was hard for men to get off work for so long but eventually agreed to the SARFB's itinerary and to playing four test matches, where they would have preferred three.

There is no record in the Board's minutes of discussion of the inclusion or exclusion of Maoris, but then much of the tour was arranged "through other channels". The Board could report that in their negotiations with the NZRFU "no difficulties of any kind have arisen. On all points the New Zealand Union have met us in a most generous spirit, which augurs well for the success of the tour."

38

Since last they had met, the Springboks had had an easy series win over the British Lions in South Africa.

The All Blacks had been more active. They lost to New South Wales in Sydney in 1922 and beat them at home in 1923 and 1925. On their long, 38-match tour of three continents in 1924-25, an All Black team called the Invincibles beat New South Wales, Ireland, Wales, England and France and won two matches in Canada. In 1926 the All Blacks beat New South Wales again, in Australia. The All Blacks had also prepared thoroughly. Late in 1927 there were trials at Napier, Wanganui, Auckland, Palmerston North, Westport, Dunedin and Christchurch, after which the six selectors, under the chairmanship of Ted McKenzie, picked a North Island team to play South Island in Wellington. The South won 31-30, and the selectors then named 13 players to go to South Africa. Then they had another trial and announced the next 16 players – the 29 players who would sail to South Africa the next year. The first casualty was Bert Cooke, a brilliantly fast three-quarter. He withdrew for business reasons, which was surprising as he was a man of many jobs, none grand. His place was taken by Sid Carleton.

The manager, appointed in December, was to be Bill Hornig, an outfitter from Wellington. Like H C Bennett of South Africa in 1921, he did the job on his own. The captain was first appointed in April 1928 – Maurice Brownlie, the inspiring Hawke's Bay forward, at a time when Hawke's Bay held the Ranfurly Shield and had included their massive 58-8 victory over Wellington in their list of successes. Mark Nicholls, significantly in the light of later events, was appointed vice-captain.

The Prime Minister of New Zealand, George Coates, the Mayor of Wellington, G A Troup, and the president of the NZRFU Henry Manoy, sent the team off with a function at the Grand Hotel on 10 April and they sailed, first class, on the *Marama* on Friday 13 April 1928.

In his address to the team the Prime Minister said: "No team that has been selected to represent New Zealand has ever given to both public and press such satisfaction as the team we are honouring this evening. The people of New Zealand have every confidence in them."

And Maurice Brownlie assured New Zealand: "Whether we win or lose it will be our endeavour to bring nothing but credit to the Dominion."

After a rough voyage over the Tasman Sea, they changed to the *Euripides* in Sydney, trained as best they could every day on board and reached Durban on 21 May where a jazz band was playing "merry tunes". They were entertained by a burlesque group and enjoyed a rendition of "I'll be a Springbok till I die". They were supposed to sail on to Cape Town, but the good ship *Euripides* discovered a leak and the team was forced to go by train to Johannesburg and from there down to Cape Town for the first match two days later, 30 May. It was a long journey.

There would be many long journeys. When the SARB discussed this matter, they realised it was a lot to ask. But J D de Villiers observed that the 1924 Lions found "the travelling on our comfortable railways a god-send to them", as it "provided a rest for the team".

People, including General JC Smuts and Mrs Smuts, packed Newlands on a perfect Wednesday afternoon to watch the All Blacks beat Western Province Country, these days Boland except that they then included Paarl, 11-3, a dull match, not surprisingly after such a journey. On the Saturday 25 000 people, including the Earl of Athlone who was the Governor-General, packed into Newlands to watch them lose to Cape Town Clubs. Both teams scored a try but the Clubs got a dropped goal, not by Bennie Osler who was injured during the match but by Willie Rousseau who had been moved from the wing to centre.

The referee that afternoon was Theo Pienaar. But then the All Blacks met almost all the 1921 Springboks on their tour. One, Sarel Strauss, went with them wherever they went.

The All Blacks took the train on the 28-hour journey up to Kimberley and on the way came close to changing New Zealand rugby. They gave up the 2-3-2 scrum formation and decided on 3-4, still keeping the rover. The first attempt against Griquas was not convincing. After two attempts they reverted to their diamond formation. Scrums would be a problem for New Zealanders for decades to come.

They were unconvincing against Griquas on the grassless ground in Kimberley and lost their next match when they met Transvaal, the first touring team to play at Ellis Park. Mark Nicholls remarked on the vast height of the goal posts and the fact that they were painted white. In Pietermaritzburg they were also tall but painted in "huge bands of black and white".

It was not the only remarkable feature of the match. Right in front of the Grand Stand Manie Geere and Bunny Finlayson came to blows, after which the referee, highly respected Jock Finlay, ordered the All Black off the field, though many thought his actions retaliatory and not the worst of the afternoon. Geere played on and the All Blacks were no match for Transvaal.

Finlayson's great-grandson also played for the All Blacks against the Springboks – the great Ian Jones of the Nineties.

Two defeats in four matches were not a great start to the tour, even making allowances for the strenuous travelling they were doing.

Then they won the next four in a row, starting against Orange Free State in Kroonstad.

The All Blacks went back to Johannesburg and beat Transvaal, minus Manie Geere, 5-0. Geere's absence did not mean a chummy match. Lionel Rabinson, the referee, was obliged to give both captains a stern warning.

The victory greatly heartened the All Blacks. Maurice Brownlie said: "We have now found our feet. We have overcome the altitude and we should go on improving in each match. I feel sure that we will have a successful tour."

On 30 June 1928 the All Blacks and the Springboks met for the first time on South African soil, and they did so on a cricket ground – Kingsmead in Durban, at a time when there was no King's Park. The score that day was not a cricket score but big enough to be a record. Mark Nicholls called the match "a total eclipse".

New Zealand, for reasons which are still mysterious, left out Mark Nicholls. He believed that he was the victim of a South Island clique. Others believed that his coarseness had told against him. In contrast South Africa chose Bennie Osler, who is still a legendary tactical kicker. He used them all – the punt for the line, the place, the drop at goal, the grubber, the diagonal kick, the cross-kick and the kick back into the box.

The man who kicked off the first-ever test between South Africa and New Zealand on South African soil was Maurice Brownlie, captain of New Zealand.

Bennie Osler was at his best at Kingsmead and a less resolute group of rugby players than the proud All Blacks would have suffered a bigger hiding. It was nonetheless 17-0, still South Africa's biggest victory over New Zealand and that was despite having to play the whole of the second half without Brooke Duffy, who was injured early in the first half. New Zealand, thrashed 36-16 in the scrums, were simply not in the game but they had one hero – Dave Lindsay at fullback.

That day majestic Bennie Osler set a world record for a test by scoring 14 points. He kicked two dropped goals and two penalties. Jack Slater on the wing scored the only try, a fine one when Osler went round the blind side. Osler had the advantage of playing behind a dominant Springbok pack who confidently chatted amongst each other during the match.

There was no doubt that the Springboks were the better side and that the All Blacks were courageous.

The match was to have been broadcast by wireless and there was national upset when it did not happen, supposedly because the post office would not allow the wireless station use of their facilities. The outcry worked, for the other three tests were broadcast. The first-ever broadcast of a rugby match had happened in South Africa and the pioneer of such broadcasting was Archie Shacksnovis, himself no slouch as a player.

The amount of rail travel the All Blacks did was enormous. They went from Durban on the Monday after the first test and arrived in Kimberley on the Thursday. On the way they had just over a day in Bloemfontein when they went shooting. They left Kimberley on the Sunday, spent time in Mafeking which still had significance as the place of the siege in the Anglo-Boer War, and arrived at Victoria Falls on the Wednesday. From there they went back to Bulawayo and then back to Johannesburg. After the Western Transvaal match the All Blacks left Potchefstroom at 2.40 a.m. and reached Johannesburg four hours later.

They drew with Northern Provinces in Kimberley and then had an easy win over Rhodesia. The All Blacks loved Rhodesia, especially the Matopos with its rugged grandeur and cheeky baboons, the grave of C J Rhodes, the "great Empire builder", the Shangani Memorial and World's View. The Victoria Falls were thrilling and the victory over the hospitable, enthusiastic Rhodesians easy even on the red dirt of the Athletic Ground in Bulawayo. They headed for the second test in good spirits.

At Ellis Park, the All Blacks were a different proposition from the first test. Johannesburg had an attack of test fever. A huge crowd turned out, some coming from Nairobi. J B M Hertzog, the Prime Minister, J H Hofmeyr, the Administrator of the Transvaal, and Sir W Solomon, the acting Governor-General, were there.

Both sides were fit. New Zealanders would claim that the All Blacks were confident, the Springboks overconfident. Each side scored a penalty goal and each side scored a dropped goal but the All Blacks won 7-6, which may sound odd. In those days there was a thing called a Goal from a Mark, and that counted three points whereas a goal dropped in general play counted four points.

Phil Mostert, a forward remember, kicked a dropped goal from a mark 40 m out and South Africa were leading 6-3 when, with ten minutes to go, Archie Strang got the ball from a scrum and from an acute angle, let fly with the drop that won the match, and left the series squared at 1-1.

Till we meet again!

The great difference in the All Blacks was in the scrummaging where they decided to use Ron Stewart, normally a loose forward, as a loose-head prop. The All Blacks would go down in their funny 2-3-2 formation

42

and then Stewart, the rover, would get down as a loose head, at a time when all players in the front row were considered hookers. Writing in 1958 Winston McCarthy said: "There's no doubt in my opinion that the two-fronted scrum is a much better, much more compact scrum – a better scrum – than the three-fronted scrum." New Zealand, it seemed, were the only country in step!

Charlie Lambe of Transvaal wrote after the match: "Test matches are not always spectacular because of the policy to sacrifice open tactics to the spirit to win at all costs. But this was carried to an extreme by the Springboks yesterday, and appeared to be uppermost in their minds, more especially after the sides had crossed over. The result was that these tactics, beside sounding the death-knell of spectacular play, proved South Africa's undoing. Like bad investors they speculated on a very narrow margin – sat on their lead, but sat too long." It may sound only too familiar a lament. The Springboks tried to step up the level of their activity but it was too difficult and too late.

In much better heart the All Blacks reeled off six successive victories as they went about their travels, including a thriller against Orange Free State in Bloemfontein.

There was a big crowd at the Ramblers Ground that day, and in the trees around about and on the roof of the Presbyterian Church. The All Blacks won 15-11, but the home side gave a good account of itself and could have won, though the All Blacks were upset with Hennie Potgieter's try. The mobile lock also kicked a penalty goal and a conversion. Playing scrum half for Free State that day was Bram Fischer, their "brainy and plucky" scrum half, later a leading member of the Communist Party in South Africa. He was the grandson of a former Prime Minister of the Orange River Colony and played for Orange Free State first when he was little more than 19.

And so they came to the friendly but windy city of Port Elizabeth for the third test. They had an easy win over Eastern Province and then came the test. Seven thousand people came by special trains from the surrounding towns. Up they all went to leafy St George's Park where the Crusader Ground was. For some the trees provided a good and cheap view as the two teams lined up, each giving a war cry.

This time Bennie's boot was quiet but the Springboks scored three tries to two and won 11-6 in a fast match played in excellent conditions.

Phil Mostert broke from a line-out and led a frantic Springbok dribbling rush downfield and when Carleton passed to Lindsay, who was under severe pressure, the ball bounced off the fullback's shoulder and

43

Philip Nel fell on it for the opening try, which Osler converted. Manus de Jongh with a broken nose got a try while the All Blacks scored two for the half-time score of 8-6 to South Africa. Both sides had good chances to score in the second half but only the Springboks did, when they wheeled a scrum on the All Black line and George Daneel fell on the ball for the try.

It was, as a spectacle, the best test between South Africa and New Zealand up till then and one of the best of all time.

Round the coast the New Zealanders went, stopping for a visit to the Cango Caves, an ostrich shoot and victory over South Western Districts in Oudtshoorn, before going on to Newlands for the fourth test of the series. To this day it is known as the Umbrella Test. The heavens opened on Newlands, the wettest of South Africa's rugby grounds by quite some way.

Before that they played Western Province in the Newlands mud and lost 10-3. The Western Province selectors did some bizarre things that day. At 11 a.m. they selected Bennie Osler and Pierre de Villiers as the halves. At noon they changed to Geoff Gray and Pinky Hill of UCT. Twenty minutes before the kick-off they got Osler and De Villiers down from the stand and told them they were playing.

New Zealand led 3-0 at half-time and then Osler took over.

Back the New Zealanders went to the Arthur's Seat Hotel in Sea Point. They had a week to think about things.

New Zealand made a significant change. For the first time in the series they brought in Mark Nicholls, and he celebrated his selection in style. In the weather it was a contest of two kickers, Mark Nicholls vs Bennie Osler, and Nicholls won hands down. Both sides scored a try, but Nicholls kicked two penalty goals and a dropped goal to Osler's conversion, and the All Blacks won 13-5.

The WPRFU tried to help in the wet. They mopped and spread sawdust. They tried to cover the schoolboys with tarpaulins, but the cold front left things sopping wet and miserable.

New Zealand had the wind when Osler kicked off and two Nicholls kicks took New Zealand to the Springbok line where Boet Neser penalised the home side and Nicholls gave New Zealand a 3-0 lead after three minutes.

Play seesawed and two All Blacks were warned, one of them Stewart who was again coming up to form the loose head. Bennie Osler kicked ahead, J C van der Westhuizen hoofed it on and fell on the ball ahead of Bert Grenside for a try at the posts. Osler gave South Africa the lead for the only time in the match.

A Mark Nicholls drop bounced back into the field of play and Robilliard picked up and nearly scored. Ian Harvey dribbled over the line and Jackie Tindall managed to flykick the ball away. Robilliard was pulled down inches from the Springbok line, and then, on the stroke of half-time, Nicholls kicked a penalty goal.

With the wind in the second half the Springboks attacked mightily but eventually the All Black forwards, on even terms in the scrums for the first time in the series, got back into the game. They broke from a line-out in a dribbling rush and Tuna Swain scored. Nicholls, who had started the scoring, ended it with a dropped goal from a scrum on the Springbok 25. The Springboks attacked for the last five minutes but the All Blacks held, to square the series.

And the toast was: Till we meet again.

After the match Nicholls wrote: "The game will always live as an example of what determination and confidence can achieve with the biggest odds facing a team." And Theo Pienaar, the 1921 captain and a touch judge that day, said: "We were beaten in all departments of the game by a side that proved in convincing manner that it was able to rise to an important occasion." And Maurice Brownlie said: "The result, I think, is a fair and happy one for both sides." And he added: "In all our matches we have found South Africans most worthy foemen."

There was an extra match afterwards, between the All Blacks and Southern Universities, played under New Zealand's restricted kicking laws and refereed by Jim Burrows, the All Black hooker. The match was a lot of fun, won 14-9 by the All Blacks, as about three thousand students sang intervarsity songs.

In the rain and wind on 7 September a large, cheering crowd said farewell to the All Blacks after three months in South Africa, and on 21 September, the *Ceramic* reached Albany in Western Australia. Finally on 9 October the All Blacks got home.

TOUR STATISTICS (SOUTH AFRICA ONLY)

P	W	D	L	Pf	Pa	Tf	Ta
23	16	1	6	353	153	67	18

TESTS

4	2	0	2	26	39	3	5

The series was drawn but the All Blacks' overall record was not as good as the Springboks' in 1921.

The New Zealand Touring Team of 1928:
H T Lilburne (Canterbury), S R Carleton (Canterbury), B A Grenside (Hawke's Bay), D F Lindsay (Otago), F W Lucas (Auckland), A C C Robilliard (Canterbury), C A Rushbrook (Wellington), T R Sheen (Auckland), L M Johnson (Wellington), N P McGregor (Canterbury), M F Nicholls (Wellington), W A Strong (South Canterbury), W C Dalley (Canterbury), F D Kilby (Wellington), G T Alley (Canterbury), C J Brownlie (Hawke's Bay), M J Brownlie (Hawke's Bay), J T Burrows (Canterbury), J Finlayson (North Auckland), S Hadley (Auckland), L H Harvey (Wairarapa), W E Hazlett (Southland), J Hore (Otago), R G McWilliams (Auckland), G Scrimshaw (Canterbury), E M Snow (Nelson), R T Stewart (South Canterbury), J P Swain (Hawke's Bay), E P Ward (Taranaki)

TOUR RESULTS

DATE	VENUE	OPPONENTS	SCORE
30 May	Newlands	Western Province Country	11-3
2 June	Newlands	Western Province Town	3-7
6 June	Kimberley	Griqualand West	19-10
9 June	Johannesburg	Transvaal	0-6
13 June	Kroonstad	Orange Free State	20-0
16 June	Johannesburg	Transvaal	5-0
30 June	Potchefstroom	Western Transvaal	19-8
23 June	Pietermaritzburg	Natal	31-3
30 June	Durban	South Africa	0-17

Date	Venue	Opponents	Score
7 July	Kimberley	Northern Provinces	18-18
14 July	Bulawayo	Rhodesia	44-8
21 July	Johannesburg	South Africa	7-6
24 July	Pretoria	Pretoria	13-6
28 July	Bloemfontein	Orange Free State	15-11
1 August	Burgersdorp	North Eastern Districts	27-0
4 August	East London	Border	22-3
8 August	King William's Town	Border	35-3
11 August	Port Elizabeth	Eastern Province	16-3
18 August	Port Elizabeth	South Africa	6-11
22 August	Oudtshoorn	South Western Districts	12-6
25 August	Newlands	Western Province	3-10
1 September	Newlands	South Africa	13-5

CHAPTER 5

A Champion at Last

Q.: What is the greatest team to leave New Zealand?

A.: The 1937 Springboks.

That joke originated in New Zealand and dates back to 1937. That year the deadlock was broken.

The Springboks of the Thirties were a mighty lot indeed, many of them still household names in South African rugby. According to one of them, Dr Danie Craven, they should never have lost a match. They did, of course, and he always blamed it on overconfidence.

They went to Australia, and lost there – to New South Wales a week before the first test, but they won both tests. In all they played eleven matches in Australia, the same number as Hannes Marais's Springboks in 1971, but then the 1937 Springboks went on to the main part of their tour – New Zealand where they played another 17 matches. Marais's team came straight home.

There had been pressure on the selectors to choose the Springbok team at the end of 1936, as had been done for the 1928 All Blacks, especially as there had been a Currie Cup tournament in 1936 and a North-South match had been played at Ellis Park at the end of the season. Instead, the selectors decided on trials at Newlands in April 1937.

Nearly a hundred players came to trials. Some 38 of them came at their own expense. Eventually Bill Schreiner took the selectors to the Civil Service Club and there they chose the 29 players for the big adventure of taking on New Zealand on their own fields. The team selected, the selectors went over to the Hotel Metropole and late that night announced the team from a balcony on the first floor. There were question marks against the fly halves and the centres. In fact the backs, ironically as it turned out, were regarded as being untalented, apart from Gerry Brand. And there was some surprise at the choice of aged Philip Nel as captain ahead of Danie Craven. Nel, who had been captain in 1933, became only the second captain to lead the Springboks in more than one season. There were just so few tests in those days.

The Springboks left from Durban on the *Ulysses* on 17 May 1937, seen off, amongst others, by Paul Roos, the 1906 captain who had sailed up from Cape Town to see them off. He said to them: "My final words to you are that you keep yourselves throughout the tour in the pink of condition, because you have a duty to perform, first to your hosts who have invited you there, and secondly to your own country, which is sending you overseas. The message I bring you from the South African Board is that you should go forth, my boys, and win your spurs."

To keep fit, the players did exercises, under the guidance of Lucas Strachan or Henry Martin, jogged, played cricket till they lost all three balls overboard, and stoked coal. Once six of them moved 69 tons of coal in four hours – or so the story goes. And there was much planning for the tour ahead and they chose a selection committee of Nel, Craven, Strachan, Boy Louw and Gerry Brand. The portly manager, Percy Day, had social and administrative duties to perform which did not have too much to do with the playing of the game. He was allowed to preside at selection meetings but did not have a vote. Oddly he did not even stay for the whole tour. He left the team to Alec de Villiers at Gisborne after buying a racehorse, which people said was the real purpose of his being on the tour. The team preferred Alec de Villiers!

They got to Fremantle on 30 May and had a series of three easy matches as they edged their way around the south of Australia in the land of Australian Rules. When they played in Adelaide, a crowd of 25 000 people watched a club match of Aussie Rules, but only 2 000 watched the Springboks play South Australia and even then they played while horse racing was broadcast over the loudspeaker system.

As with the Springboks of 1993, the 1937 Springboks found arrival in Australia's rugby country after the fleshpots of the land of Aussie Rules a rude awakening and they crashed to New South Wales 17-6 in the rain and the mud as the great Cyril Towers cut them to ribbons. In the tests Jimmy White, one of that special tradition of deadly Springbok tacklers, mowed Towers down early. They won the second test as well. In fact in this one they were well ahead till a Wallaby felled Pierre de Villiers and the rest of the game was on a war footing and ended with the Springboks only nine points ahead.

On 17 July 1937, the night of the second test at Sydney Cricket Ground, the Springboks set sail on the *Wanganella* for New Zealand where a nation was licking its lips as it lay in wait for the team that had not done too well in Australia. The Battle for the Crown was about to begin.

The welcome was enthusiastic as they arrived but they did not have a gradual introduction. On 24 July they faced Auckland.

The Springboks started the New Zealand campaign with a prophetic thrashing of Auckland at densely packed Eden Park – 19-5, five tries to one – and all of New Zealand trembled, as well they might. The Springbok backs, especially Louis Babrow, were magnificent.

But soon they were brought down to mud. From firm Eden Park they went down to Rugby Park in Hamilton, and the sort of conditions that laid low the next Springboks to visit New Zealand, in 1956. There they played a combination of Waikato, King Country, where there was a little boy called Colin Meads, and Thames Valley. They won. Each side scored a try but Freddie Turner added a penalty goal, and the match ended with the Springboks defending their three-point lead desperately and grateful when the home team miscued a fairly easy penalty kick which could well have levelled the scores.

Down they went to the southwest corner of North Island, to play Taranaki where the men of 1921 had played a pointless draw. This time the Springboks opened the new Rugby Park with Mount Egmont's classic cone rising quietly and snowcapped over the hedge on the hillock to the left of the main stand. The captain of Taranaki was Jack Sullivan, who was to play such a prominent rôle in New Zealand's rugby and in relations between the two countries. On this occasion he was an enterprising centre who snapped up whatever trifles the Springboks left unconsidered. Before the war he was offered a contract to play rugby league for Bradford Northern for what was then a huge sum – £5 000. Well, it was a huge sum – enough to buy five big houses in Cape Town at the time.

But as far as score went it was a comfortable win for the Springboks in a fast match. Yet again, as in 1928, scrummaging was proving decisive. The Springboks won the scrums 37-9, an incredible difference and an impossible one in modern rugby. But New Zealand took heart because the moderate Taranaki pack had beaten the Springboks in other aspects of play. Again the Springbok backs were too good for their New Zealand opponents.

There was nought for New Zealand's comfort in the next match when the Springboks travelled east to Palmerston North and produced a remarkable display at the Showgrounds, beating Manawatu 39-3, six tries to one, on a heavy ground with Craven at centre and Flappie Lochner at scrum half, which seemed a weird arrangement. In fact they changed places at half-time when the score was 3-0.

Down they went to Wellington, coached by Mark Nicholls. They were received by the Prime Minister, Michael Savage, other members of government and sportsmen, including 52 former All Blacks.

The match at Athletic Park, watched by 30 000 people, played on a firm ground on a windy afternoon, was a triumph for the Springboks. They won 29-0, six tries to nil, and D O Williams scored a hat trick.

The whole of New Zealand was in panic with the first test a week away. Only a mindless patriot would have bet on the All Blacks. But those men patriotic enough to bet on the All Blacks would nevertheless have had good reason to, for nothing in sport is predictable and secondly because the Springboks are the world's worst favourites. The All Blacks, expected to win, will usually do so. The Springboks, expected to win, will regularly and sometimes spectacularly not do so.

Every one of the All Black backs was making his debut. The Springboks went up to Masterton in miserable weather and came back to Wellington miserable. Wellington too turned miserable and the Springboks did funny things with selection.

They chose Craven at fly half and captain and, shades of 1921 and 1981, left out their skipper, Phil Nel. Gerry Brand, the star of the team, was crocked and Freddie Turner played fullback.

Each side scored a try, but the All Blacks deserved their 13-7 victory.

The day was wet. The crowd was enthusiastic and the All Black forwards were magnificent. For most of the match they played with only seven forwards and how those men marauded! Behind that pack Dave Trevathan outplayed Craven who looked ponderous.

After a Trevathan penalty goal, the Springboks missed a couple but they first scored a try when D O Williams beat three men on a 25-yard run for the corner. New Zealand went ahead 6-3 when Jack Hooper broke away and slick play ended with John Dick scoring in the corner.

There was no doubt that the All Blacks were the better side. Their forwards had terrorised the bigger Springboks and Trevathan had done unto South Africa as Bennie Osler had done unto New Zealand.

In a three-test series, defeat in the first test leaves a side, especially the visitors, with a massive hill to climb. The Springboks in their next match, against mediocre opposition at Blenheim on the north of South Island looked as if they had no heart for the climb. The stuffing had been knocked out of them.

Their next match was against redoubtable Canterbury, conquerors of

51

the 1921 side. In fact they had not lost to a touring team for fifty years. This time the Springboks came good. The forwards were wonderful and Tony Harris, so fast off the mark, was brilliant at fly half. In fact this match made the tour. The Springboks recovered and won 23-8, a hiding in those days.

Over the Springboks went to Greymouth and a strange occurrence. It is not unusual for opposing captains to shake hands, but usually it is before and after the match. This time it happened during the match. Philip Nel was captaining South Africa and Ron King, the All Black captain, was captain of the West Coast-Buller combination. During the match Nel objected to a headlock that King put on him, and the two captains had words. The referee, A B Rowlands of South Canterbury, got the two of them to shake hands.

South Canterbury were a tough proposition in Timaru on a day when Boy Louw, most loyal of Springboks, played hooker to give Jan Lotz a rest. The Springboks won easily, but it took time and effort to get on top.

There was a week till the second test in Christchurch and most of the team went up to Mount Cook.

This time the Springboks picked a more sensible team. Craven was at scrum half with Tony Harris at fly half and Nel was back in the pack and restored to leadership.

This time the Springboks were tense and focused. They were down 6-5 after Jack Sullivan had scored two tries. Ron Rankin was laid out and Boy Louw was so concussed that he was almost useless and spent the rest of the match giggling, collapsing in the tunnel on his way to the dressing room after the match, while Ebbo Bastard was also weakened by a bump on the head.

Then the referee penalised New Zealand and Philip Nel gave the ball to Gerry Brand with the instruction for him to "make a plan". He goaled it and South Africa led 8-6. They also scored next when Bastard picked up a wayward pass meant for Louis Babrow and dived over. South Africa won 13-6.

One left and all to play for.

In 1921 the Springboks went to Invercargill to play Southland and they were the holders of the Ranfurly Shield. The same was true in 1937.

The match in 1937 was strangely out of character with the nature of the game and the scores of the day. Both teams threw the ball around and Southland scored more points against South Africa than any other New Zealand team. They scored 17 points. They lost because South Africa scored 30, but the game was immense fun.

Up the South Island the Springboks came to fanatic Dunedin and Otago, where the street signs are in blue and gold because those are Otago's colours. Otago had lost the Ranfurly Shield to Southland while the Springboks were in New Zealand. Again the ground was hard, South Africa was enterprising and Otago were not negative. The Springbok victory was massive – 47-7. The Springboks were cheerfully and confidently riding the crest of the wave.

And so the Springboks left South Island, crossing over Cook Strait from Lyttelton to Wellington and then travelling up by train to Napier on the south of Hawke's Bay. There they played Hawke's Bay in a tough match in which Craven's skill saved the Springboks' hides and the Springboks won 21-12. They played badly in their next match when Poverty Bay, Bay of Plenty and East Coast combined to form opposition, but they won 33-3 at Gisborne.

Then came the crucial third test.

In the history of tests between South Africa and New Zealand there have been two that have stood out as watershed matches, outstanding in their decisiveness. The first of those two was the third test played at Eden Park, Auckland on 25 September 1937. The second was played at Ellis Park on 24 June 1995.

The tension of the week before the third test in 1937 was at breaking point. There was speculation, hope and anxiety. Philip Nel wondered if test rugby was really worth it "because of the strain imposed on the men and the exaggerated importance of victory". And there were loads of advice. The most famous piece of advice to reach the Springbok camp came from Paul Roos, a cable with three words: SCRUM, SCRUM, SCRUM. Which is what the Springboks did, opting for scrums instead of line-outs as the laws of the day allowed. It worked for them on the day, despite incurring a rash of scrum penalties.

In 1928 strict Maurice Brownlie gave his men the week off prior to the crucial fourth test, and it worked. Philip Nel made his 1937 side work hard, mentally and physically – and it worked.

During the week Louis Babrow came to the Springbok selectors and told them that he could not play, at a time when injuries were a plague. One who would not be able to play was powerful Jimmy White.

They asked Babrow where he was injured.

He explained that he was not injured. That week there would be Yom Kippur, the most sacred day in the Jewish calendar, when Jews would not play sport.

The Springboks were aghast. Injuries apart, Babrow was their most potent weapon at centre. They explained their problem and told him to think again.

Back he came later and said: "I'm a Jew, aren't I?"

They agreed and felt that that was what was creating a problem for the present.

He said: "I'm a South African, aren't I?"

They agreed but were unsure of the depth of his patriotism.

He said: "No, hang on. That means I am a South African Jew. The game will be over before Yom Kippur starts in South Africa. I'm playing."

He played all right, and with him in the centre was Flappie Lochner instead of Jimmy White, the only change in the team that had won the second test.

The All Blacks made two changes to their backs. Back from injury came Brushy Mitchell, and Pat Caughey came in on the right wing while Jack Sullivan switched to the left. The only change to their pack was young Ron Ward of Southland for Rankin. Some thought it strange that they were more worried about the backs than the forwards when the forwards had been the ones beaten at Lancaster Park.

It was not the best of days for running rugby on slippery Eden Park but it was also not a day of clinging mud. The Springboks were determined to run. It would be hard to find a better team performance in tests between the two countries. Behind their magnificent pack the Springbok backs were full of verve and ideas. They said of Gerry Brand that he missed kicks, but never an important one. Kicks were not important this day and he managed only one.

Dave Trevathan scored two penalties for New Zealand who were never really in the game as the Springboks swung in with five tries, every one a gem.

A few minutes after the start Lochner went slashing between Hooper and Mitchell about 25 yards out and Babrow flashed over for the first try.

Again the backs were in action and Babrow slashed through, swerving out to the right touchline. He cross-kicked and the ball bounced over the New Zealand goal line where any of several Springbok forwards could have scored. The one who actually did was Ferdie Bergh whose record as a try-scorer for South Africa was eventually broken by John Gainsford. Brand converted and the Springboks led 8-0.

The Springboks kept on running and the All Blacks battled to keep D O Williams out.

Half-time came and the Springboks led 8-3.

During the week preceding the test, there was a fever of anxiety throughout New Zealand. Much was made of the Danie Craven dive pass, in the same vein as the panic in South Africa about Jonah Lomu's power before the World Cup Final in 1995. The length of his pass was a source of wonder.

The second half had not been long under way when the Springboks opted for a scrum instead of a line-out. Craven signalled Harris away. Harris moved wider. Dave Trevathan moved out to mark him. Craven signalled wider still. Harris moved out farther. Trevathan went with him. Craven signalled again with an impatient gesture. Harris shrugged his shoulders and went out a lot wider. Mystified, Trevathan followed him.

Craven fed the scrum. Jan Lotz heeled. Craven picked up and flipped the ball to Freddie Turner who came racing in from the blind-side wing. There was a huge gap for him and he went slashing through it. Flappie Lochner jumped to take his lobbed pass and he fed Babrow who raced for the line, dived and scored in the corner. 11-3.

Five minutes later Williams went down the left wing with his pumping knees and past three All Blacks to make the score 14-3. The crowd at Eden Park was silent. Afterwards the *Auckland Star* reported: "It was a great match. Never before has Eden Park held such a tremendous crowd. But it was a crowd without inspiration, without enthusiasm. There was a tumult of shouting when the teams took the field, there was half-hearted enthusiasm until South Africa scored the first try. Thereafter the great crowd watching New Zealand beaten time and again for possession, became as lifeless as the New Zealand pack itself."

Babrow should have passed with two men outside him and was tackled by Jack Taylor. Lucas Strachan picked up and hurled a long pass to Freddie Turner who scored in the corner. 17-3.

Trevathan goaled his second penalty six minutes from the end, and that was that.

It was an astonishingly easy win, something like New Zealand's victory in the fourth test in 1965 – complete and glorious.

At the end of the match, Harry Simon, the All Black scrum half, came to Louis Babrow and said: "I believe you're a bloody Jew?"

Babrow, already tender in conscience, was about to act in anger when Simon said: "So am I."

Oddly there was one more match to play – up in the mud against North Auckland, now Northlands, at Whangarei. And it was the donkey cart after the Lord Mayor's show, even worse, for although the home side was reputedly weak, there was the worst fighting of the tour and the Springboks won 14-6. The tour was over.

The deadlock had been broken. For the first time in three series there was a winner. But the toast would always be, Till we meet again. The links that had been forged would be special and they would become closer again through war.

TOUR STATISTICS (NEW ZEALAND ONLY)

P	W	D	L	Pf	Pa	Tf	Ta
17	16	0	1	411	104	87	17

TESTS

3	2	0	1	37	25	8	3

The South African Touring Team of 1937:
G H Brand (Western Province), F G Turner (Transvaal), D O Williams (Western Province), P J Lyster (Natal), J A Broodryk (Transvaal), A D Lawton (Western Province), L Babrow (Western Province), J L A Bester (Western Province), S R Hofmeyr (Western Province), J White (Border), D F van de Vyver (Western Province), T A Harris (Transvaal), G P Lochner (Eastern Province), D H Craven (Eastern Province), P du de Villiers (Western Province), M M Louw (Western Province), S C Louw (Transvaal), H J Martin (Transvaal), C B Jennings (Border), J W Lotz (Transvaal), P J Nel (Natal), A R Sherriff (Transvaal), M A van den Berg (Western Province), W F v R v O Bergh (Transvaal), W E Bastard (Natal), B A du Toit (Transvaal), L C Strachan (Transvaal), G L van Reenen (Western Province), H H Watt (Western Province).

TOUR RESULTS

Date	Venue	Opponents	Score
24 July	Auckland	Auckland	19-5
28 July	Hamilton	Waikato- King Country- Thames Valley	6-3

DATE	VENUE	OPPONENTS	SCORE
31 July	New Plymouth	Taranaki	17-3
4 August	Palmerston	North Manawatu	39-3
7 August	Wellington	Wellington	29-0
14 August	Wellington	New Zealand	7-13
18 August	Blenheim	Nelson-Golden Bay-Motueka-Marlborough	22-0
21 August	Christchurch	Canterbury	23-8
25 August	Greymouth	West Coast-Buller	31-6
28 August	Timaru	South Canterbury	43-6
4 September	Christchurch	New Zealand	13-6
8 September	Invercargill	Southland	30-17
11 September	Dunedin	Otago	47-7
15 September	Napier	Hawke's Bay	21-12
18 September	Gisborne	Poverty Bay-Bay of Plenty-East Coast	33-3
25 September	Auckland	New Zealand	17-6
29 September	Whangarei	North Auckland	14-6

CHAPTER 6

War Again

THE ALL BLACKS were scheduled to tour South Africa in 1940. Lots and lots of them went to Africa at that time, but to the north. The tour was cancelled because of World War II.

South Africans also went Up North, as the war zone was called. The two countries met and inevitably rugby football broke out.

There is a lot of free time, even at times of battle. There is even more free time in pubs, and there is seemingly endless free time in prisoner of war camps. And when they had free time South Africans and New Zealanders played rugby, amongst themselves, against each other and against others. And for many they were test matches.

There was also The Book. It was a joke and a misnomer, but famous nonetheless. "Who wrote the book?" they would ask. The South African version of the book would show a fine physical specimen of a South African soldier teaching puny and moronic New Zealanders the game of rugby football. The New Zealanders retaliated with their version, in which a fine physical specimen of a Kiwi would teach puny and moronic South Africans the game. It made for good fun and camaraderie. The South Africans and New Zealanders got on much better than they did with anybody else, including the Australians. South Africans and New Zealanders would meet in pubs and soon a scrum would develop. They scrummed bars to bits from Benghazi to Bologna and on to Brighton.

And then there were more formal matches, especially in Egypt and Italy between teams of South African and New Zealand divisions. Leading South Africans in these matches were Louis Babrow, Ebbo Bastard, Jimmy White and Pat Lyster of the old brigade and Felix du Plessis, Cecil Moss and the Fry brothers of the brigade to come.

In November 1941 the 2nd New Zealand Expeditionary Force beat the South African Division 8-0 at Bagguish. They played in the sand with manned anti-aircraft guns keeping watch over them. The South Africans complained that, contrary to the agreement, the New Zealanders played in boots while they were barefooted. The referee that day was Father Jesse Kingan of the Marist Fathers in Wellington.

At about that time the Second Echelon left New Zealand for the Middle East, but because Italy had entered the war and there was a real threat that Britain would be invaded, they were diverted to England. En route they stopped off at Cape Town and under the captaincy of Eric Tindill, the double international whom the Springboks would meet in unhappy circumstances in 1956, they lost 9-6 to Combined Universities at Newlands. Interestingly, there was playing for Tindill's team one Frank Solomon, an All Black in 1931-32, the last of the wing forwards or rovers – that New Zealand invention when they packed 2-3-2 and had a rover standing out. That was not what made Solomon's appearance on Newlands turf unusual. What did was that he was born in Pago Pago, Samoa. He played for the Maoris in 1927. He would not have been allowed to play in South Africa for the All Blacks of 1928, 1949 or 1960.

In June 1942, shortly before the fall of Tobruk, Louis Babrow captained a South African team that lost to a New Zealand team, captained by Jack Sullivan at Maadi about nine miles from Cairo, where the 2nd New Zealand Expeditionary Force had encamped in February 1940. In the match Pat Lyster was injured and Jack Sullivan, who was marking Louis Babrow, so badly injured that his rugby career came to an end. The South Africans in turn won at Qassasien in December that year, the dates suggesting that rugby was more important than the formality of having seasons.

Weakened by the departure of the South African 6th Division for battle in Italy, the South Africans nevertheless engaged in a test series with England, Wales and New Zealand for the rugby crown of the Middle East.

The South Africans were not expected to do well. But they had Attie van Heerden as a selector and Charlie Newham as their captain. Before 18 000 spectators on a field at Alamein, they beat the Artillery School and then went on to beat England and New Zealand before drawing with Wales which led to a decider which South Africa won 9-6. The best-known player on the South African side was Billy Anderson, one of the greatest players of his age and one of the best never to have played for South Africa.

The Springboks were the Champions of the Middle East.

But in February 1943 the New Zealanders beat the Rest of Egypt 10-3 in the Municipal Stadium in Alexandria, and there were eleven South Africans in the Rest team. Earlier they had thrashed the Rest of Egypt

22-0, a score that would have been higher except for the tackling of the South African fullback, one Van der Walt.

An interesting match took place in Egypt, one which could not have happened in South Africa. A New Zealand team played a team from the Cape Corps. The Cape Corps was made up of Coloured troops, all of whom were noncombatants, because nonwhites were not allowed to bear arms. They played the same New Zealand side that had previously beaten a South African side. The match was drawn 12-all.

In Rome Louis Babrow was doing much to organise rugby. Trials were held and on 30 December 1944 the South Africans beat a New Zealand 2nd Division team 8-3 at the Foro d'Italia. In the South African team were many good players including Springboks George Smith and Louis Babrow and the postwar Springbok captain Felix du Plessis.

In 1945 Bombardier M M Louw went scurrying around in a jeep with urgent orders from headquarters. The names, ages, weights, heights and playing histories of all promising rugby players in the various units were to be delivered to HQ as a matter of urgency.

The reason for this frantic rush was a dispatch from General (later Sir) Bernard Freyberg, VC, commander of the New Zealand Division, challenging the South African 6th Division to a rugby match – if they still played rugby.

Four days after Boy Louw's desperate journey 60 trialists moved into a hotel in Rapallo in Italy's lake district. They were soon being licked into shape with PT in the morning, coaching in the afternoon and a match practice every second day. Each man was given half a bottle of beer a day with an extra bottle on Wednesdays and Saturdays, supplies permitting. This training camp lasted a fortnight. The trials were held. Then the Kiwis came, with truck loads of supporters.

The referee was R E Prescott, the former England prop. South Africa, with future Springboks Cecil Moss and Stephen Fry, future Junior Springbok Hannes Morkel, the son of Gerhard Morkel of 1921 fame, and other notable players, won 30-5, and there was much talk about The Book that night. The Kiwis challenged again and the Springboks, as South Africa's troops were generally called, travelled this time, down to Florence where they again won, 23-3.

The 6th Division played other matches before meeting New Zealanders again, this time in England and this time the New Zealanders won 9-6. And then they played other matches till eventually they were allowed home from the war.

At that time New Zealand had a 2nd New Zealand Expeditionary Force team which played 33 matches in Europe, winning 29 with two draws and two defeats. They played England, Wales, and France, losing only to Scotland. Of their team, Charlie Saxton was a 1938 All Black and sixteen others later became All Blacks.

When they got home to New Zealand they played another five matches against provincial teams. Sadly they did not clash with the SA 6th Div. In that New Zealand team were Driver Bob Scott, Private Johnny Smith, the great centre who was barred from South Africa in 1949, Driver Wally Argus, Lieutenant Fred Allen, Major Charlie Saxton, debonair Sergeant Lachie Grant, Private Jack Bond, Lieutenant Neville Thornton, Corporal Eric Boggs, Trooper Jim Kearney, Lance Bombardier Ron Dobson, Private Bill Meates, Major Jack Finlay, MC, Trooper Kiwi Blake, Captain Pat Rhind, Private Johnny Simpson and Private Keith Arnold, who was called Killer because of his tackling.

New Zealand also chose a Combined Services team that played in London. Amongst others they played the South African Air Force. They included All Blacks in their numbers as well – Bob Stuart, Ray Dalton, Morrie Goddard, who twice played for England in wartime internationals, Roy Roper and Ian Botting.

There was also a remarkable tournament in Stalag IVb which housed some 700 South Africans amongst the 10 000 prisoners of war in the camp.

Leagues started by huts and then national teams. The South Africans held a trial match before their newspaper, the *Union Express*, announced the team which would be captained by Fiks van der Merwe, a fitness fanatic as his name suggests and a Springbok against New Zealand in 1949.

They made themselves jerseys with dye, bartered for chocolate in food parcels, and the simple clothing of the Red Cross parcels – green jerseys with a big golden Springbok on the badge.

Their first match was against the Anzacs whom they beat 21-0, and on they went to victory over England, Scotland and a combined team from England, Scotland and Wales. The deciding match for the championship was against Wales. So keen were the men to have smart Springbok jerseys for the match that they had to swop much chocolate for material to make them. As a result it was a physically weakened team which took the field for the big match which the South Africans won 3-0 through a try by Fiks van der Merwe.

It was, of course, astonishing to many Europeans that troops could stop fighting and take part in something that looked even more violent than warfare. And at one stage in Egypt a rugby match was used as a decoy two days before the Battle of Alamein. Louis Babrow was asked by the commander-in-chief by order from Field Marshal Montgomery to stage a game. Of course, once South Africans and New Zealanders got going, it was a real game, so real that to the Germans it seemed as if there were dissent in Allied ranks. The match was played behind the Alamein railway station and was watched by about ten thousand men.

While homogeneous New Zealand was united in fighting Hitler and Mussolini, there was division in South Africa between those supporting the war effort and those opposed to such support. This division was nasty in the Western Province and bitter in the Eastern Province. Major Danie Craven took a team of servicemen – prominent players, including Tony Harris, George Smith, Jimmy White, Jack van der Schyff, Billy Anderson, Felix du Plessis, Johnny Bester and Hannes Morkel – around the country in the hope and expectation that the spirit of rugby would triumph over the spirit of political divisions, but he was wrong. Rugby forged unity amongst like-minded people, not otherwise.

He tried to achieve the same again during apartheid times and many people believed that rugby, being so important in the fabric of Afrikaner life, would be able to destroy apartheid. They were wrong.

CHAPTER 7

Rugby at War

PEACE OF A SORT settled onto the world after Victory in Europe and then Victory in Japan. Soon battlefields were swopped for rugby fields.

As with the Anglo-Boer War, there were two Rugby Wars, the second more serious than the first. In all hostilities lasted from 1949 to 1956, with acrimony lingering beyond that.

Victory was important. War had told the world that. The winner took all. He had the moral high ground as well as fame, glory and spoils. The vanquished had nothing. *Vae victis*!

In 1949 the All Blacks came to South Africa with high hopes, regarded in New Zealand as a great side. They went home disgraced and bitter. A proud man will not stand being stripped and mocked. And furthermore they felt that the whole thing had been unjust.

Home the All Blacks went to their islands to seethe and nurse their wrath, feeding it and developing it into a powerful force, ready to be unleashed in 1956.

Boy Louw knew the importance of the conflict when he walked into the Springbok dressing room in 1949 to warn the Springboks that they were about to enter battle. The fight for the crown was on again, all over Southern Africa.

The All Blacks were to have come to South Africa in 1940, but could not. Then they were to have come in 1947 but asked for a postponement. In May 1948 they decided that at the end of that year they would choose a team to tour South Africa in May of the following year, which may well have been mistake number 1.

During 1948 they went through a series of no fewer than 16 trials. In April 1949 the Springboks had trials and picked a short list and got it wrong for July of that same year. The All Blacks may well have made mistakes in 1948 for 1949 as well.

New Zealand had, as is its custom, three national selectors but there

63

were also selectors for North Island and South Island. The selectors would have a busy year.

After the North Island-South Island match in Wellington, the chairman of the NZRFU, Alan Belcher, broadcast to the nation at 6 p.m.: "Here are the names you have been wanting to hear." And he read out the New Zealand team. Jim Parker was named as manager with Alex McDonald as his assistant. Both were former All Blacks.

Of the chosen team Wally Argus, the best of New Zealand wings, pulled out for business reasons and was replaced by Ian Botting.

The team assembled in Wellington on 8 April. The first match was on Union Day, 31 May. That may have been mistake number 2. They had six days to wait in New Zealand before they even sailed.

On 14 April they set sail on the *Tamaroa*, bound for Fremantle, for a match in Perth, and then Cape Town, which meant that they did not have to change in Sydney. On board Red Delamore and Neville Thornton tried to keep them fit and they polished up their version of McNamara's Band and performed *Sleeping Beauty* with Des Christian in the title rôle and Fred Allen, the captain, as Prince Charming.

They arrived in Cape Town on Tuesday 10 May, still three weeks ahead of their first match. That was undoubtedly mistake number 3.

They got a great welcome, amongst others from the Prime Minister, D F Malan, and the Mayor of Cape Town, Alderman C O Booth. More important from their point of view, they were met by Bo Wintle, the man who did his best to teach them to scrum and did it so well that they eventually outscrummed the Springboks. Originally when they set out, they believed that their scrummaging would be the equal of the South Africans', a false belief.

They went off to Hermanus, then a small holiday resort on the Indian Ocean east of Cape Town. Danie Craven believed firmly that the All Blacks lost it there, through succumbing to the good life. That was mistake number 4.

At Hermanus they spent an hour a day learning Afrikaans, possibly in view of the new Nationalist government, possibly to help them with Springbok calls on the field, possibly to improve their social activities.

From Hermanus they came back to Cape Town for some practice, several social occasions and sightseeing. Later the All Blacks would complain about refereeing but the All Blacks had made several mistakes before the tour even got under way.

There was vast enthusiasm for the start of the tour as the daily activities of the All Blacks were recorded, whetting the appetite for what was to

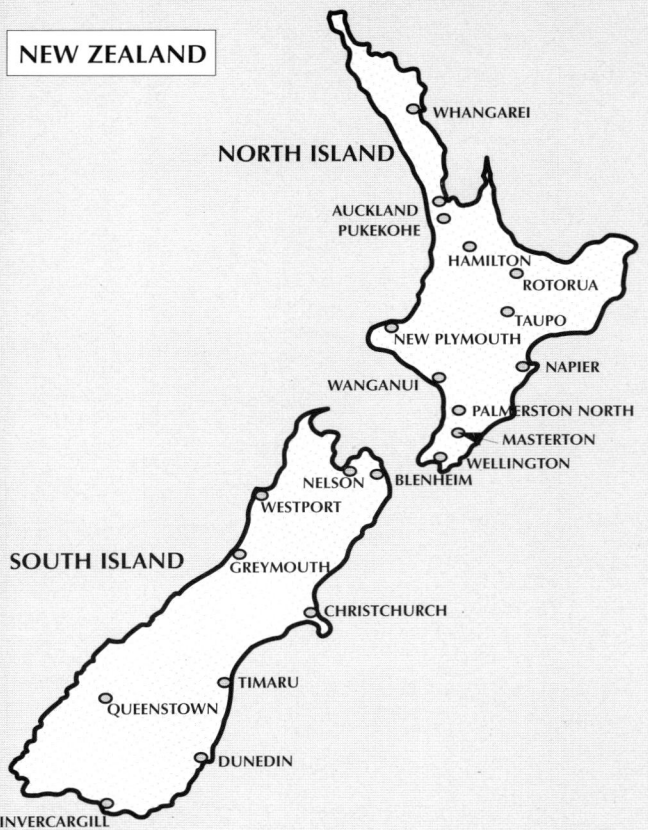

NEW ZEALAND

NORTH ISLAND

WHANGAREI

AUCKLAND
PUKEKOHE

HAMILTON

ROTORUA

TAUPO

NEW PLYMOUTH

NAPIER

WANGANUI

PALMERSTON NORTH

MASTERTON

WELLINGTON

NELSON

BLENHEIM

WESTPORT

SOUTH ISLAND

GREYMOUTH

CHRISTCHURCH

TIMARU

QUEENSTOWN

DUNEDIN

INVERCARGILL

The North Island is approximately 500 miles (770km) long.

It is roughly a thousand miles (1 500 km) from Cape Town to Johannesburg.

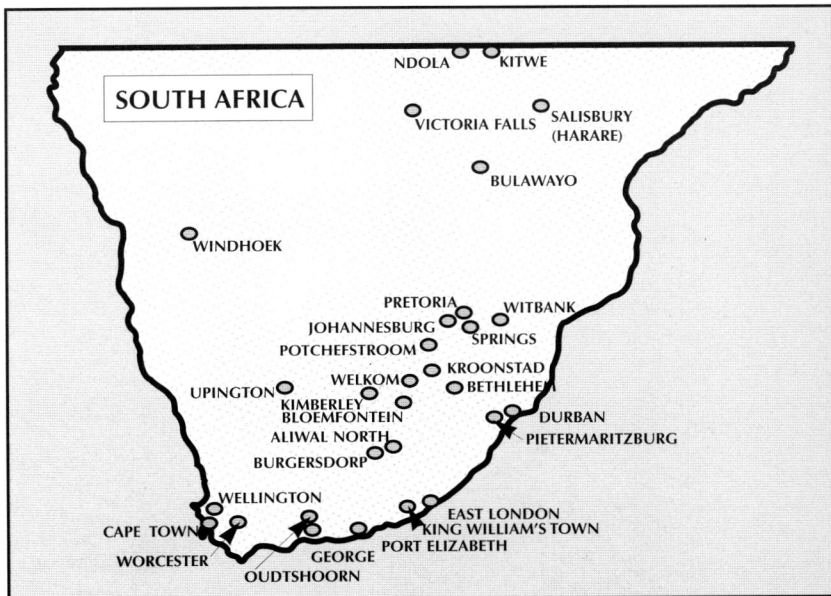

SOUTH AFRICA

NDOLA   KITWE

VICTORIA FALLS   SALISBURY (HARARE)

BULAWAYO

WINDHOEK

PRETORIA   WITBANK

JOHANNESBURG   SPRINGS

POTCHEFSTROOM

KROONSTAD

UPINGTON

WELKOM   BETHLEHEM

KIMBERLEY
BLOEMFONTEIN

DURBAN

ALIWAL NORTH

PIETERMARITZBURG

BURGERSDORP

WELLINGTON

EAST LONDON

CAPE TOWN

KING WILLIAM'S TOWN

WORCESTER   GEORGE   PORT ELIZABETH

OUDTSHOORN

Imperial Services Team on tour in South Africa in
1919
Back Row: Sgt A P Singe, Sgt A H West, Sgt A A Lucas,
Sgt S J Standen, Sgt D McK Sandman, Sgt W L Henry, Sgt H G Wittington, Sgt E A Belliss
Third Row: Lieut J E Moffitt, Sgt J A Bruce, Sgt A Gilchrist, Lieut G J McNaught, Staff-Sgt E J Naylor,
Sgt R W Roberts, Staff-Sgt E W Hasell, Staff–
Sgt E L J Cockroft, Sgt-Major J Ryan
Second row: Sgt J Kissick, Sgt E Ryan, Lieut E W King
(assistant manager), P W Day (SARFB representative), Lieut R W Baumgart (Manager), Staff-
Sgt C Brown, Staff-Sgt R Fogarty, Sgt L B Stohr
Front row: Sgt-Major J G O'Brien, Sgt M Cain,
Sgt W R Fea, Sgt W A Ford, Staff-Sgt P W Storey

Dave Gallaher, the first captain of the All Blacks in
1905, in the uniform he wore in South Africa during
the Anglo-Boer War.

The Springboks cross the Southern Alps, by carriage and on foot.

Everybody is friends at the end of the first test in 1921. On the left is the All Black captain, George Aitken, on the right Boy Morkel, the Springbok captain, and in the middle, biggest of the three, is the referee, Ted McKenzie.

Attie van Heerden, Olympic sprinter, goes waterskiing in the third test in 1921.

The boot that won the match. Mark Nicholls kicks New Zealand to victory in the Newlands wet in 1928.

Brothers in arms – Stan and Bennie Osler when they faced the All Blacks together in 1928.

A tale of two generals as Prime Minister J C Smuts meets Maurice Brownlie.

The 1937 touring team, the only team to have won a series between South Africa and New Zealand away from home.
Back row: T A Harris, D F van de Vyver, S R Hofmeyr, J White, A D Lawton, L Babrow
Third row: W E Bastard, J W Lotz, J L A Bester, G P Lochner, H J Martin, D O Williams, J A Broodryk
Second row: C B Jennings, S C Louw, M A van den Bergh, W F v R v O Bergh, G L van Reenen, A R Sherriff, B A du Toit, H H Watt
Seated: F G Turner, P J Lyster, P W Day, M M Louw, P J Nel, D H Craven, A de Villiers, G H Brand, L C Strachan
Front: P du P de Villiers

Danie Craven dives to set his backs in motion at Eden Park in 1937.

They led the Springboks in 1937 and they look worried about it: Danie Craven, Gerry Brand, Lucas Strachan, Boy Louw and Philip Nel

Johnny Dick scores for New Zealand.

All Blacks on the rampage as the Springboks scamper back in defence in the first tes in 1937. Tori Reid leads the charge as Craven, Pierre de Villiers, D O Williams and Jai Lotz are anxious to defend. The All Black on the left is Ron King, the captain.

Ferdie Bergh scores a try from a cross kick in the Springbok victory which stunned Eden Park and the whole of New Zealand in 1937.

come. And when it came, Parliament took the afternoon off so that members could go to Newlands. Things would not be all that different in 1995.

Their very first match was a rude awakening for the All Blacks. They played Western Province Universities at Newlands. Dennis Fry kicked off and for the first 22 minutes the All Blacks played expansive rugby to lead 11-0. The trouble was that they did not increase their score and by the end of the match were lucky to have a two-point lead which they had clung to for the last twenty minutes of the match. And there were people who believed firmly that Basil Butler had scored a try for the students by diving on a Fry diagonal kick ahead of Peter Henderson and they tried to use photographic evidence to prove Ralph Burmeister wrong.

It was an exciting match, and one man stood out for New Zealand, as he would throughout the tour, Bob Scott, the fullback. Time and again he hurled back the Universities' attacks. Time and again on tour he saved the All Blacks. Their record at the end of the tour was, by their standards, a poor one. It would have been, by any standards, an abysmal one had Bob Scott stayed playing rugby league and not been available for the All Blacks.

It was the last exciting rugby the All Blacks played till they had an unofficial match against Town Clubs at Newlands while waiting to sail away.

The All Blacks went inland to Koch country, to take on Boland with Chris and Willem Koch and relentless Piet Kriel in a heavier pack than the All Blacks' and tiny Mike Cronje, Buks Marais and Piet Neethling amongst the backs. On a glorious day the All Blacks won a dour match 8-5.

The early itinerary for the Forty-niners was much easier than that for the 1928 All Blacks. They simply edged their way east – to Oudtshoorn, where they played with the ostriches, received a kiwi made of ostrich feathers and visited the Cango Caves; then Port Elizabeth, where Morrie Goddard broke his wrist and a section of the crowd rioted; then East London after a nine-hour drive with a stop for lunch in Grahamstown; and then, after a stay-over in Kokstad where they laid a wreath on Ebbo Bastard's grave, Durban before turning left into the Transvaal. But it was not as simple a journey as it sounds.

In East London, they met Basil Kenyon, whom Danie Craven thought the greatest of all Springbok captains. Basil Kenyon of Transkei was captain of Border. Under him Transkei became the Border club champions, something unheard of and not to be repeated in post-Kenyon times. He was without a doubt a fine leader of men.

Border beat New Zealand 9-0 at the BRU Ground in East London on 15 June 1949, the biggest defeat ever of the All Blacks by a provincial team in South Africa, strange as it may seem.

65

After the match Jim Parker said: "The Border defence was the best I have ever seen in my life." Fred Allen said: "It was a magnificent game played in a magnificent spirit. We were beaten by the better side." And the Border president, A M Roy, whose nickname was Fatty, said: "I am speechless. The unexpected has happened."

Border had beaten the All Black pack and had tackled well after Jimmy White had spent time at practice teaching them to tackle. That was enough for victory.

Defeat was followed by a dull victory over Natal. Jim Parker blamed the mediocre performance on the hospitality and the humidity. That night the All Blacks called in Bo Wintle, an amiable man who had propped for Western Province from 1935 to 1944. They asked him to teach them how to scrum. They were out on the field being taught that same Sunday morning.

Their first opportunity to try out their new technique was against Western Transvaal, and already improvement was obvious. In fact it was the best All Black performance on the tour. Up till then they had been regarded as too bad to be true.

In Johannesburg they played a young Transvaal XV, captained by Piet Malan with his lifelong friend Pa Pelser on the other flank. Of those behind the scrum four would later play for South Africa. But their most important meeting, as later events would show, was with Eddie Hofmeyr, a young referee, who would remain a bogeyman forever in the history of New Zealand rugby.

This would be the first quiet shot in Rugby War I, its Sarajevo. It was a quiet shot as the All Blacks won 6-3, but they did find Eddie Hofmeyr pernickety.

Not all of their problems were Hofmeyr's fault by a long chalk. In the first half the All Blacks spent only four minutes in the Transvaal half and led 3-0 because they goaled a penalty.

In Kroonstad, where Danie Craven, who was following the All Blacks with keen interest as he prepared to coach the Springboks, helped the All Blacks with their scrumming, Bob Scott kicked nine points and the All Blacks drew with the Orange Free State. Then they went to Springs to play the recently founded Eastern Transvaal, and the Red Devils opened their account in splendid fashion by beating the All Blacks 6-5, two penalties to a goal – and the referee was blamed. There were 27 penalties in the match – 15 to New Zealand, 12 to Eastern Transvaal. But the referee, Tommy Stevens of Eastern Transvaal, ruled a forward pass when Boggs passed to Elvidge who went over in the last minute of the match.

Down they went to Newlands and Western Province. In 1924 Cove Smith's Lions beat Western Province. Since then the All Blacks, the Wallabies and the Lions had come that way and failed to lower the flag of South Africa's most tradition-rich province. This time the match changed lots of people's ideas.

The first test would be played at Newlands the week after the Western Province match. The selectors had their minds made up. The Springbok team was chosen but they would wait till after the Western Province match.

Province lost. The score was only 6-3 but the All Blacks were more convincing than that. Border and Eastern Transvaal had won but the mighty Western Province had lost. Gathering his selectors about him, Bill Schreiner took them off to the Olympic Sports Club in Rondebosch where they met in the privacy of the card room to pick their team. Out went Chum Ochse, Otto van Niekerk and Dennis Fry. Van Niekerk never did become a Springbok and Fry never played a test. Only three Western Province players made the side – big Ballie Wahl of the enormous pass, Bubbles Koch and Tjol Lategan in the centre.

When they announced their team, it was the first team of entirely new Springboks since the first test in 1891. Felix du Plessis's Springboks were all brand new.

What a day that was at Newlands! The whole of Cape Town had been in a fever of excitement in the week leading up to the test. Thousands queued through the night. The gates were shut and people scaled the old galvanised iron fences. When they could not see they got a ladder and climbed up onto the roof of the South Stand then popularly called the Malay Stand. When the police came to dislodge them they fought the police until forced to yield. Newlands was packed. In those simple, austere days after the war, rugby was a passion, a test an experience beyond thrill, a test match with the All Blacks an ecstasy.

Hannes Brewis kicked off for South Africa and within the first minute Jack van der Schyff missed a comparatively easy penalty kick at goal. As events turned out it was a significant miss, as were the others he missed in the first half, because Bob Scott got one over and Peter Henderson charged down a clearing kick by Van der Schyff for the All Blacks to be leading 8-0, a massive lead for the times, and a numbness grasped the spectators.

Just before half-time Felix du Plessis and Floors Duvenage were discussing who should take a possible penalty kick at goal when Lachie Grant was "miles off-side". Prop Okey Geffin from the Transvaal took the ball in his hands and, mesmerised, placed it for the kick at goal, a rôle to which he was not unaccustomed. He measured back his stride with care, hitched his shorts to his armpits and kicked the goal. There was a penalty again when Neville Thornton indulged in something New Zealanders call rucking and, surprisingly, Du Plessis gave the kick to Van der Schyff, who missed again. From a scrum Kearney dropped a sweet goal.

Half-time came and the score was 11-3. There was lots of gloom and despondency about Newlands.

Then came the famous/notorious second half. During that half, New Zealand did not score a point. South Africa crept up steadily, penalty by penalty, and all by Okey Geffin. It was excitement beyond life for the crowd, but, oh, the controversy it spawned!

The half was barely going when Eddie Hofmeyr penalised the All Blacks at a ruck after Ballie Wahl had chipped ahead for Cecil Moss. Geffin goaled. Eddie Hofmeyr penalised the All Blacks at a line-out, and Geffin goaled. 11-9. You had to be there to feel it as hope suddenly surged amongst the South Africans, and the New Zealand contingent sank into silent anger.

After Jack van der Schyff had barged Peter Henderson out at the cornerflag and Fred Allen had missed with a drop attempt, the Springboks attacked. Van der Schyff dropped. Johnny Simpson and Neville Thornton were on top of him and charged the attempt down. In those days there was none of the tolerance that said it was not a knock if it came off your hands in charging down a kick. In 1949 it was a scrum.

At that scrum the All Blacks were penalised and Geffin goaled. 12-11. It was time to throw arms and hats and anything else in the air. Policemen threw up their helmets and did handstands on the side of the field. The Springboks were leading.

Still it was not the end.

Bob Scott kicked at goal and the ball scraped past the right-hand upright. Let Winston McCarthy, who was there as a commentator, sometimes called the Screaming Skull, and ended up the cheerleader of New Zealand bitterness, describe what happened next as Tjol Lategan footed a dropped New Zealand pass towards their 25: "Boggs and Moss raced after the ball, and in his enthusiasm Boggs placed his hand on Moss for the Referee to quite rightly penalise the winger."

Eddie Hofmeyr said afterwards that he had considered a penalty try at the time. Fred Allen said that if he had awarded a penalty try he would have taken his team off the field. That would have been a pretty how-d'ye-do.

Geffin goaled and broke the world record – fifteen points in a test match. South Africa won 15-11.

Not that it was convincing. Not that the New Zealanders would accept any explanations that Eddie Hofmeyr might give. And not that they had seen the end of Eddie Hofmeyr.

In a grouchy mood the All Blacks headed for the Transvaal where the crowd threw bottles at the All Blacks. Jan Lotz made his final appearance at the age of 39 and outhooked Has Catley in a serious way. Catley was also a veteran at that stage. They had actually played against each other in 1937. Transvaal beat New Zealand in most measurable aspects of play but lost 13-3 and deserved to do so.

The All Blacks left that same Saturday evening for Rhodesia, reaching Bulawayo on the Monday morning. From there they went by train to Victoria Falls, getting there early on Tuesday morning. They wandered around and then got back on the train, arriving at Bulawayo on Wednesday morning. That afternoon they played Rhodesia.

Can you believe it? The All Blacks claimed that they were never the same again, and there was more travelling to come. But that stretch of four nights on the train was bizarre. They left straight after one match and arrived just in time for the next.

Coached by Roger Sherriff of the 1937 Springboks, Rhodesia won. Two of their stalwarts were men from the Western Province – Salty du Rand and the rejected centre Ryk van Schoor, both of whom were playing for Inyazura, both of whom would make their mark in international rugby. This was at a time when the Romsley Tobacco Company attracted good players and the club at Inyazura was powerful at a time when tobacco was booming in Manicaland. Ryk van Schoor made his mark on the All Blacks in 1949 and Danie Craven was there to see him do so. He laid into Fred Allen in jarring fashion while his centre partner Waldemar Brune of Mufulira made life a misery for Red Delamore.

There is no point in going all that way for one match. On the Thursday the All Blacks were back on the train, arriving at Salisbury on the Saturday. They left Salisbury again on the Sunday, suffered a collision in the middle of the night which flung them from their bunks and arrived in Pretoria in the early hours of Wednesday morning. Of eleven successive nights, they had spent three in beds and eight on trains. They may have had justification for their complaints! And Charlie Willocks had so injured his shoulder when he tumbled from his bunk that he had to miss the second test.

They did not win the second match against Rhodesia either. The grass was green but the sun was hot and the final score 3-all, thanks to a magnificent try by Bob Scott from five yards inside his own half.

Having got to Pretoria, the All Blacks were required to play, luckily for them, only on the Saturday. There was in this match an important first encounter. Jaap Bekker and Kevin Skinner met at Loftus Versfeld and already there was trouble, for which the referee penalised Skinner. Seven years later they would be at it again. The referee would be a different person from the penalty-happy Mr A C (Apie) de Villiers who was at Loftus Versfeld when the All Blacks beat Northern Transvaal.

Northern Transvaal were a good side, with Basie Viviers at fullback, Hansie Brewis and Fonnie du Toit as halves, Jorrie Jordaan and Jaap Bekker in the front row, Willem Barnard at lock, Louis Strydom and Fiks van der Merwe on the flanks and Ernst Dinkelmann at number 8. All of those were or were to be Springboks.

Brewis kicked a penalty goal and Northern Transvaal led 3-0. Scott kicked a penalty goal and the scores were level. Scott kicked another and the half-time score was 6-3. It was also the final score.

The second test was at hand. Second test, and the hairs on the neck started to rise. Two nations were enthralled at the prospect of the great battle at Ellis Park.

South Africa made significant changes in terms of the next few years. In came Fonnie du Toit at scrum half, Ryk van Schoor came in to centre, Salty du Rand for Fiks van der Merwe and Chris Koch to prop in place of Hoppie van Jaarsveld. All of the newcomers became remarkable Springboks. The other significant change was Ralph Burmeister as the referee. Tests one and three were dour; tests two and four were lively. Hofmeyr refereed one and three, Burmeister two and four.

An enormous crowd came to the old Ellis Park – 72 000 of them, paying £30 000, records for rugby union at that time. And this time South Africa beat New Zealand hands down.

New Zealand led 3-0 through a Bob Scott penalty. Geffin equalised. The next score was one of rugby's exquisite moments.

Remember New Zealand had a watertight defence. The great Hennie Muller dashed for the line but was tackled and a scrum formed 10 yards from the line, South Africa's ball. Fonnie du Toit passed to Hansie Brewis on the right and the fly half shaped to drop at goal. Jim Kearney moved in to block the kick. Brewis checked and in an electric shudder of genius swung round the back of the scrum to the left. He shaped to pass but there was nobody to pass to. He looked to stab a punt at the cornerflag and then there was a gap. Genius shuddered again, and he darted through the gap for 20 yards. As he placed the ball neatly over the goal line, the only All Black touched him, a tentative hand from Bob Scott.

It was one of the great fly-half tries, all the greater for being so surprising, as Piet Visagie's was in 1970.

At half-time the score was 6-3.

Chris Koch caught Larry Savage, and Salty du Rand snatched the ball free and gave it to Hennie Muller who passed to Hansie Brewis who straightened and gave Tjol Lategan the most sympathetic of passes. Lategan slid inside Bob Scott and was over to score in the left hand corner as spectators charged out onto the field to hug him.

Kearney kicked a drop when Brewis failed to find touch and the New Zealanders were only three points behind. Not to be outdone, Brewis added a dropped goal from a scrum. South Africa won more convincingly than 12-6 suggests.

The All Blacks went on, some to the Kruger Park, the rest to Pretoria where Morrie Goddard returned and they enjoyed a comfortable victory over Northern Universities.

They travelled to the Diamond City, and a tough 8-6 victory over Griqualand West and Morrie Goddard was again brilliant.

Then they went on a wander across the country. From Kimberley, the All Blacks went by train to Bloemfontein and then down to Aliwal North, and their biggest victory of the tour, 28-3 over North Eastern Districts.

They came back to Bloemfontein and an unflattering win over Orange Free State, and from there down to humid Durban, and Eddie Hofmeyr. For the third test the All Blacks again exercised their choice and again the All Blacks picked Eddie Hofmeyr to referee the test.

The All Blacks did a strange thing. They chose a fly half, Neville Black, at scrum half ahead of the two scrum halves on the tour – Bill Conrad and Larry Savage, neither of whom was up to scratch.

The Springboks picked a mammoth pack, certainly by the standards of those times. In came Flip Geel to lock and Bubbles Koch moved to flank. It was a match played in humidity by mastodons – not a thrilling spectacle, and again Eddie Hofmeyr was the centre of controversy.

Winston McCarthy said: "There is no doubt that the better team lost. Nevertheless it was one of the poorest International games that I have seen. Certainly the first half was brighter than the second, but I never wish to see again such purposeless rugby as was provided in the second spell. In-so-far as the New Zealanders were concerned, I have every sympathy with them in that they were 'scared' to do anything purposeful, but the Springboks, with two tests in hand and a lead of 9-3, should have been able to produce better Rugby had they been capable of doing so."

Geffin kicked three penalties to a try by Morrie Goddard. He had come into the team in the place of the captain Fred Allen who had been dropped. The score meant that the Springboks had won the series, the only time either of the teams had won three successive series.

The All Blacks went by *Pretoria Castle* back to East London, which they thoroughly enjoyed despite the drought, for the return match with Border, and humble Border did what humble Rhodesia had done – played the All Blacks twice without defeat. Having won the first, Border drew the second 6-all. It was exciting, the Border defence was magnificent and their display was rewarded with the selection of two of their players for the fourth test – speedy Carrots Geraghty on the wing and Basil Kenyon as Springbok captain.

The selection of Kenyon was a tough one, for it meant dropping Felix du Plessis, captain for the crucial first three tests and ending the great man's career, for though he played perhaps his best rugby in 1951 he was considered too old and not chosen for the marvellous tour to the UK, Ireland and France, for which Basil Kenyon was chosen as captain.

It was a short journey from friendly East London to friendly Port Elizabeth for the final test, the best match of the series, possibly because the frantic battle for the crown had, by then, been decided.

For the Springboks the final victory was success beyond their dreams. For the All Blacks, defeat was bitter – a whitewash followed by the long journey home to face recriminations.

Either side could have won the test and the backs got a grand chance to play. The All Blacks scored two tries, through Peter Johnstone, who opened the scoring in the match, and Ron Elvidge, who, with Bob Scott's conversion, closed the scoring for the series. Fonnie du Toit got the Springboks' only try. Hansie Brewis kicked a drop, Geffin a penalty and a conversion. South Africa won 11-8.

The All Blacks went round to Cape Town where they played a fun match according to the New Zealand kicking laws and allowing substitutions for injured players, which enabled Bob Scott to come on and rescue his side from defeat and force a draw. The gate money from the match went towards sending the South African athletics team to the Empire Games the following year.

Harry Frazer, the All Black lock, announced that he was going to marry Ethel Blythe of Johannesburg, whom he had met on the tour.

Then on 25 September 1949 the All Blacks sang "Now is the Hour", the South Africans sang "Sarie Marais", and the All Blacks sailed from Cape

72

Town on the *Dominion Monarch,* and Fred Allen added to ocean rugby memorabilia by dropping his boots overboard.

Whitewashed, the All Blacks still scored more tries than the Springboks in the series – four to the three of South Africa. The difference between the two teams was unfairly reflected by the 4-0 result in the series, a massive divide.

But there would be retribution as a proud nation gritted its teeth and girded its loins for the coming of 1956.

TOUR STATISTICS (SOUTH AFRICA ONLY)

P	W	D	L	Pf	Pa	Tf	Ta
24	14	3	7	230	146	43	8

TESTS

4	0	0	4	28	47	4	3

The New Zealand Touring Team of 1949:
J W Goddard (South Canterbury), R H W Scott (Auckland), E G Boggs (Auckland), I J Botting (Otago), R R Elvidge (Otago), M P Goddard (South Canterbury), P Henderson (Wanganui), W A Meates (Otago), F R Allen (Auckland), N W Black (Auckland), G W Delamore (Wellington), K E Gudsell (Wanganui), J C Kearney (Otago), W J M Conrad (Waikato), L T Savage (Canterbury), E H Catley (Waikato), D L Christian (Auckland), P J B Crowley (Auckland), R A Dalton (Otago), H F Frazer (Hawke's Bay), L A Grant (South Canterbury), L R Harvey (Otago), P Johnstone (Otago), M J McHugh (Auckland), J R McNab (Otago), N H Thornton (Auckland), C Willocks (Otago), N L Wilson (Otago)

TOUR RESULTS

Date	Venue	Opponents	Score
31 May	Newlands	Western Province Universities	11-9
4 June	Wellington	Boland	8-5
8 June	Oudtshoorn	South Western Districts	21-3
11 June	Port Elizabeth	Eastern Province	6-3
15 June	East London	Border	0-9
18 June	Durban	Natal	8-0
22 June	Potchefstroom	Western Transvaal	19-3
25 June	Johannesburg	Transvaal XV	6-3
29 June	Kroonstad	Orange Free State	9-9
2 July	Springs	Eastern Transvaal	5-6
9 July	Newlands	Western Province	6-3
16 July	Newlands	South Africa	11-15
23 July	Johannesburg	Transvaal	13-3
27 July	Bulawayo	Rhodesia	8-10
30 July	Salisbury	Rhodesia	3-3
6 August	Pretoria	Northern Transvaal	6-3
13 August	Johannesburg	South Africa	6-12

Date	Venue	Opponents	Score
17 August	Pretoria	Northern Universities	17-3
20 August	Kimberley	Griqualand West	8-6
24 August	Aliwal North	North Eastern Districts	28-3
27 August	Bloemfontein	Orange Free State	14-9
3 September	Durban	South Africa	3-9
10 September	East London	Border	6-6
17 September	Port Elizabeth	South Africa	11-8

CHAPTER 8

Referees

"WHEN YOU COME to us, we cheat you and beat you. And when we go to you, you cheat us and beat us." This was John Gainsford's simplistic view of contests between South Africa and New Zealand and he was expressing it in New Zealand.

Referees would protest, of course. They would claim honesty and objectivity. But it is a fact that visitors, regardless of where and the referee's origins, will be penalised more than the home team and that fifty-fifty decisions will go in favour of the home team.

It was ever so and there have ever been arguments about refereeing. After all the longest dispute at international level was that between Scotland and England, which started in 1884 and was not resolved till 1889.

It happened in the first test, back in 1871. It will happen in the last test – there will be complaints about referees. These complaints were certainly loudest in 1949, 1956 and 1976, but they have not been silent even in the days of "neutral" referees – not for those who remember Norling anyway.

South Africa was leading New Zealand 5-0 at Carisbrook in the first test between the two countries, in August 1921. The All Blacks were on the Springbok 25 when Ces Badeley kicked an up-and-under towards the Springbok goal posts. Gerhard Morkel moved back but allowed the ball to bounce and it bounced away from the big veteran. Charlie Meyer and Henry Morkel raced for the ball and dived. Moke Belliss, the Wanganui forward, also dived. The referee Ted McKenzie of Wairarapa in New Zealand decided that Belliss's dive was the successful one. Mark Nicholls converted and the scores were level.

The South African report on the match read: "The try scored by Belliss caused some dissatisfaction. With this exception the refereeing was very satisfactory. New Zealand was awarded 12 free kicks during the game, and the Springboks nine."

In the second test there was also a disputed try, but this time the Springboks won and the dispute was more muted.

Again South Africa was leading 5-0. Ted Roberts broke down the midfield and passed to Moke Belliss. Belliss was tackled but Les McLean picked up and scored. The dispute? In those days and for the next three decades, the ball after a tackle had to be played with the foot before the hands were brought into play. It sounds a cumbersome law but it did keep the players on their feet if they wanted to keep on playing, and playing the ball with the foot after the tackle and scooping it up in the same swooping movement became an art. The referee at Eden Park that day, Albert Neilson of Wellington, who had fought in South Africa during the Anglo-Boer War, awarded the try and New Zealand levelled the scores. The Springboks chose him to referee the third test nonetheless. He was later president of the Wellington RFU and secretary and treasurer of the NZRFU between 1926 and 1950.

The 1928 series was almost weird. There were no complaints at all about the refereeing, not in the tests anyway. One man refereed all four tests – V H Neser of Pretoria whose nickname was Boet or Noppies, who played cricket for South Africa and for many years after he had stopped refereeing held the record for a South African test referee – nine tests in all. Mind you, there was a belief in the Lions' camp in 1924 that he was a cheat!

Mark Nicholls even said of Lionel Oakley's refereeing in the Griqua match: "Mr Oakley, the referee, was never unduly severe and helped the game go ahead merrily to the evident delight of all." For the opposite reason he liked Jock Finlay less, for in the Transvaal match he "whistled no less than 200 times, 94 times for scrums, 75 line-outs and 22 penalties". Of the Western Transvaal match he said: "Mr. Nic J du Plessis, the 1921 Springbok forward, was the referee. He penalised us thirteen times and gave us one free kick. On two occasions he overruled the New Zealand touch judge and on another occasion he reversed one of his own decisions. He was extremely strict and kept a tight hold on the game." He had reversed his decision after awarding the All Blacks a "try" when he saw the touch judge with his flag up.

Nicholls observed at the end of the tour: "There are several differences in South African and New Zealand knock-on ideas. Our tendency is to be too liberal, and theirs is the very opposite."

That's all the sweet voice of reason.

On that tour the All Blacks were presented by the home union with a panel of three local referees from whom to choose. For the tests the Board gave them a panel of five for each test. They just kept choosing Boet Neser, who was later a judge.

There were no complaints in 1937 either when the Springboks went to New Zealand and won, no comments even about the refereeing. Obviously the referees are better when you win!

Then came 1949 and the start of real bitterness, as acrimonious, nasty and base as sporting acrimony can get.

In 1949, the Springboks won the test series 4-0, which meant that they had then beaten New Zealand six times in a row. That was not good for New Zealand and in fact the 1949 whitewash, while an interesting statistic, was not good for rugby between the two countries, first because the difference between the two teams was not really that great but most of all because the humiliation to New Zealand bred bitterness.

Travelling with that team as the official broadcaster was Winston McCarthy, a man of many words. His bête noire was Eddie Hofmeyr. The All Blacks' bête noire was Eddie Hofmeyr. As a result New Zealand's bête noire became South Africa and its rugby. When the 1956 Springboks got there New Zealand was on a war footing.

In 1949 South Africa won the first test 15-11 after being behind 11-3 early in the second half. New Zealand scored the only try of the match and added a dropped goal and two penalty goals. South Africa scored five penalty goals. Geffin kicked five penalty goals out of five.

The man to listen to is Winston McCarthy, the voice of the 1949 All Blacks. He dubbed the first test the penalty Test.

The scrum was in the eye of the controversy. It had in previous series been the All Blacks' Achilles heel. On this tour they tried hard to get it right, and they had an astonishing hooker in Has Catley. McCarthy claimed that Craven set the referees on Catley. "If a foot struck the ball before it was legitimately in the scrum it followed, naturally, that Catley must have been the culprit, even though both hookers 'had a go'. Yes, following Has Catley's success in this Test, he was a marked man."

It was probably the way Catley "hung" in the scrums, lowering his body to the ground, more than his footwork, which was the object of disapproval. Certainly he hooked in ways that would be regarded as bizarre and illegal today.

McCarthy spent a lot of time analysing the penalties in both tests. He had no complaints about three of them. "But there were two I could never agree with." And so he tabled his complaints and who said what. There was the penalty against Grant for obstruction when he swung out from the flank to help with the hooking in the front row, and another against the scrum half Savage well after Catley had heeled in the scrum. Then he complained about the award of the scrum when the ball became unplayable in a ruck/maul/pile-up.

After the third test, McCarthy again complained about two penalties. The first was against Catley for hooking the ball before it had touched the ground. McCarthy claimed that Geffin afterwards owned up to being the player who had hooked on the full. "Therefore the penalty should not have been awarded to South Africa. I am as sure in my facts with this statement as any that I have ever made in connection with Rugby football, and despite subsequent denials by certain South African Press correspondents, Geffin did make this statement to members of the New Zealand team."

About the second penalty he wrote: "Mr Hofmeyr's decision on this occasion was one of the worst, and certainly one of the most amazing, I have ever seen in my experience of Rugby football. This is what happened: Thirteen yards inside the All Black half Henderson threw the ball in from touch and, as often happened in this game, a scrum resulted. South Africa got the ball and scrum half Du Toit sent it in to Moss, who had come in from the wing to first five-eighth position; he grubber-kicked through, and ten yards short of the New Zealand 25 and right in the centre, Meates, who had followed across field when he saw Moss racing into the fly half position, attempted to pick the ball up but missed it. Muller then got the ball at his toe and when he saw Scott standing in the centre of the 25 he kicked to Scott's left. Scott, anticipating the Muller move, swung round and in three strides had reached the ball and grabbed it in a magnificent take. He swung around and kicked to his right hand touch, which he found, incidentally. It was then that the whistle blew for a penalty against Scott for using Meates as a 'shield' in order that he might dodge Muller!! The fact that Mr. Hofmeyr had seen Scott in many games beating single-handed five or six opponents did not register with him on this occasion . . . It was one of the most sickening decisions that I have seen in any football, let alone in an International."

McCarthy's conclusion: "There is no doubt that the better team lost."

Later he would put down biased refereeing as one of the reasons for the All Black defeat. His comment on the first test a decade later is different. In that match at Carisbrook the Lions scored four tries and Don Clarke kicked six penalties. The All Blacks won 18-17. McCarthy wrote: "All praise to Don Clarke for his fabulous kicking. Black marks for the Lions for making the penalties possible." The fatuous New Zealand remark was: "We won within the framework of the rules." Vivian Jenkins wrote: "Then came the triple deathblow by Clarke. 'We wuz robbed,' I say, and I don't care who knows it. For once I am with the boxers." The referee that day was Allan Fleury of Otago.

What McCarthy said and implied about South African referees in 1949 was mild compared with what appeared in the *Southern Cross*, a Labour Party newspaper in New Zealand which is no longer in existence. The paper claimed to have read letters home from All Blacks in which they complained that the referees in South Africa were cheating them. What the *Southern Cross* had to say got back to South Africa, in much the same way as Charles Blackett's racist reports in New Zealand became public in 1921. The opposition tried to discuss the matter in the New Zealand parliament, but the Speaker would not allow it.

The All Black management and the players denied any such complaints.

In 1956 the Springboks, who had as their assistant manager Dan de Villiers, one of the test panel referees in 1949, did not hide their complaints. After the Canterbury defeat Danie Craven contemplated making a formal complaint on the refereeing. He contemplated it out loud – to Terry McLean who was writing a column for *Die Burger* at the time. McLean told South Africa about Craven's anger at referees in New Zealand. It did not take long for McLean's remarks to be translated back to New Zealand which went into an apoplexy of anger. The news was reported in New Zealand that Craven had lodged a formal complaint about the referees. The New Zealanders called it sour grapes, and the Forty-niners could not conceal their mirth. They called it justice.

Cuth Hogg complained to Craven who shovelled blame McLean's way. Newspaper men, referees and traffic policemen were not Craven's favourite people.

At Lancaster Park the scores were tied when a ruck developed. It went on and on. Some said it went on for over a minute. It ended when the referee Hugh McNeill of Hawke's Bay, who had denied the Springboks a try when they pushed Canterbury over the line at a scrum, blew his whistle and awarded a penalty to Canterbury for something Daan Retief or, as he thought, Salty du Rand had done. And everybody knows that if you wait long enough at a pile-up/ruck a penalty will happen.

Reg Sweet recalled: "All in all it seemed to me to have gone on interminably long even by New Zealand standards, and I watched several South African players stand clear in perplexity, obviously wondering what to do next, then join in again as the only obvious course of action while referee McNeill put his whistle to his lips, removed it, replaced it and went through the motions a third time. In the end he shrilled it, and indicated Daan Retief as being off-side."

The whole business of the rucks was a problem. In South Africa the

80

1949 All Blacks had been penalised for falling down to form a wall to protect the ball. In New Zealand they were allowed to do it and the Springboks could not get to the ball. Furthermore rucks lasted longer and there was an acceptable New Zealand custom of using boots on players on the ground to "ruck them out of the way" or to discourage them from being in the way. This has not changed all that much!

The aftermath was really nasty. Dana Niehaus eventually cabled his newspaper in South Africa suggesting that the 1960 tour be called off. And when Craven got back to South Africa he was all for a cessation of relations between South Africa and New Zealand.

Craven claimed that he went to the 1957 IRB meeting intent on telling the New Zealanders that there would be no more rugby contact between the two countries. The IRB put Craven and Hogg into the same room with orders to sort out their differences. It did not take them long to shake hands, and afterwards Hogg accompanied Craven to France where he was getting the 1958 French tour organised.

There were also stories in 1956 that New Zealand referees watched film of Springboks in the line-out to see where they could penalise them, and the axe fell upon bullocking Jan Pickard – for "jumping on the run". There was certainly much publicity about the Pickard jump and straight after it John Pring penalised Pickard the first time he went for the ball in the Wellington match.

Where Eddie Hofmeyr had penalised obstruction in 1949 and incurred the wrath of the All Blacks, so the New Zealand referees ignored obstruction and incurred the wrath of the Springboks. Jeremy Nel and Theuns Briers were both taken out when they had moved into scoring positions in the Canterbury match without getting any support from McNeill.

One thing is certain – neither the referees nor the managements of the various teams did the right thing when it came to controlling the violence. Kicking and punching were the order of too many matches, and not a soul was sent off. The first Springbok sent off was James Small in 1993 – for impolite conversation with a referee. The naked violence of 1956 incurred not a sending off.

Craven may have been vilified in New Zealand for speaking up. But his team were grateful. He said he had to choose between personal popularity and loyalty to his team. He chose the latter, and to an extent it worked. There were not again the bitter complaints from the Springboks that had marred the earlier matches.

To be fair to him, too, Craven chose Frank Parkinson for the first two tests, even though he had refereed the Waikato match which the Springboks had lost and the first test which the Springboks had lost. The others on the panel for the first test were Eric Tindill and Stan Whiteford of Canterbury who had been the dominant figure on the field in the Hawke's Bay match. This time Bill Fright, who refereed the Southland match, was on the panel in place of Whiteford. The Springboks stuck with Parkinson and won. Fright said of Parkinson's performance in that test: "It was the only time I saw Frank Parkinson fail. He was technically perfect." The statement is open to dubious interpretation!

The Springboks chose Fright for the third test, ahead of Whiteford and Wolstenholme. That was the day when Kevin Skinner introduced himself to Chris Koch with the words, "How do you want it today, Cockroach?" and punched him.

At no stage did Fright consider sending Skinner off. In fact he was proud that he did not send a player off in seventeen years of first-class refereeing.

Bill Fright also refereed the fourth test, but this time it was Hobson's choice for the Springboks. They did not want Fright at all. They wanted Wolstenholme. The history of the Canterbury Rugby Referees' Society says: "The New Zealand union and the appointments' committee made sure Fright would have the fourth test. The rest of the panel was John Pring and Tindill, and the Springboks had made it clear they wouldn't have a bar of Tindill or Pring again, so they complained they had no choice in the matter. 'They were still fighting for Bernie Wolstenholme till mid-day on the Wednesday, with me sitting in Canterbury on standby.'" The "me" quoted is Bill Fright.

In wondering why such a talented bunch of Springboks lost in New Zealand, Winston McCarthy wrote: "As was asked of the 1949 All Blacks, was it injuries? Biased refereeing? Inadequate goal-kicking? And as the answer came for 1949, so it can be repeated – yes, all of those." On tours he said: "And this tour of 1949 was the biggest shocker of all time – well, I would say the only one that shocked anybody more than the 1949 All Blacks in South Africa was the 1956 Springboks in New Zealand."

Back in South Africa there was not great sympathy for Craven. In an editorial the *Cape Argus* wrote: "Sportsmen generally will agree that blaming the referee can often be interpreted as an excuse for a lack of strategy, the last psychological loophole when there has been defeat."

In New Zealand, whenever Craven said referees, the New Zealanders said 1949.

In 1949 Bob Scott kicked badly. In 1956 the Springboks simply had no reliable goal kicker, especially after the surprising selection of Basie

Viviers had meant leaving Jack van der Schyff out. All sorts of kickers were tried – Viviers, Pickard, Johnstone, Dryburgh, Claassen, Nel and Ulyate. With a really good goal kicker the Springboks could have won the series – as would have happened in 1994.

Before the Springboks played the combination of Thames Valley, Counties and Bay of Plenty, a group of cyclists put on a rugby match on the dirt track around the field. They had a referee who caricatured all Craven's complaints about referees in New Zealand.

The bitterness of 1949 and 1956 largely evaporated in 1960, though this may have been the result more of New Zealand tolerance than satisfaction with the refereeing. T P McLean, the most level-headed of rugby journalists, said: "The All Blacks were brilliantly done by two incredibly fine referees, Mr Ralph Burmeister, who controlled three games, and Mr H P A Hofmeyr, who had charge of the difficult match with Northern Transvaal and whom the All Blacks would have greatly liked to play under at any other convenient time. They were also exceedingly well done by in other matches by such as Dr E A Strasheim – though he did tend to speak in Afrikaans – who had the first test, by Dr A A Gordon, who had the match with Central Universities, and by Mr Chris Ackermann, who refereed the match with Combined Western Province Universities. They also encountered a number who, if not capable of setting the Thames on fire, made honest and workmanlike jobs of difficult tasks." That said, the New Zealanders would have preferred panels drawn up by the SARB for all provincial matches and taken from the best referees in the country, rather than panels of local referees for each match.

He also said: "The All Blacks professed to be happy with the refereeing and they went to great pains to conceal any criticisms they might have of particular individuals . . . But, as with all of the great rugby expeditions since the end of the Second World War, the All Blacks, too, felt that referees were ruling against them more than they were against home teams and it was because of the fear of South African referees that the great tragedy of the tour, the adoption of an almost wholly defensive approach to the game was considered, tested and adopted."

The problem of the number of penalties would not be alleviated by the introduction of unattached referees, nor would it obviate controversy and the accusation of bias. It is a statistical fact that home teams are less penalised than visiting teams, regardless of what the place of origin of the referee is. And the biggest refereeing controversy in matches between South Africa and New Zealand happened in 1981, when the referee was a Welshman!

The referee the 1960 All Blacks liked least was W H Badenhorst of Transvaal whose nickname was Bofbal. He refereed the match between the All Blacks and the Junior Springboks. In a grim foreshadowing of the controversies of 1976, he disallowed a penalty kick at goal when the ball, about to be kicked by Tony Davies, rolled over for a second time. Badenhorst then objected to Russell Watt's ill-mannered protest.

The big debate in 1960 was the McMullen "try" in the first few minutes of the fourth test in Port Elizabeth. The match was only five minutes old when Frank McMullen gathered a loose kick and set off 40 m down the field on a brilliant run, speeding between Dick Lockyear and Hennie van Zyl. He checked his pace and then accelerated to the left and Lionel Wilson. The goal line was ahead and there was nobody in front of him

Keith Oxlee dived and ankle-tapped McMullen who fell prone on the ground with the ball under his chest. Lying there he arched his body and launched himself across the line and grounded the ball. Without hesitation, Ralph Burmeister penalised McMullen, a decision which would be forever notorious in New Zealand. McMullen got up and flung the ball to the ground in his anger/disappointment. McMullen was not tackled within the definition of the Law because he was not held. The Law of the day which applied to him read that he had to "IMMEDIATELY play the ball or get up or roll away from the ball." Burmeister ruled him out of order and penalised him.

Terry McLean regarded Burmeister as a Homer. It was, I am sure, meant as a compliment, but Homer was in fact blind! Terry Lineen stated that Burmeister was one of the best three referees he had played under in 20 years of international rugby throughout the world. Tom Pearce did cry about the McMullen "try" when he got home though.

There was a disputed try in the first test in 1965. When Kel Tremain picked up the ball to score the first try on a day when the All Blacks won 6-3, it had just gone a good yard forward from Mick Williment as Dawie de Villiers tackled him. Pat Murphy awarded the try. In those more sensible days, the Springboks recognised his award as an error and chose him as the referee for the next two tests as well.

Pat Murphy, by the way, was nearly replaced in the second test when he hurt a knee ligament. In the third test his knee flared up again, and he was replaced by Alan Taylor, the referee who was a touch judge while Tommy Bedford ran the other touch. At the time Taylor had refereed only three representative matches. In 1981 he tried to persuade the Canterbury Referees' Society to disassociate itself from the tour and later became a marcher.

84

The 1965 Springboks did not get publicly upset about referees.

In 1970 the All Blacks, under Ron Burk, followed the example of the 1965 Springboks and there were no groans about the refereeing.

After the clash between Syd Nomis and Fergie McCormick at Newlands in 1970, Wouter du Toit, the chairman of the SA Referees' Society, suggested that the referees for the remaining tests should be instructed to be on the lookout for dirty play.

Craven was furious: "Utter nonsense! We never have and never will give directives to the referee in any Test match. Leave it to him, for heaven's sake, and let us accept gracefully the result this far as it appears on the board, that is one test each."

This new-found diplomacy would not outlast the 1976 All Black tour. It would not even outlast the unattached referees of the Eighties.

J J Stewart had harsh words for Schubel O'Reilly after the ghastly match in Upington and said: "And I will never return to your stinking country."

The choice for tests was limited, partly through the All Blacks' own doing. Apparently they decided before the tour that they would not use Piet Robbertse and Steve Strydom because they were revealed to be members of the Broederbond. Afterwards they would claim that the only reason they chose Ian Gourlay was that he was English-speaking and clearly not a Broederbonder. After the first test, they went off Gourlay anyway.

The referees who made up the test panel were Gourlay, Strydom, Bezuidenhout and Robbertse. They actually wanted Max Baise for the second test, and were refused. They liked Johan Gouws but he was also not on the panel.

Gert Bezuidenhout refereed the second test and there were no All Black complaints. On the contrary they chose him for the third test. They did not like him all that much when he disallowed Sid Going's kick at goal when the ball rolled over twice and they objected to the Springboks' power scrumming and tried to counter Johan Strauss's strength by sticking two heads against him. There were doubts about Dawie Snyman's dropped goal, but the truth was the Springboks deserved to win.

The All Blacks saved their wrath for later.

It spewed out after the fourth test, for which they also chose Gert Bezuidenhout, the headmaster from Johannesburg. The Springboks won 15-14.

Ten minutes into the second half, Bryan Williams got the ball on the blind side on about the halfway line, kicked ahead, gathered the ball and passed inside to Kevin Eveleigh. Eveleigh passed back inside to Bruce

Robertson. Chris Pope shaped to tackle Robertson who kicked towards the goal line. Just as he set off in pursuit, Johan Oosthuizen held him back. Peter Whipp came across and dotted the ball down.

Gert Bezuidenhout awarded a penalty kick. Andy Leslie and Ian Kirkpatrick demanded a penalty try, that might well have won them the match. There Gert Bezuidenhout stood, lonely in that towering arena. His loneliness would go on for a long time after the match. If this decision was a mistake, it was not his only mistake in the match, nor was he the only one to make a mistake. Ten minutes before the end Bezuidenhout penalised the All Blacks at a line-out, always a lottery in any match, and Gerald Bosch, whose record for kicks at goal in the series was only eight successes out of nineteen attempts, kicked the winning points. The All Blacks' success rate was also poor. On that tour they first learnt how to kick around the corner! In their first two matches they missed fifteen successive kicks at goal.

After the match an enraged J J Stewart, who was frequently enraged on the trip, said: "There was no possibility that the referee was going to let us win this afternoon."

They were still complaining, nearly two decades later in New Zealand. Gert Bezuidenhout was still remembered with bitterness – along with Eddie Hofmeyr and, significantly, Ken Rowlands.

The last name is significant because he was an unattached referee. And that leads us to 1981 and Clive Norling. You would have been hard pressed to find a Springbok supporter who believed that Norling had not cheated.

After the test in 1976, Danie Craven took Gert Bezuidenhout to task and said that he, too, believed that he should have awarded a penalty try, by which time the match was long over, Bezuidenhout had no chance to change his decision, the score stayed, and Bezuidenhout would be forever a hurt and sad man.

But the biggest irony of the lot is that for the 1976 series the South African Rugby Football Board offered the New Zealand Rugby Football Union unattached referees, that is referees from a neutral country, and the NZRFU turned it down! The sick theory behind their refusal was that that would give them the right to use home referees for the Lions tour in 1977, because they needed victory after defeat by the Lions in 1971. The other theory was that they did not want Australian referees.

They did use home referees in 1977 and did beat the Lions who "had reservations" about the refereeing in New Zealand. In fact it was an unhappy tour ending with an unhappy speech by George Burrell, the Lions' manager. It was a tour on which the Lions felt New Zealand was on a war footing following the Lions' victory there in 1971.

An amusing argument in 1976 concerned the use of sand to tee up kicks at goal. The New Zealanders made a great fuss about this and there were threats of serious objection during the war psychosis which led up to the first test. The first side to kick at goal during that first test was New Zealand. And Bryan Williams, the kicker, called for sand, teed up the ball and kicked at goal, thereby ending one argument for the duration of the tour.

The first time unattached referees were used in tests between South Africa and New Zealand was in 1981 – at Lancaster Park in Christchurch when Laurie Prideaux of England was in charge. Clive Norling refereed the last two tests of the series, and there were bitter, loud, long complaints about his refereeing in the third test – at least the way it ended.

Nothing was said after the second test when the team that clearly deserved to win won clearly. The complaints came after the third test. There were no complaints about the missed knock that occurred as Gary Knight scored his try. Most people accept refereeing errors, especially early in the match. Their complaints centred on the closing minutes of the third test, the long second half, a great but bizarre test made ludicrous.

The Springboks came roaring back after being 16-3 down and the score was 22-18 when a scrum was awarded deep in New Zealand territory. It was also well into injury time.

Wynand Claassen asked Clive Norling how much time was left. He told Claassen it was the last scrum. Rob Louw, playing flank, was not sure what the tall Welshman had said and asked him how much time was left. Quite distinctly Norling said: "This is the last scrum of the match."

The Springboks scored and levelled the scores, and the match went on and on. Six and a half minutes after the "last scrum", Norling awarded a scrum to South Africa.

Divan Serfontein wanted to put the ball in when the scrum slewed. The All Blacks had done well during the series in disrupting the Springbok scrum by shoving early and twisting the scrum. In fact in that match only one Springbok scrum had not wheeled towards Serfontein and every time Serfontein had stopped and appealed to the referee who had had the scrum formed properly. It happened again and Serfontein stood back, unable to put the ball in. This time Serfontein was not allowed to have the scrum properly set. Norling awarded a free kick against South Africa for foot-up, something he had not done previously in the match though there had been cases of "flashing" by hookers earlier.

Mark Donaldson, on at scrumhalf for injured Dave Loveridge, took a tap kick and ran to his left and slightly forward. He passed to Rollerson who was tackled by the forwards some 12 metres ahead of the original mark.

The whistle went and Norling changed the free kick into a penalty, which Hewson goaled.

People will swear forever that time had long elapsed when he awarded the scrum, that he should have penalised Andy Haden for twice punching Flip van der Merwe in the face just before the scrum, that the free kick should not have been awarded, that Donaldson had run well over 5 m before he passed to Rollerson which would have put retreating Springboks onside. And they will tell you sadder stories about comments made by the referee after the match.

In 1983 Norling awarded a penalty try to the Wallabies when they played Argentina in Sydney. The award was for a deliberate knock-on, some 20 m from the Argentinian goal line. Afterwards Norling locked himself in his dressing room to avoid reporters. Rodolfo O'Reilly, the Pumas' coach, said of the penalty try: "It was the invention from the showman."

Unattached referees did not solve the problem!

In 1986 refereeing was again the cause of the storm when the Cavaliers toured South Africa.

The Cavaliers objected to the tolerance by the local referees of lifting in the line-outs. After the very first match Ian Kirkpatrick, the former All Black great who was the manager of the Cavaliers, made it known that he would not have Fransie Muller again after Muller had refereed the first two matches, both of which the Cavaliers won by a solitary point.

They liked Wynand Mans even less when they lost to Transvaal. They accused Wynand Mans, who had toured New Zealand as a Springbok in 1965, of exacting vengeance for his visit to New Zealand.

They were cross with Mans at Newlands as well, when he was the touch judge in the match between the Cavaliers and Western Province. Mans twice indicated foul play by the Cavaliers. Andy Haden, the captain that day, went up to Mans and told him he was an arsehole! Haden threatened to take his team off the field.

But the visitors' vitriol was reserved for Ken Rowlands of Wales. Again it was what happened at the end that really counted. There were no complaints when they lost the first test and their try was a penalty try. There was no complaint when they were lucky enough to win the second test. There was no complaint when they got a hiding in the third test. The complaints came loud and bitter when they lost the fourth test.

Wayne Smith was remarkably rude to the Welshman during the match. After the final whistle Hika Reid charged at Rowlands with his shoulder. At the function afterwards Andy Dalton said in his speech: "In International rugby I have never publicly criticised a referee. I have always demanded honesty from a referee. But when I think what our guys have been through to get here, I think sadly that we got less than that today."

Ian Kirkpatrick, the Cavaliers' manager, said: "Some of the decisions were incredible . . . I would say Rowlands was definitely whistling it pro-South Africa in this game." And Jock Hobbs, captain in Dalton's place, said: "We were penalised out of the game."

Naas Botha reminded the Cavaliers of the Norling affair and Dalton's lack of sympathy for the Springboks at the time and advised them that "cowboys don't cry".

Rowlands, from Ynysybwl in Wales, had had probably the most difficult assignment a referee has ever had – four tests involving the same two teams on successive Saturdays.

Ironically the headline of *Die Burger* after the second test was: "Blaser Help All Blacks Wen." (The referee helped the All Blacks to win). The headline was wrong on more than one account.

There is no doubt that winning and losing is the major problem at the heart of the matter. The Springboks in the World Cup Final of 1995 did not complain when Ed Morrison did not award Ruben Kruger's try, though it was clearly a try. But then the Springboks won. Had they lost it might well have been a completely different matter.

The Springboks detested Sandy O'Neill of Australia when they just lost to the All Blacks in 1992 but, amazingly, thought Dave Bishop was wonderful when the Wallabies smashed them in the wet at Newlands in the same year. Even Craven praised Bishop. And the Springboks could not stand Jim Fleming of Scotland when they gave England a hiding at Twickenham in 1995. It would suggest that winning and losing is not the only problem.

The All Blacks were unhappy in 1992 when they found that there would be a South African touch judge along with an Australian touch judge. Eddie Tonks was furious. T P McLean, reporting on the match, said, amongst many other things: "The Kiwis kicked up bobsy-die when, at Ellis Park, they observed Botha in conversation with Freek Burger, the Afrikaner touch-judge." An Afrikaner touch judge? Not just a touch judge or a rugby touch judge. There may be a touch of paranoia somewhere.

They say of the Welsh that you do not beat them, only score more points than they do. It may not apply only to the Welsh. Losing, it may always be easiest to blame the referee. Perhaps it will ever be so, whether he is unattached/neutral or not.

Questions were asked about the method of appointment whereby a match was allotted to a country, and that country could then choose one of its referees for the match – according to their own machinations and not necessarily according to the requirements of the teams involved.

In 1994 Ireland were allotted the first two tests between South Africa and New Zealand, Wales the third. Ireland and Wales would then decide which referee they would send from their respective countries.

Ireland had two experienced men in Owen Doyle and Steve Hilditch, and a series between South Africa and New Zealand is tough enough to demand the most experienced of hands. Instead they sent Brian Stirling who must have found the Dunedin test hateful, just for the problems in the scrums alone. He got those right in the second test, with the result that it was a better match for everybody, including Brian Stirling.

Wales had Derek Bevan, acknowledged as the best referee in the world, but instead they sent Bob Yeman whose only test before the third test in 1994 was Ireland vs Romania.

It would seem more fitting that some body, chosen for its good sense and practical knowledge of refereeing at the highest level, should be chosen to appoint the best referees to the toughest matches. In 1994 the Springboks would have been happier to have had Colin Hawke and Dave Bishop, both New Zealanders from South Island, to referee the tests. So much for unattached!

CHAPTER 9

Vengeance

"IT'S ALL YOURS, New Zealand."

Those were Danie Craven's warm and generous words to the whole of New Zealand after the fourth test in 1956 when New Zealand became the first team to take a rubber off South Africa for six decades.

The warm and generous words hid the tight cold grip of bitterness around his heart.

The cause of the bitterness?

Defeat? The nasty side of rugby football? The sense of being cheated? The blow to the ego?

All of these are possible.

No South African had ever had the carte blanche that Craven had had. He had been declared manager. Then he was elected president of the SARFB and he took over the coaching. He was the lot – president, manager, coach – and, make no error, he would have dominated selection. And the end of this autocracy was the first failure for 60 years.

The trouble started early and persisted. Not all the trouble was made in New Zealand. It started before the team was even picked.

There were trials at Newlands. Salty du Rand was the man most likely to captain the Springboks. Jan Pickard, also an ex-Matie and a man with remarkable leadership qualities, was also a candidate. On the Wednesday of the trials week Pickard's weaker side had beaten Du Rand's more fancied side.

That evening there was fun in Pickard's room in the Avalon Hotel. Du Rand remonstrated with Pickard and an argument ensued. Du Rand, whose wife, ironically, came from Cardiff, accused Pickard of forsaking his Afrikaans heritage by playing for an "English" club, Hamiltons. Pickard told Du Rand that he could not take a hiding, whereupon Du Rand smacked Pickard and broke his nose.

The next day Craven got all 120 trialists together and in front of them

Salty du Rand apologised and the two men shook hands.

The selectors rushed to change their team which was now in need of a captain and into it they brought Basie Viviers, a friendly man, who had been good for team spirit on the 1951-52 tour but not really good enough to command a place in the test side, which would be a problem on the tour. Viviers had been dropped from the Orange Free State team in 1955 and then moved to Western Transvaal but had still not been amongst the 82 players invited to trials in 1956. His selection reduced the 1956 team's ability to kick goals.

The team assembled in Johannesburg and there was much emphasis on fitness, with bars on the soles of forwards' boots to simulate the heavy-footedness expected in the mud of New Zealand. Little scrum halves carried heavy forwards in the quest for fitness at the Wanderers, Rand Leases and Ellis Park. Muscle trouble instead of fitness ensued in some cases.

They were the first South African team to fly abroad. They left Johannesburg on a Qantas Super-Constellation on the morning of 8 May and arrived in Sydney on the morning of 11 May. They spent 26 hours in Mauritius and had a match practice at the Dodo club and then stopped on West Island of the Cocos Islands to refuel. And while they were there Jaap Bekker climbed a coconut palm to pick a fruit.

Over the Indian Ocean on the way from the Cocos to Darwin, Peewee Howe looked out of the window and noticed that a propeller was not turning. There was tension on the flight but it was relieved by the antics of Clive Ulyate, the clown prince of South African rugby, with his monocle and Poona tales.

Craven believed that the air trip was a bad omen for the tour, and in 1969 the Springboks were back on board a ship for Southampton.

The injuries got worse as the tour went on. Basie van Wyk broke a leg and could not play on the tour though he cheerfully went on with the team. Jan du Preez also broke a leg. The replacements for the two were James Starke and Theunis Briers.

Ian Kirkpatrick broke a shoulder. Basie Viviers, Johnny Buchler, who played only four matches in New Zealand, Wilf Rosenberg, Pat Montini, Brian Pfaff, Tommy Gentles, Salty du Rand, who broke his hand, Dawie Ackermann with a torn cartilage, Clive Ulyate and Melt Hanekom all battled with injuries. At one stage 13 of the thirty players were on the injured list. It was the tour that "invented" the hamstring, which was an unknown bit of rugby anatomy up till then. The team founded a Survivors' Club, which had only seven members by the end of the tour – Bertus van der Merwe, whose baby son died while he was in Australia, Jan Pickard,

Jeremy Nel, Chris de Wilzem, Popeye Strydom, Chris de Nysschen and Piet du Toit.

The Springboks were unimpressive in beating the Wallabies 9-0 in both tests, and then they headed on a five-hour flight across the Tasman to a nation in waiting.

Spiro Zavos, a New Zealander, describes the mood in New Zealand: "A type of crusading fever swept the country as the Springboks made their triumphant way through Australia, edging ever closer to New Zealand. Old timers emerged to give warnings about how tough, rough, nasty, shrewd and overpowering the South Africans were likely to be. The atmosphere when Danie Craven . . . and his team finally landed in New Zealand resembled that of France when the first German troops stepped foot on its soil in 1939. There was fear, loathing for past humiliations, anxiety, awe, a fierce desire for revenge and above all a determination to win at all costs." One of the people whipping up the war spirit was Winston McCarthy who said of Craven: "This is a man who speaks with three tongues in his cheek."

They had a huge welcome in Auckland and all along the railway line there were people to welcome them till they came to an even bigger welcome in Hamilton, the city whose provincial team is called Waikato, whose mascot is a cow called Mooloo. Hamilton welcomed the Springboks with a brass band which played Vat jou Goed en Trek, Ferreira, a banner which announced KUIER LEKKER, BOKKE and a procession of rugby floats. Cowbells rang, girls jumped on the team's bus to get autographs, work stopped for the week, and the Springboks walked straight into a massive punch.

A week after playing in Sydney they met Mooloo and mud on Rugby Park in Hamilton, and the spirits of the whole of New Zealand soared.

With the wind at their backs, Waikato tore into the Springbok forwards. There was going to be no repeat of 1921, 1937 and 1949. New Zealanders were proud of their manhood and were not going to come apart up front. From the kick-off they swamped Harry Newton Walker and their forwards swarmed in. Inside a minute they had scored when Malcolm McDonald surged over in the corner for a try.

Welcome to New Zealand, South Africa!

A young fullback, called Don Clarke, dropped a goal with his left foot from 40 yards out. Rex Pickering scored a try and Clarke converted and added a penalty goal. At half-time Waikato led 14-0.

The welcome was threatening to get even warmer.

Then Jeremy Nel broke, gave to Peewee Howe and Tom van Vollenhoven, who had a disappointing tour, scored in the corner. Jan Pickard, captain that fateful day, converted. The Springbok backs swung into action again and Jan du Preez scored a magnificent try under the posts. 14-10.

Waikato won. Injuries could hardly be an excuse because the winners had played an hour of the match with only 14 men. New Zealand was already a harsh reality for the Springboks. There would be no easy pickings.

That night Jan Pickard handed over a springbok head to Waikato. The head is given to a nontest team that beats the Springboks, a tradition dating back to 1912 when Billy Millar's team gave one to Newport. On this tour it had not lasted even one match.

Rain was pouring down when the train stopped at Whangarei station but there were 3 000 people standing in the rain to welcome the mighty Springboks. Rain would be part of the tour that wet, wet winter. Whangarei had more than double its annual rainfall.

In 1937 the Springboks had marvelled at the height of the Whangarei goal posts and the depths of its mud. The mud was deeper in 1956. He who could score would win. Pat Montini dribbled the ball over the North Auckland line and the Springboks won 3-0. But again the Springbok forwards took a pounding.

Life was not going to be easy as they travelled back to Auckland. Life was not easy on the field and not easy off it either. The team had good spirit and was extremely well behaved – for any group of men let alone a rugby team. But they were accused of clannishness, of rudely switching to Afrikaans and not mixing with opponents. Mixing with opponents is a more important part of New Zealand rugby than it is of South African rugby, and Craven was at pains to keep his men away from boozy gatherings. On the other hand they were nonpareil in their visits to schools. One particularly happy group were the children of Mount Street Home for handicapped children who came to see the team and were given an autographed rugby ball for a fund-raising drive. For Jaap Bekker the happiest news on the tour was that a polio victim he had visited had walked again. Terry McLean said of them: "The effect of such kindness upon the boys and girls of the country was prodigious." And they kept on giving their autographs, so much so that McLean, who travelled everywhere with them said: "No team, no amateur team, should ever be called upon to shoulder such a burden."

Life on the field was tough because the New Zealanders were good and determined, the weather was foul, the South Africans found the refereeing unfriendly, their forwards were not good enough and they found the New Zealand rucking frightening, and the crowds at grounds were astonishingly hostile.

94

The Auckland match, won 6-3 by the Springboks, was a disgrace, on a day when the playing conditions were excellent. In the Springboks' favour they survived even though they were reduced to six forwards when two went out into the back line to replace injured backs.

Down they went to Palmerston North and another great welcome on a Sunday evening, which helped to get the tour back on the rails. They went on to Wellington and a narrow victory in a great match when handsome Dawie Ackermann was a star and injury time went on and on as the clock at the ground stopped and locals reckoned the referee John Pring allowed the close match to go on seven minutes longer than he should have.

The Springboks won up in Maori country and then had a big win in the north of South Island. That took them down to Dunedin to face Otago where both sides scored a brace of tries but the Springboks won 14-9. It was "our toughest match", according to Craven, and again there were complaints about the referee, I L Armishaw of South Canterbury, who penalised the Springboks 20 times and Otago nine times, and turned down three possible tries by the Springboks.

In Dunedin the replacements, Theuns Briers and James Starke, joined the team.

Rugby fever never and nowhere runs higher than it does in Dunedin when a test match is due. There was a whole week to prepare for it.

The Springboks prepared with grim intensity for the first test, with hard practice, strict curfews, lots of talk, mental preparation.

The All Blacks were full value for their victory, their first in seven tests against the Springboks. The Springboks stuck to a dour stereotyped pattern of hoofing the ball downfield while the All Blacks were livelier and more varied. The decisive moment came from a Jarden try. He intercepted a pass between Dawie Ackermann and Peewee Howe when the Springboks looked certain to score, and set off up the field for a try which he converted. At the end that was the winning score – 10-6 to New Zealand, two tries to the All Blacks to Peewee Howe's scrambled try for South Africa who ended with only six forwards against New Zealand's seven.

It was Ron Jarden's match. His display was one of the great wing three-quarter displays in the history of international rugby.

First blood in the series went to New Zealand. For the fourth time the home team had won the first test. In all series between South Africa and New Zealand, the home team has won the first test.

There were injuries to both sides in this match. Jan du Preez broke a leg, Dawie Ackermann damaged a cartilage, Mark Irwin damaged a rib and the

95

three of them left prematurely. Robin Archer injured a rib but played on in pain. Afterwards Mr D C Jolly, a past president of the Otago RFU and one of the seven toastmasters at the aftermatch function, proposed the replacement of injured players. It would be a long time coming.

The show had to go on, and the Springboks came back up South Island to Timaru, Willie Wolseley and a comfortable victory over the Hanan Shield provinces despite injuries and unhappiness – yet again – with the referee. Willie was an elegant goat, South Canterbury's mascot.

Next stop was Christchurch and controversy. For Craven's Springboks it was a black hour as Canterbury, the Ranfurly Shield holders, were awarded a dubious penalty and won the match 9-6.

Afterwards Craven complained bitterly about the refereeing and the team claimed this had a cathartic effect. Whatever the effect they then won five matches in a row, starting with a happy visit to Westport where each Springbok was given the title deeds to a square foot of New Zealand at Cape Foulwind, the first bit of New Zealand sighted by Abel Tasman.

In Invercargill Craven was "arrested" in the name of "Lord Rugby, Governor of New Zealand" for submitting to Waikato Woolamooloo Jersey and to Canterbury Lamb, and taken handcuffed in a vintage car to the police station. Craven paid a fine of £1, which went to the Crippled Children's Society. They went back up to Wellington for the second test, and this time they picked some of the more "competitive" men – Ian Kirkpatrick, Paul Johnstone and Jan Pickard. Pickard played at number 8 and he took it as his job to protect his friend Tommy Gentles.

The wind blew at Athletic Park, which was no surprise. Basie Viviers won the toss and gave New Zealand the wind, a surprise in New Zealand but standard practice in South Africa. The New Zealanders believed that you took the elements while they were available and sought to get an unassailable lead. The Springboks believed that so much time in a match was spent settling down that the wind advantage was wasted in the first half and that the psychological advantage of turning over with the wind was too good to be ignored.

The Springbok forwards came in hard this time. At the very first scrum they crunched the All Blacks' front row and the new loose head Frank McAtamney rose into the air. Half-time came and all New Zealand had was a three-point lead, thanks to a try by Ross Brown.

The second half belonged to the Springboks. It was barely started when Tommy Gentles went round the blind side of a scrum and fed Daan Retief who burst over to score in the right-hand corner. Basie Viviers, back into the side because Roy Dryburgh was crocked, converted from touch and the Springboks were ahead. They never looked like losing their lead and could have won handsomely if they had succeeded with even half of their kicks at goal and Ian Kirkpatrick would claim he scored a try which was disallowed. Eventually Gentles broke again and fed Salty du Rand who scored.

After the match Jaap Bekker collapsed in the changing room and was taken to hospital where he woke at 3 a.m. and had to be told what the score was. The hospital recommended a lay-off of two weeks. Bekker did that and was on the field again for the third test.

The second test victory was not a pretty win, but a convincing one. And it left the All Blacks haunted by the ancient spectre of Springbok scrum-maging.

Their solution would remain a controversial one forever. They called back Kevin Skinner, the Forty-niner who had retired from rugby, the ex-heavyweight boxing champion. He rallied to his nation's call. God might or might not defend New Zealand but Kevin Skinner certainly would. Back he came from an 18-month retirement, left his farm like Cincinnatus and was drafted into the All Black side to bolster the front row.

Before the third test could happen the Springboks went north from Wellington to Wanganui with its bright sunshine and the procession of vintage vehicles. For the Springboks, relieved by victory, it was a skittishly happy visit.

Playing, ominously, for the Wanganui/King Country combination was a youngster who would have a massive impact on rugby football and on matches between South Africa and New Zealand, Colin Earl Meads, then just 20 years of age. Not only did he play but Colin Meads scored one of his team's two tries. With Roy Dryburgh at fly half, South Africa scored eight and won the match 36-16.

They went further west to New Plymouth and Mt Egmont with people at every stop to greet them. At the village of Hawera two thousand people were at the station to cheer them on their way, singing Sarie Marais for them.

They say that if you can see Mt Egmont it is going to rain, but if you cannot see it, it is raining. You could not see it that Saturday when the Springboks played Taranaki and, as in 1921, drew with the home team. Each side scored three points, a try to Jan Pickard and a penalty to John Bayly, but in truth Taranaki gave the Springboks a torrid time.

Back the Springboks went to the South Island and the third test at Lancaster Park, the scene of Canterbury's disputed victory.

New Zealand made three important changes. In came Don Clarke at fullback, Kevin Skinner at prop and Peter Jones on the flank.

South Africa lost and the score flattered New Zealand who scored two tries in the last two minutes.

The Springboks were cross because Don Clarke's conversion was not over but was given over and counted two points, and the Springboks should have been leading 10-9 with two minutes to play and not forced to take risks to pull the game out of the fire.

But most of all they were angered by what they perceived to be Kevin Skinner's calculated assault on their props, at a time when Craven had insisted that the Springboks clean up their act and had given the example by dropping Ian Kirkpatrick, accused of kicking an opponent and photographed doing so, Jan Pickard who had trampled and taken pugilistic retribution for being held in the line-out in New Plymouth, and Paul Johnstone who had objected to having his jersey tugged repeatedly by Morrie Dixon.

In the first line-out Skinner punched Chris Koch. Eight minutes later Koch swung at Skinner and missed, but was penalised and Don Clarke's second penalty gave New Zealand a lead of 6-0.

Then Tommy Gentles, pounded by big Peter Jones and without Pickard to protect him, dropped the ball and Ponty Reid footed the ball ahead, collected the bounce, fed Bill Gray who passed to Morrie Dixon who headed for the line and a great try.

That was when Don Clarke kicked the conversion that missed and counted two points! The touch judges both raised their flags but Bill Fright, the referee, was not sure at all and chatted to the Christchurch touch judge, Keith Noonan, who told him it was over while Ian Kirkpatrick, the Springbok centre who was touch judge that day, admitted sticking up his flag only because the other touch judge had done so. "It was his pole," Kirkpatrick said. After all he had been overruled by the referee John Pring in the close Wellington match when even the Wellington players thought Jan Pickard's penalty kick was over, though John Pring thought that the ball had crossed over the top of the goal posts. And so it came to pass that New Zealand got two extra points in the test in Christchurch.

Half-time came and the All Blacks led 11-0.

In the second half Skinner switched sides in the scrum and his attentions from Chris Koch, suitably subdued, to Jaap Bekker who ended the match with a bloodied face.

Dawie Ackermann picked up a fly hack by Ron Jarden, did a switch with Clive Ulyate and suddenly the defence opened up. Ulyate slung a long pass to Tom van Vollenhoven. As Dixon challenged him, Van Vollenhoven passed to Butch Lochner who scored. Basie Viviers converted from touch. 11-5.

Bill Fright called the skippers together and gave them a stern talking to. The next one to fight would be sent off.

Tommy Gentles broke sharply on his own 10-yard line, as few scrum halves could do better. He passed to Dawie Ackermann who gave to Jaap Bekker who charged ahead at surprising speed. Bekker passed to Salty du Rand who gave to Wilf Rosenberg who dived over for a try near the posts. It was one of the great test tries. 11-10.

The All Black forwards at this stage were on top and the only hope for the Springboks was for their backs to try to break out. A risky business.

When Gentles dropped the ball, the All Blacks footed through and Jarden leapt, caught the ball and scored. Then Jones grabbed a ball dropped by Rosenberg and gave to Dixon who gave to Tiny White who scored, and it all looked a comfortable win for New Zealand 17-10. Danie Craven said afterwards: "We have no excuses. We were badly beaten at forward and they upset our backs."

The Springboks trudged up to Wellington and New Zealand Universities surprised everybody by scoring four tries to two and winning 22-15 in a fast and furious match on a bright, sunny afternoon. Many horrible things happened on the tour that were no good for rugby football. What happened at Athletic Park on that afternoon was good for rugby. Afterwards Basie Viviers said: "Thanks very much for a magnificent game. The better side won, make no mistake about that."

Then came the Maori match – and much trepidation. There was trepidation on rugby's side that there would be a resurgence of the bitterness of 1921, that the violence that had characterised so much of the tour would be seen as racist violence and further sour relations between the two countries.

The worst fears did not materialise.

Perhaps the Maoris had also approached the match with trepidation that these ferocious racists would vent their fury on them.

Whatever it was, the Maori challenge fizzled out and the Springboks won an astonishing 37-0 victory before an Eden Park packed with 60 000 expectant spectators. Theunis Briers scored three of the Springboks' seven tries. Afterwards Tiny Hill said: "Those forwards were frightened." And he meant his own men.

In that Maori side there were All Blacks – Pat Walsh, Bill Gray who captained the Maoris that day, Tom Katene, Keith Davis, Albert Pryor and Tiny Hill. There was nothing wrong with the pedigree of the team.

The next day the Springboks went to a marae at Ngaruawahai and ate pork, puha, whitebait, oysters and toheroa in King Koroki's dining room.

Guide Rangi said of the match: "We are not depressed. You were too good. We were well beaten, but we Maoris say these things pass with the wind."

When the Springboks played a combination of Thames Valley, Counties and Bay of Plenty at Rotorua with its geysers and thermal springs, Maori traditions and sulphurous smells, Kevin Skinner played. There was talk that he would not finish the match. He finished the match and walked quietly off at the end as the Springboks stumbled to an unconvincing 17-6 win, but not before Salty du Rand had called him a coward.

At the end of the match, Du Rand asked Clive Ulyate to drop out high in Skinner's direction. The Springbok forwards homed in on him. Skinner, fully aware of the possibilities of the tactic, stood aside, hands in the air to draw the referee's attention to his noncombatant status.

Four days later Skinner was again in action against the Springboks with Harry Newton Walker on the loose-head side in place of Chris Koch.

There were 62 000 people in Eden Park that sunny day for the fourth test, the biggest crowd ever. In fact it is one which cannot be repeated in present times as the size of the ground has, along with many others since the coming of television, been reduced.

This was the battle for the crown. If 1928 had happened again the series would have been drawn. The All Blacks were determined that this would not be 1928 in reverse. The Springboks wanted it to be 1928 in reverse. There was no place on the field for anybody faint of heart – if such could ever get onto the field when Springbok and All Black meet.

Basie Viviers missed a kick. Don Clarke missed a kick. Don Clarke kicked from 62 yards away on that windless day and only just missed. Then South Africa did something naughty at a scrum and Don Clarke goaled. 3-0 to New Zealand. Dryburgh, playing wing, missed. Clarke, whose defence had saved the All Blacks time and again, missed a kick.

That was the situation at half-time but it had in fact been a half full of movement.

Ron Hemi came away from a line-out with the ball at his feet. Peter Jones, whom Daan Retief once described as "the greatest forward in the world", footed the ball ahead and it bounced high. Basie Viviers was waiting for it. Peter Jones came charging at Basie Viviers, hands up for the ball, and with a huge right hand Jones plucked a bouncing ball from in front of the Springbok fullback and strode massively more than 30 yards for a try that made the score 8-0. "I ran harder than I had ever run in my life," he said later.

Skinner punched Walker and Dryburgh missed a kick at goal. Clarke kicked a penalty goal from 48 yards out. 11-0.

Then with three minutes to go fighting erupted as Tiny White lay on the ground writhing from the agony in his back.

Then Theunis Briers ran down the wing, kicked ahead and James Starke was close to scoring but lost the ball. Peewee Howe counterattacked and gave to Roy Dryburgh who swerved his way for a try which Viviers converted.

And Bill Fright, who refereed four of the Springboks' matches, blew the final whistle at a ground bathed in ecstasy. There was no doubt that New Zealand deserved to win this one. The score in their favour was 11-5.

Danie Craven was given the mike and made one of rugby's most famous statements of generosity: "It's all yours, New Zealand." And Basie Viviers said: "We were beaten by a better team." Happily the crowd sang Auld Lang Syne and Now is the Hour.

Peter Jones, wearing a blazer on his bare torso was asked to address the crowd and, in one of rugby's immortal quotes, said: "Well, ladies and gentlemen, I hope I never have to play as tough a game as today's. I'm absolutely buggered." It was broadcast to the nation.

It was all New Zealand's. The victor takes all.

There would be bitter moments to come, but never the equal of those of 1956.

Three days after the fourth test the Springboks flew from Whenuapai, Auckland's airport, leaving behind a satisfied nation and 28 parking tickets and taking with them disappointment and the prospect of rejection on their return.

That was, until 1992, the last encounter between South Africa and New Zealand devoid of politics.

TOUR STATISTICS (NEW ZEALAND ONLY)

P	W	D	L	Pf	Pa	Tf	Ta
23	16	1	6	370	177	79	28

TESTS

4	1	0	3	29	41	6	7

The South African Touring Team of 1956:
J U Buchler (Transvaal), S S Viviers (Orange Free State), K T van Vollenhoven (Northern Transvaal), P G A Johnstone (Transvaal), R G Dryburgh (Natal), J G H du Preez (Western Province), T P D Briers (Western Province), W Rosenberg (Transvaal), P E Montini (Western Province), A I Kirkpatrick (Griqualand West), J J Nel (Western Province), C A Ulyate (Transvaal), B F Howe (Border), B D Pfaff (Western Province), T A Gentles (Western Province), C F Strydom (Orange Free State), H P J Bekker (Northern Transvaal), A C Koch (Boland), P S du Toit (Western Province), H N Walker (Western Transvaal), A J van der Merwe (Boland), M v d S Hanekom (Boland), J A du Rand (Northern Transvaal), J T Claassen (Western Transvaal), C J de Nysschen (Natal), J A J Pickard (Western Province), C J van Wyk (Transvaal), D S P Ackermann (Western Province), C J de Wilzem (Orange Free State), G P Lochner (Western Province), J J Starke (Western Province), D F Retief (Northern Transvaal)

TOUR RESULTS

DATE	VENUE	OPPONENTS	SCORE
9 June	Hamilton	Waikato	10-14
13 June	Whangarei	North Auckland	3-0
16 June	Auckland	Auckland	6-3
20 June	Palmerston	North Manawatu-Horowhenua	14-3
23 June	Wellington	Wellington	8-6
27 June	Gisborne	Poverty Bay-East Coast	22-0
30 June	Napier	Hawke's Bay	20-8
4 July	Nelson	Nelson-Marlborough-Golden Bay-Motueka	41-3

Date	Venue	Opponents	Score
7 July	Dunedin	Otago	14-9
14 July	Dunedin	New Zealand	6-10
18 July	Timaru	Hanan Shield	20-8
21 July	Christchurch	Canterbury	6-9
25 July	Westport	West Coast-Buller	27-6
28 July	Invercargill	Southland	23-12
31 July	Masterton	Wairarapa-Bush	19-8
4 August	Wellington	New Zealand	8-6
8 August	Wanganui	Wanganui-King Country	36-16
11 August	New Plymouth	Taranaki	3-3
18 August	Christchurch	New Zealand	10-17
22 August	Wellington	New Zealand Universities	15-22
25 August	Auckland	New Zealand Maoris	37-0
28 August	Rotorua	Bay of Plenty-Thames Valley-Counties	17-6
1 September	Auckland	New Zealand	5-11

CHAPTER 10

Fighting

As IT WAS in the beginning, is now and ever shall be.

Rugby wrings its hands in anguish about the fighting. Pious statements of contrition are made with a firm purpose of amendment. And yet the fighting goes on, and when rugby men meet they talk with glee about the great fights of yesteryear, and spectators will remember the fighting long after they have forgotten the score or even who won the match. The hooligan's game is not always played by gentlemen.

There was fighting in 1921 when the Springboks played Otago and Boy Morkel threatened to take his team off the field. From there till Ian Jones's punch on James Small in the World Cup Final of 1995 the problem of activities outside of the gentlemanly requirements of the Laws of the Game has persisted.

There was ugliness at Ellis Park in 1949 when the All Blacks played Transvaal. One moment of it was amusing.

Johnny Simpson, the tough All Black prop, was knocked to the ground, jumped up and saw everybody standing still.

"What's going on?" he asked belligerently.

"We're waiting for the ball," he was told.

"Forget the ball," he snarled. "Let's get on with the game."

Listen to the sweet voice of Winston McCarthy on the fighting in that match: "It was caused by Dannhauser paying too much attention to Simpson while the latter was not in possession of the ball. Being red-blooded, Simpson did not take kindly to Dannhauser's attentions and did the obvious thing; he made one mistake, however, he missed with his uppercut. The action brought a roar and a shower of bottles from the crowd. Play was held up for five minutes while bottles and broken glass were cleared from the field by the players, the police and some spectators . . . A little later in the game, Dannhauser was again in evidence. On this occasion Conrad was the victim, and he was laid out quite flat in the Transvaal 25.

No action was taken by the spectators over this incident!"

Listen to him again when Northern Transvaal played the All Blacks at Loftus Versfeld and Kevin Skinner and Jaap Bekker met for the first time. "There was an incident during the game, when Skinner took a man-sized swipe at front-ranker Bekker. The Referee spoke to both players and a penalty was awarded against the New Zealander. After the match I was speaking to the Referee, and he said to me, 'It is a pity that the spectators do not watch the game closely. When Skinner punched Bekker and the crowd roared, they apparently did not see what Bekker had done to Skinner just previously; he had pounded the New Zealander in the ribs with both hands, and it is only natural that Skinner would retaliate.' I said, 'So, seeing that there were faults on both sides, you gave a scrum?' 'Oh no,' he replied, 'I penalised Skinner!'"

To get objectivity in the recordings of the fighting is impossible, and that is the case when the worst of it happened, in 1956 when the Springboks were villains to the New Zealanders and the New Zealanders, above all the archfiend, Kevin Skinner, were the villains to the hard-done-by Springboks.

Bottle throwing was foreign to New Zealanders, though Basie Viviers did have one thrown at him in the third test in 1956. The thrower and his friend were removed by the police.

In 1956 fighting broke out in the ugly third match of the tour, when the Springboks played Auckland at Eden Park. It was then that the referee and the managements of the teams, failed to strike a blow which could have changed the ugly nature of violence which would continue through almost the whole of the tour.

The fighting started early. The referee, Eric Tindill of Wellington, was not inexperienced. He had refereed two tests in 1950 and another in 1955. Furthermore Snowy Tindill had played for New Zealand at both rugby and cricket. He did not send anybody off, and in those days, before additional powers for touch judges, the responsibility was solely his. The Springbok management did not, apparently, chastise anybody. The New Zealand authorities also took no action. There was no meeting of concerned people to get the matter sorted out. Perhaps everybody was being kind and hospitable and saying: "It's a man's game." They in fact were doing the game a disfavour.

The crowd were hostile and not impartial, which is understandable. When Geoff Parry of Auckland used his boots on a prone little Tommy Gentles, there was no upset. When a Springbok used his boot on Parry, there was loud booing. Two Auckland players kicked Johan Claassen and the crowd did not boo. But they booed when Claassen, the Springboks' unsuccessful goal kicker on the day, kicked at goal, then a most unusual occurrence, now part and parcel of almost every ground in the world. It was the spirit of Ellis Park 1949 all over again, though without the bottles.

John Graham played in the match and recalled: "People stopped thinking. It was bloody sad – we stopped thinking and got stuck into each other. The physical confrontation went on for the whole game. My abiding memory is of the nastiness of it."

He also blamed the Springboks.

Johan Claassen was more sinned against than sinning. His greatest sin was that he was better than any New Zealander in the line-outs, and for his trouble he got a punch on the nose that broke it in Wanganui.

When, at the dinner after the Auckland match, Craven suggested that such violence should cease, his statement received much publicity and for a while things quietened down.

All that is fine. At the centre of the storm was Kevin Skinner. There will not be a Springbok supporter in 1956 who will not die believing that Skinner was a villain, the Al Capone of rugby football. Not long before Craven died, he said of Skinner: "That is one man, in my opinion, who will never be welcome in South Africa."

Terry McLean, the doyen of rugby writers, discussed the matter briefly: "On the one hand it was said that Skinner warned Koch three times in scrummages and that Koch replied, 'We'll see,' when asked if he was going to give up a particular form of illegality. On the other hand, it was plainly evident that Koch was injured in a line-out in the first minute, before a set scrum had taken place. It was the second line-out. This tended to confirm the story that the All Blacks had gone onto the field determined to check the Springbok practice of getting through to the wrong side of the ruck after a line-out for the sake of kicking the ball back to their scrum half, and that Skinner had already discussed the matter with Koch."

Terry McLean, often virtuous, found all this mildly amusing.

Afterwards, the All Black centre fly half, Ross Brown, said: "I wouldn't like to go through that series again. It went beyond sport. We were playing for national prestige. It honestly took me three months to recover. I didn't sleep properly for about three months – those tests upset me so much." He was not available for the All Black tour in 1960.

In 1970 Winston McCarthy met Jaap Bekker who showed him a tooth. "See that tooth?" Jaap asked. "I was with Kevin Skinner and I told him to let me have a look at a gold ring he was wearing. He took it off and I put it in my pocket and told him it would go into my front tooth when I got

106

home to South Africa, the same tooth he broke off in the third test. Yes, the gold in my tooth came from Kevin's ring. Bekkers can't be choosers."

Neither Koch nor Bekker ever squealed about the treatment they received. As in all the series down the years it has been largely nonplayers who have done the squealing.

Ironically in 1994 Kevin Skinner returned his All Black tie to the NZRFU in protest at the continued selection of prop Richard Loe whom Skinner regarded as too dirty to play for New Zealand.

Sadly but perhaps fittingly, the series ended in a massive brawl with Tiny White carried off after receiving an evil boot in the back. The boot was said to belong to tortured Jaap Bekker. Fortunately White's injury turned out not to be serious and he attended the dinner after the test.

The 1960 tour of South Africa was child's play in comparison with the violence of 1956. But there were squabbles all right.

One broke out around Ton Vosloo, then a journalist and much later the managing director and chairman of Nasionale Pers and one of South Africa's most powerful men. In *Die Landstem,* Vosloo reported Whineray as saying he would use his fists on Piet du Toit if the rugged Bolander played in the tests. Tom Pearce was raucous in his denial of this, threatened Vosloo with legal action and banning from the All Blacks' hotels and matches! Peace was declared later.

There was, it is true, fighting at Boet Erasmus Stadium, which in 1995 was still a scene of violence during the World Cup, as it was when England visited in 1994.

It started quietly enough with Terry Lineen and Bienkie van Deventer, centres of all harmless people, having a go. But it became serious when the All Blacks objected to Doug Holton's scrumming. Roger Boon was shoved upwards and brought his knee up into the face of Freddie Hansen. Holton went to his hooker's assistance as props feel obliged to do and used a balled fist. Eric Anderson also used a balled fist. Ian Clarke kicked Hambly Parker, and so on and so forth.

The fighting went on well into the second half till Ken Carlson, or some moral force, brought order and for the last quarter of an hour rugby broke out.

The most priceless comment on the match came from Tim Mason, the 1947 All Black who migrated to Cape Town and then to Port Elizabeth. He said: "It is a long time since I have seen two teams retaliating to such an extent." Who retaliated first?

In his speech after the match, Nev MacEwan, the captain of the day, said: "It was the thirteenth match of the tour on the thirteenth day of the month and we had a technical knock-out in the 13th round." The two teams got on happily and without grudges from the final whistle onwards.

An interesting incident on that tour happened in the Transvaal match. John Wessels, the Transvaal hooker, had the ball partly trapped under his arm at a ruck which the All Blacks were intent on winning. Ron Horsley, the least angelic of the All Blacks on the tour, had several goes at his arm with his boot, occasioning medical treatment for Wessels and much booing from the crowd. The local press also voiced disapproval. T P McLean's attitude was: "Horsley was striking for the ball. The relevant law allows this." There is, when it comes to rucking, a cultural difference between New Zealand rugby and the game played in the rest of the world. To the New Zealanders any part of the body, apart from the head, is fair game for foot treatment if it impedes the sacred delivery of the ball.

Then there was tough stuff in Boland Stadium when the powerful local front row took on the All Blacks. The Boland front row that day was Chris Koch, Bertus van der Merwe and Piet du Toit. They believed that Wilson Whineray could not take it and that Hemi injured his ribs because his captain pulled out of a scrum. After that match big Tom Pearce had no complaints. That was the way he liked rugby to be played. "You can keep the flossy stuff," he said. Ron Hemi was replaced on the tour by Roger Boon.

The last test had its tough bits too, when Keith Oxlee was trampled on, when Briscoe was dropped with a short left hook and when Russell Watt got the warning word for lashing out at Hennie van Zyl with his boot.

The 1970 tour started quietly. It is true the All Blacks suffered bad injuries to Ian MacRae against Griquas and Colin Meads and Alan Sutherland against Eastern Transvaal, but there was no open warfare till they got to Transvaal.

The injury to Meads was crucial to the tour. Not a man of unblemished or angelic record, Meads may or may not have been the victim of violence rather than accident.

It started even before the game. Jannie le Roux, the frequently controversial president of the Transvaal RU, announced before the match: "The All Blacks may win the game, but Transvaal will win the fight." The leaders of the fight were certainly Transvaal, with prop Piet Bosman in the van.

The tough match of that series was the second at Newlands, surely one of the most physical tests ever played. Afterwards Ian MacRae, the strong All Black centre said: "Gee, it was hell out there in the foxholes."

<u>The list of casualties is impressive:</u>
Piston van Wyk: 6 stitches in his lip
Syd Nomis: 2 teeth knocked out and others loosened
Mannetjies Roux: painful kidneys and suspected cracked vertebrae
Dawie de Villiers: injured jaw
Fergie McCormick: 5 stitches in a scalp wound
Alan Sutherland: 6 stitches in a face wound
Ian MacRae: 5 stitches in a hand wound.

It was the Twenty-two Stitch Test.

There were of course other minor injuries.

The worst moment of them all, called shocking by Alex Veysey of New Zealand, happened in the sixth minute of the second half.

The All Blacks were on the attack in front of the Grand Stand when Syd Nomis intercepted. Fergie McCormick was in front of him and he chipped ahead, on about the halfway line. He raced to get round McCormick, but did not. McCormick, back turned, smacked out with his arms and collected Nomis in the teeth with his left elbow. Nobody in South Africa liked McCormick for the rest of the tour, especially when he let it be known that he had done it deliberately. He was afraid that Nomis would otherwise have scored.

Ron Burk felt that McCormick should have been sent off the field. There was hysteria about the whole incident, which most people would not even have seen as they would have been following the ball. And the referee penalised McCormick anyway. The one man who went in to bat for McCormick in the turbulent times afterwards was Danie Craven, who told the press to lay off him. When the press produced a series of photographs of McCormick, back turned, they apologised and some heat was taken off the nuggety fullback. The Springboks did not forget as easily and went for McCormick in the third test, after which he was dropped.

The match was only four minutes old when fighting started. A minute later the forwards were at it again. Johan Spies put his knee into Chris Laidlaw. Grizz Wyllie swung a punch at Jan Ellis. There was a terrifying ruck on the Springbok line at which Dawie de Villiers was trampled and Piston van Wyk left lying prone, eventually to be helped from the field with blood streaming from his face.

The All Blacks were ugly when they played the Gazelles, South Africans Under 23, and big men like Meads, Wyllie and Sutherland laid into the younger men. It was this diplomatic team's least edifying display.

It was a tough series. By comparison the 1976 series was gentle, though certainly not pure and innocent. It, too, had its unpleasant moments.

In the second test John Williams took a clout on the nose and had it shattered. South Africa showed many pictures of him with his nose covered and his sorrowing wife walking ahead of him. In the third test Moaner van Heerden stood on Pole Whiting's head and his ear needed six stitches. New Zealanders were shown this over and over again, and were up in arms about it. South Africans would produce a litany of players destroyed by All Black boots in 1976 "rucking". It was all bad for rugby. For New Zealanders, Moaner van Heerden was the brutal face of South African rugby, accused also of kicking Going who rose from the ground and piled into big Moaner van Heerden. And for some strange reason the erratic Kit Fawcett hit Morné du Plessis. It was the most violent of the tests in that series.

The All Blacks followed their defeat in the third test with a Monday match against North Western Cape and South West Africa – long names but short on playing strength and the All Blacks emerged from the match without any credit whatsoever. The fighting started early, with Billy Bush and Hennie Coetzee at each other. Later, so the story went, Billy Bush was actually ordered from the field for stamping on a player on the ground and then chasing Coetzee some 10 m to punch him besides the contact which his fist made with the referee's cheek. But the players, led by Frank Oliver, persuaded Schubel O'Reilly to allow him to stay and the referee, mindful of the need to be hospitable, allowed him to stay. Not that the All Blacks were grateful. In fact afterwards, when O'Reilly said he would give up refereeing, the All Blacks felt that it would be a good riddance.

According to O'Reilly he did not send Bush off as there was no reason to do so. He had no reason to send Bush off as it was Bush's first act of silliness and that he did not punch anybody but charged at Coetzee. O'Reilly warned and penalised Bush. O'Reilly did not retire then. He did so in 1979 when he sent off Naas Botha in a club match, just before Botha was due to play for Northern Transvaal. O'Reilly found it unacceptable that Northern Transvaal officials, including the president, were angered with him and not Naas Botha who had previously been warned in the match. Schubel O'Reilly went off to play bowls instead.

The player worst wounded in this battle was Kevin Eveleigh who took Chris Saayman's boot in the face and had to be replaced by Ken Stewart. Eveleigh's wife Joy was so upset she called for the cancellation of the tour.

J J Stewart labelled the match the most disgusting he had seen in years.

Not long afterwards there was more fighting in Kimberley. After a warning Jimmy Young laid into Frank Oliver who did not turn the other cheek. Young was sent off by Tinkie Heyns and went off. The two captains, Van As Jordaan and Andy Leslie, whose plate was broken by a punch in the mouth, pleaded Young's case but there was no suspended sentence. That evening Frank Oliver sympathised with Jimmy Young.

The final test also had its hairy moments, and Keith Murdoch, for punching in a scrum and after it, and Jazz Muller for kicking a player on the ground, were lucky to stay on the field. After all the referee, Bert Woolley, had sent off Lion John O'Shea for less in 1968.

There were outbursts of nastiness in 1981 but nothing like the controversy that surrounded the violence, apart from other aspects, of the 1986 Cavaliers' tour. In fact the worst bit was in the first test when Gysie Pienaar took umbrage at Bernie Fraser's unlawful attack on him and struck out at the wing who struck back. Soon lots of players were striking. When it ceased Laurie Prideaux called the captains and Fraser and told them they were being really stupid "in these difficult times for rugby". Things went better after that.

The most notorious act of violence happened after only 37 minutes of play on the tour. It was not the only act of violence, nor in a sense worse than many acts of mob violence which would occur on the tour. It was a solitary, highly effective punch which caused a wave of revulsion to flood throughout most of South Africa as the deed was shown over and over again on television.

Against Northern Transvaal at Loftus Versfeld in Pretoria, in the 37th minute of the first half, an aggrieved Burger Geldenhuys rose from the ground and set off in pursuit of any Cavalier, set on vengeance.

Ahead of him was the Cavalier captain, Andy Dalton. From behind Geldenhuys swung a round-house punch at Dalton. It connected with his jaw and broke it. That was the end of Dalton's tour. It was also the end of Geldenhuys's test hopes for the year. On 26 May, a month after the punch, Dalton was able to eat again.

It was not the only fighting in that match. Uli Schmidt punched Gary Whetton, and the referee said to him: "Uli, jy's gelukkig, ou pêl." (Uli, you're lucky, old chum.) The statement was broadcast to the world over Veldore (Field Ears).

The worst fighting of the tour was in the night match at King's Park when the Cavaliers played Natal, the match after defeat in the first test. The fighting started at the very first scrum. It was worse at the line-out soon afterwards. After that things came to some sort of order, but it was the worst fighting ever seen in South Africa in a match involving a touring team.

111

In the fourth test a decision unique in international rugby was given. Gary Knight hit Gert Smal, which was always a mistake. Gert Smal hit Knight who was unconscious for a count of twelve. When he was revived Knight along with Smal was sent to the cooler by Ken Rowlands, an instruction given to the referee by Danie Craven who did not want any of the untidiness which would accompany sending off.

During the 1994 Springbok tour of New Zealand, there was, inevitably, more fighting. Unfortunately for the Springboks they were on the receiving end of refereeing wrath.

James Small leapt for a ball in the Waikato match and collected the Waikato captain, Steve Gordon, knocking him out. Small was cited afterwards. It was not done in an amiable way.

Nothing was said to the Springboks in Hamilton on the Sunday after the match. But as they were leaving, they were handed a note that told of the decision to cite Small. Small and Jannie Engelbrecht, the manager, had to go to Wellington for a hearing at which Small was "censured". He thereby achieved an unenviable double of being the first Springbok sent off in a test match when Ed Morrison had sent him off at Ballymore in Brisbane in 1993 for verbal abuse, and of being the first Springbok cited.

Apparently the citing was led by Stan Hickford, president of Waikato, who reported the matter to David Howman, the New Zealand watchdog in this matter, who found no reason to cite any New Zealanders. Presumably the rule of war applied – winner takes all, including the moral high ground.

That he was cited was odd. Neither his action nor that of Adri Geldenhuys was as violent as several others on the tour that went unnoticed and uncited, which tended to devalue the citing by calling its impartiality into question. Certainly the kick that struck Mark Andrews's head at Lancaster Park deserved some sort of censure, the same boot that concussed Balie Swart at Carisbrook in the first test – an anonymous boot to this day.

The match in Palmerston North was a disgrace. It was certainly the most unpleasant of the tour. Eventually the referee, Steve Walsh of Wellington, sent off Adri Geldenhuys for a feeble punch after the touch judge had produced his flag and reported the incident. Geldenhuys's punch was certainly not the most violent act of the afternoon. It did not compare with the efforts of Mana Otai, who captained Tonga at the 1995 World Cup. Geldenhuys's action was certainly far less violent than Gary Nesdale's use of his feet on Jannie Claassen, and when the Springboks later pointed out a punch by Mana Otai, the Manawatu lock, they were penalised for chirping!

Afterwards Gary Knight, the great All Black prop in 36 tests, said: "I feel sorry for the guy that got sent off because I know what it's like to play in a country and feel that everything is up against you. From where I sat Manawatu certainly handed out as much as South Africa did. I saw an incident where a Manawatu player walked all over a South African and right in front of the line umpire. He didn't even put his flag out. I don't think it washes."

To the Springboks the citing and the sending off were all part of the war psychosis gripping New Zealand. The worst of it was a public attack on James Small by Murray Deaker, a personality on radio and television in New Zealand.

During the tour much had been made of James Small. He was on the covers of all sorts of magazines. Much was made of his rehabilitation from drugs. Then along came Meaker who said of Small: "I am well aware that the effects of marijuana stay around for a long time. This guy is an absolute nutter." Legal steps were contemplated but fizzled out.

From Palmerston North the team went to Wellington to complete the week's hat trick of horrors. The match itself was a delight, but afterwards there was shown over and over again the horrible sight of Johan le Roux biting at Sean Fitzpatrick's ear like a crazed dog.

It is hard to imagine the indignation in New Zealand. The incident was shown over and over again. It was the Burger Geldenhuys-Andy Dalton incident magnified many times. South Africans bowed their heads in shame. Before the NZRFU had any hearing, the Springbok management decided that Johan le Roux would be sent back to South Africa where there was precious little sympathy for him.

Later in the year the portrayal of the incident was studied by New Zealand's Broadcasting Standards Authority which found that the television coverage had been unbalanced because it had not shown the whole incident.

The whole incident would have shown Fitzpatrick attacking Le Roux and shoving his head into the dirt. Attacking the man known for a short fuse?

Whatever Johan le Roux may have had in his defence and even though he had support from Andy Dalton and Andy Haden, nobody listened and he was suspended by the NZRFU until 1 March 1996 and sent home from the tour, another unenviable first for the new Springboks. He admitted guilt and later appealed against the severity of his sentence, but to no avail. The whole incident had done enormous harm to the good name of the game and above all to the good name of the Spring-

113

bok. It would be forever one of rugby's most notorious "incidents".

For the Springboks, who had been an odd mixture of friendliness and arrogant rudeness on the tour, it was a day of shame.

Sean Fitzpatrick set many records in his time. One of them may just have been creating so much mayhem without ever being sent off the field – the master agent provocateur, the angel who may hide devilish cunning. His welcome to Naas Botha at Ellis Park was a late tackle and an unprovoked punch in the first minute of the 1992 test. And he had another go at Naas Botha later in the match, with his customary impunity. But then he also punched Francois Pienaar on the nose, which may mean that he has a thing about opposing captains.

The Springboks under Engelbrecht refused to cite, which angered Louis Luyt.

The last match between the two teams, in 1995, was not without its silliness either. Ian Jones was silly when he punched James Small, probably hoping to fire the wing's short fuse, and Richard Loe was barely on the field when he stuck his boot into Mark Andrews, causing the lock to be replaced. As they had not done in 1994, the Springboks behaved.

CHAPTER 11

Back to Rugby

IT WAS BACK TO rugby – but only just. The 1960 All Black tour almost did not happen. Again the Maori question was posed. Again South Africa, then in the grip of Verwoerdism and the push towards a republic, would not have Maoris. This time New Zealand rugby had a bit more concern for its fellow New Zealanders, but in the end the desire to preserve ties with South Africa triumphed over moral considerations. The tour happened, and the Maoris stayed in New Zealand. That was the first defeat for New Zealand in 1960. New Zealand came to South Africa brimming with confidence. South Africa was still in a trough of despondency.

The Springboks had lost their first series in 60 years just four years before and then they had lost a series to France, their first home defeat in 62 years. They had tried a bit of preparation with a test against Scotland in April 1960, the first short tour in rugby's history. The Springboks had won, but they were certainly not convincing.

There was uncertainty about too many important things – halfbacks and captain amongst them.

While the Springboks were thus wobbling, seemingly out of control on a downward slope, the All Blacks had beaten the Springboks and then won a series against the British Lions, when Don Clarke outdid Okey Geffin. And the All Blacks had an established, charismatic captain in Wilson Whineray, a revered figure in New Zealand rugby long after he had stopped playing.

There was little hope in the national breast for success against the All Blacks. But down below there was a new spirit moving, a young spirit and it has ever been youth that has carried the day in warfare and on the rugby field. The Junior Springboks had gone off to Argentina in 1959 and returned full of success to beat the Rest of South Africa. A new team was being born.

On their way to South Africa the All Blacks played and won five matches in Australia, including two on the same day in Sydney when they split into two teams and one played Queensland, the other New South Wales. The first try scored for the All Blacks on their 1960 tour was scored by Eddie Stapleton of Australia, for two New South Welshmen, Maurie Graham and the great Eddie Stapleton, filled in for injured players. The All Blacks arrived in South Africa confident and determined. The whole of New Zealand had confidence in them. The whole country had a mission – to win in South Africa.

Red Conway, the New Zealand loose forward, was afraid he would miss the tour because of a septic finger. He had it amputated to get it to heal more quickly and to avoid affecting the rest of his body.

South Africans may have feared them, but they turned out to welcome them warmly – 10 000 people at Jan Smuts Airport in Johannesburg on the afternoon of Sunday 22 May 1960. The All Blacks then went off to Vereeniging to get acclimatised for the tour. It would not be as long or as softening as the Hermanus stay of 1949.

The All Blacks opened their tour on 28 May 1960 against a universities side, as they had done in 1949. This time they played Northern Universities in Potchefstroom instead of Southern Universities at Newlands, and this time the All Blacks soared to victory, 45-6, eight tries to nil. And Don Clarke's booming boot added to South Africa's nervousness. He had a similar effect in 1960 to the effect Jonah Lomu had during the World Cup in 1995.

All of this élan evaporated at their next stop as the All Blacks went down to the coast and played Natal in the steamy cauldron of King's Park. Natal, captained by Brian Irvine and including Roy Dryburgh and Nick Labuschagne, had one plan – to shift the game laterally as far as possible to make the big All Black forwards move about in the heat as much as possible. And on the flank they had Percy Hall, who wrestled professionally as Mr X. His job was to keep Peter Jones in check, which he did with devastating effect.

The crowd was partisan and passionate beyond good manners, Don Clarke missed seven kicks and in the end only a refereeing error in their favour earned New Zealand a draw as Don Clarke loomed up on the blind side, took a big forward pass and was nonetheless given the try. Natal 6, New Zealand 6. It was a match Natal could and probably should have won.

Drawing was not a good result for the All Blacks because they lost confidence in their backs, and with good reason. It seemed that New Zealand believed that for victory over South Africa they needed to win at forward.

All their effort, concentration and thought had gone into the pack, and the backs were left to hazard. If the 1949 match with the Varsities was a decisive shock for New Zealand, so was the Natal match in 1960. Off they went again on their wanderings – to big wins over Griqualand West in Kimberley; South West Africa in Windhoek where the Administrator welcomed the tourists as the "1906 Wallabies"; Boland in Wellington on a day when Piet "Spiere" du Toit annoyed Wilson Whineray by overpowering the All Black captain in the scrums and Ron Hemi injured ribs and the Koch brothers, Willem and Chris, played against their second All Black touring team; Western Province Universities at Newlands in a match when the expected champagne turned to flat beer; and Northern Transvaal at Loftus Versfeld.

The last was a win of great proportions and it came a week before the first test. The All Blacks were gloriously on course and would be peaking just in time. After all, the Northern Transvaal match was, as has become a cliché, "the fifth test". New Zealand won 27-3, three tries to one, and two of those tries were scored by the awesome Big Fisherman, Peter Jones. The All Blacks were in ecstasy after the match. They even loved and admired the referee – H P A Hofmeyr of Western Transvaal, a teacher at Potchefstroom Boys' High and known generally as Hoffie. They thought him the best referee in South Africa though he never did get to referee a test match.

But still the South African public and press found the All Blacks and their rugby unattractive. The *Sunday Times* wrote: "Anyone who thinks the All Blacks play unattractive rugby because of an overwhelming desire to win at all costs is making a mistake. The explanation is far simpler. They play unattractive rugby because they don't know how to play any other."

The All Blacks were favourites to win the first test, but that did not stop people packing into Ellis Park for the opening test of the series and it did not stop them getting right behind their team. All afternoon long the noise of battle rose. The result was in fact never in doubt. It was victory as clear-cut as could be and it went to the Springboks.

The All Blacks blamed prematch tensions, which may just have affected the Springboks as well, and the altitude for their lethargy. Altitude has ever been a bogey for visiting teams. South African teams never mention it as an excuse for victory, and Western Province, Eastern Province and Natal are still expected to do well at Loftus Versfeld and Ellis Park. Ellis Park is higher (364 m higher) than Loftus Versfeld where the All Blacks had performed so well, not a massive difference. And half of the Springbok forwards came from sea level and seemed lively enough. And it was the All Blacks who put in the great finish in Bloemfontein in the third test, which suggested that they could cope with altitude. The fact was that the underdogs had played much better than the top dogs and in the process Hennie van Zyl had scored two glorious tries.

From a scrum Dick Lockyear passed to Keith Oxlee. In from the blind side came Michel Antelme. Oxlee dummied to his left and then shot the ball inside to the wing. Antelme sailed through a gap. Ralph Caulton covered and went for Antelme who skipped John Gainsford with a long pass to Ian Kirkpatrick. It was two against one – Kirkpatrick and Hennie van Zyl against Don Clarke. Upright Van Zyl scored behind the posts.

The Springboks won a maul. In came Antelme from the blind side wing again some 40 yards from the New Zealand line. He did not get as far this time but far enough to get his backs past the New Zealand defenders and in no time Hennie van Zyl had the ball and went, knees pumping, down the left-hand touchline. Don Clarke came across. Van Zyl hesitated. Clarke had to see that he was not beaten on the inside. Van Zyl spurted and suddenly he was through the narrow corridor between Clarke and the touchline.

The final score was an astonishing 13-0 to South Africa, and it could have been a lot more.

The referee for the first test was Bertie Strasheim of Northern Transvaal, the son of an international referee, J J Strasheim, the only father-son combination of international referees in the world of rugby. The All Blacks chose him from a panel of four. The other three were Chris Ackermann of Boland, E W H Badenhorst of Transvaal and Piet Calitz of Western Province.

From Johannesburg the All Blacks made the long flight up to Ndola in Northern Rhodesia, as it was then called, for their first-ever visit there. The match was played in the copper town of Kitwe, and unusually the Rhodesian side had twelve players from Northern Rhodesia. The Governor General Sir Evelyn Hone was at the match. It was, from the New Zealand point of view, a waste of time, for they played remarkably poorly in a match which had no flow at all. And they missed the braai organised for them after the match as they found the food at braais not filling enough! They preferred to return to their hotel, thus causing much local upset. The New Zealanders hit back by complaining about the poor standard of South African hospitality. It was all rather shoddy.

The All Blacks then went down to Salisbury. The Rhodesians were kind. The Governor General, Lord Dalhousie, welcomed them, a dance was organised, the All Blacks were driven to the Victoria Falls and victory was easier at new Glamis Park, the Old Hararians' ground which was renamed in honour of the visit by the Queen Mother. The All Blacks won but achieved their victory without endearing themselves to the local populace. Eric Shore, sports editor of the *Evening Standard,* laid into the All Blacks. "There is no need for the All Blacks to use feet and fists as they did, unless winning meant so much to them."

After avenging the Forty-Niners in Rhodesia, the All Blacks went down to Bloemfontein in the days when the war cry VRYSTAAT was at its most popular. For the home crowd it was a match to shout about. They did not score a try and the All Blacks scored two, it's true, but Orange Free State beat the All Blacks 9-8 and Don Clarke kicked so poorly that he was replaced by Russell Watt, whose kick, a potential winner, rolled along the ground.

Playing for Free State that day was a lock forward called Louis Luyt, subsequently to have such an enormous impact on world rugby. McLean says of his performance: "He was a splendid forward, this man, and his example was being taken up more and more strongly by his team-mates."

In many ways, the All Blacks defeated themselves. They missed scoring opportunities and Don Clarke had another "Durban day", missing several kicks. Ironically it was his kicking that was to save New Zealand in a test match on the same Free State Stadium in Bloemfontein.

The next match was an occasion of rejoicing – for the All Blacks and for rugby football, for on that day the All Black backs came alive as they beat Brian Irvine's Junior Springboks 20-6, five tries to one, and all the All Black tries were scored by backs. Then came trouble – yet another Battle of Boet Erasmus in Port Elizabeth. Before a small crowd, Eastern Province and New Zealand fought. If there was a match, New Zealand won it 16-3. The only real excitement of the afternoon was the fighting. The only real rugby was played in the curtain-raiser.

Before the Western Province match the All Blacks took massive umbrage when Louis Babrow, the 1937 Springbok and chairman of selectors in the Western Province, wrote an open letter to Jack Sullivan, the New Zealand coach, asking them to stop their unattractive, "pathetic rugby". The letter appeared, preceded by much fanfare, in the Magazine section of the *Cape Times.* It looked like a Dear Jack letter, reminding him of their "stirring series" in 1937 and the matches at Maadi and the "party afterwards and the Egyptian belly dancers" and that they had both been wounded on practically the same day at the Battle of Alamein. Babrow told Jack Sullivan that "you are overall the best side ever to come to South Africa . . . but I must say you are the least attractive team I have seen in many a year." He exhorted Sullivan and his men. "What about making today [when Western Province and the All Blacks would meet] a great one. Let both sides try and play aggressive and constructive rugby and let us give the rugby public a treat."

The All Blacks gave the rugby public a treat, Western Province did not. Babrow had every right to feel embarrassed.

But he did say some true things, for example on the All Blacks: "Not a single three-quarter has enhanced his reputation here and why? Because he is thwarted and not allowed to play his natural game – he has to play to a pattern, he is told to do this and to do that."

Only a tiny crowd, for Newlands, arrived at the match. The irony was that Western Province, apparently at Babrow's instructions, played far drabber rugby than the All Blacks and got a hiding. The spark died again when the All Blacks went to Oudtshoorn and bored the friendly folk of the ostrich capital of the world.

During the tour Morrie Mackenzie of New Zealand wrote about the "horrible bulldozing football which has nearly wrecked our game and certainly tarnished the All Blacks' name." At the end of the tour the *New Zealand Herald* wrote: "We have had a surfeit of this sort of rugby: scrum, kick, line-out and ruck, and the whole dreary routine repeated up and down the touchline until one side or the other, probably out of sheer boredom, makes a fatal error."

Later the SA Rugby Board formally apologised to the NZRFU for Babrow's letter.

When they came back to Newlands for the second test, nobody would have regarded the All Blacks as favourites. The Springboks were the favourites, the worst possible position for the Springboks to be.

Both sides scored a try, but this time Don Clarke kicked like a dream – a conversion, a penalty goal and a dropped goal which travelled high and true for some 45 yards. The pass to Colin Meads for his try certainly looked well forward, but the truth was that New Zealand were full value for their 11-3 win.

There were three good features in the Springbok effort that afternoon – the gem of Oxlee's try which brought the Springboks level with Clarke's penalty goal, their grim defence and their sportsmanship at the end as they stood at the tunnel at Newlands and clapped the All Blacks off the field.

But then the match had started in that spirit when before the kick-off Wilson Whineray trotted over to Chris Koch to congratulate him on breaking the record for the number of caps – 22 in those days, one more than Salty du Rand had achieved.

Perhaps that sort of thing is no longer possible. They would both be rare gestures today. But the second test in 1960 was a good match, good for rugby football and good for the series.

Central Universities, for whom one of the forgotten men of the 1956 tour, Chris de Nysschen, did well in the line-outs, achieved a rare feat – scoring four tries against New Zealand. The All Blacks also scored four tries but Tony Davies kicked better and New Zealand won 21-12. Eastern Transvaal scored two tries against the All Blacks in Springs and New Zealand scored one, but Don Clarke kicked well and the All Blacks won 11-6. They did not deserve to win.

Willem Brits, that eager leader of men, was a deacon in the Tamboerskloof congregation of the Dutch Reformed Church. The dominee, Piet Fourie, sent him a telegram wishing him well for the match and expressing the hope that it would be enjoyable and he suggested that Willem read, for himself, a passage from Colossians. Brits took his Bible to the team in the dressing room and read to them from Colossians: "Whatever your work is put your heart into it as if it were for the Lord and not for men, knowing that the Lord will repay you by making you his heirs. It is Christ the Lord that you are serving; anyone who does wrong will be repaid in kind and he does not favour one person more than another." Then he led the Combined Services out onto Loftus Versfeld and they beat the All Blacks 8-3, two tries to nil. On the flank for the services team was one Frik du Preez, who would one day be acknowledged as one of the greatest forwards of all time. Oh, and a policeman was playing prop, J L Myburgh, whose nickname was Mof. It was a fine match.

Transvaal had nine Springboks in their team when they met the All Blacks at Ellis Park but they succumbed to the might of the All Black pack and Don Clarke's thunderous boot. The All Blacks won 19-3, shoving aside the memory of the Combined Services match. There were angry moments in the match, followed by downright nastiness at Potchefstroom when the All Blacks thumped Johan Claassen's Western Transvaal. The crowd did not wait for cause to vent their anger. Bottles were hurled from the start and not even a lunatic mind could have found any justification for such an action that day at Potchefstroom. McLean said: "South African audiences had on the whole been fair, sporting and agreeably partisan. By the average standard, the behaviour at Potchefstroom was intolerable." And then there was the report of Fred Boshier of New Zealand's *Evening Post*: "On the whole it was an orderly affair." The eye of the beholder affects reporting!

And so they went to Bloemfontein for the third test and one of the most dramatic six minutes in test match history, let alone in matches between the two countries.

There was personal drama, too. The Springbok selectors dropped the captain, Roy Dryburgh. But they did not bring in the Free State fullback Piet Botha. Instead they chose Lionel Wilson, the quiet fullback from the Western Province who came to Bloemfontein and was vilified by Free State partisans. As captain the selectors chose Avril Malan, then a 23-year-old, a great leader of men. Today he would be too small for a lock forward but he would still make a great tight-head flank with his mobility and dedication to duty. He remains the youngest Springbok captain ever.

The Springboks were winning the match comfortably. 11-3 in a test match in those days was a massive lead, and the Springboks were, one would have thought, a team of steely determination enough not to yield such a lead. The All Blacks, as statistics will prove over and over again, are a first-half team. Time and again they have been less productive in the second half.

Dick Lockyear kicked a penalty, and that was the only score in the first half. Don Clarke kicked a penalty and that levelled the scores. Then the Springboks took over. Lockyear kicked another penalty and then Ian Kirkpatrick picked up a charged-down kick and set off on a clever run, twice selling dummies before putting Keith Oxlee in for a try at the posts. The game looked won.

With six minutes to go Don Clarke kicked a penalty goal, from 60 yards out and into the light wind. It did not look like missing. The score became 11-6.

There were two minutes to go, and the All Blacks won a ruck inside the Springbok 25. Kevin Briscoe shovelled out a poor pass towards Steve Nesbit. It passed him but Terry Lineen picked it up and passed to Kevin Laidlaw who shot through a gap. Fifteen yards from the line he punted past Lionel Wilson and Frank McMullen raced after the ball, past Michel Antelme. Doug Hopwood was also in desperate pursuit of the ball.

Frank McMullen dived, scored and knocked himself out!

Six yards from the left-hand touchline Don Clarke lined up the conversion and goaled it. It was one of those great moments of iron nerve in sport. Don Clarke had big-match temperament. And he had been in bed with a cold on the Thursday before the match.

Ralph Burmeister blew his whistle, and so ended a dramatic test. It was on to Port Elizabeth and all to play for. And Tom Pearce said: "Drawing is like kissing your sister."

There were a couple of chores before then – victories over North Eastern Cape, one that brought the All Blacks no credit for they failed even to score a try though the home side did, and a handsome one over Border in East London. It was victory and deserved, but not without controversy.

The Springboks and the All Blacks met in windy Port Elizabeth to decide the series. And the wind blew.

The All Blacks played with the wind in the first half of the fourth test, and had only three points to show for it at the end of the half, the same number as South Africa had managed. The All Blacks could have had more. How loudly they would claim that they should have had more.

Early in the half Frank McMullen counterattacked from a poor South African kick and raced 40 yards for the line. He passed Lionel Wilson. The goal line was ahead when Keith Oxlee did enough to his ankle for McMullen to fall prone on the ground. He got to his knees and crawled/dived/jack-knifed/bounced/scrambled/crawled across the line. He grounded the ball in what would have been a try had Ralph Burmeister not decided otherwise. He penalised McMullen.

There were arguments forever about the rights and wrongs of the decision but it will remain forever a fact as much as Norling's penalty in 1981. It is fascinating to speculate on the course of the match and the outcome of the series had that try been allowed.

After some angry outbreaks, mostly involving Kevin Briscoe and Martin Pelser, who were the spark and the gunpowder during the series, Don Clarke goaled a penalty. And then came a crucial score. Into the gusting gale Dick Lockyear kicked a penalty goal from 32 yards out to level the scores, and that's how it stayed till half-time.

There was nothing spectacular about the second half as the wind-assisted Springboks stayed in All Black territory.

Doug Hopwood caught Don Clarke in his goal area and he was forced to concede a 5-yard scrum. The Springboks won the scrum and wheeled. Dick Lockyear feinted to pick up the ball, and there was mighty Martin Pelser powering through Don Clarke for the match's only try, which Lockyear converted.

Muscle, heart, sinew, brain and emotion were strained to the full but none of the thirty players added to the score, and South Africa had won the match 8-3 and the series 2-1. But it was not an inspiring tour.

Afterwards Tom Pearce said: "You are worthy champions of the rubber. You have won the series with honour and we leave with honour." Terry McLean wrote: "Let there be no doubt in anyone's mind that in the fourth and vital rubber match of the series, the Springboks defeated the All Blacks much more decisively than the score would suggest." And Wilson Whineray said: "We feel closer to you people than we did when we arrived four months ago." When his playing days were over, he opposed the 1981 Springbok tour to New Zealand.

The All Blacks played a dull match against a Transvaal XV while waiting to fly off home via Mauritius and the Cocos Islands where they were, frustratingly, delayed because of engine trouble. And some played with Springboks for the South African Barbarians against Natal.

When they got home, they had to play against the Rest of New Zealand, the sort of punishment the 1956 Springboks had had to endure. Like the 1956 Springboks, they won. In fact the All Blacks won easily.

Before the fourth test, two young New Zealanders had endeared themselves to the friendly people of Port Elizabeth by running round the field with a banner which read: "Totsiens from the Kiwis. See you in '65."

Till we meet again. But there were many in New Zealand who believed that this would be the last All Black tour.

TOUR STATISTICS (SOUTH AFRICA ONLY)

P	W	D	L	Pf	Pa	Tf	Ta
26	20	2	4	441	164	75	23

TESTS

4	1	1	2	25	35	2	5

The New Zealand Touring Team of 1960:
D B Clarke (Waikato), W A Davies (Auckland), R W Caulton (Wellington), D H Cameron (Mid-Canterbury), J R Watt (Wellington), R F McMullen (Auckland), T P A O'Sullivan (Taranaki), K F Laidlaw (Southland), T R Lineen (Auckland), S G F Bremner (Canterbury), S R Nesbit (Auckland), A H Clarke (Auckland), R J Urbahn (Taranaki), K C Briscoe (Taranaki), M W Irwin (Otago), W J Whineray (Auckland) (c), I J Clarke (Waikato), E J Anderson (Bay of Plenty), R C Hemi (Waikato), D Young (Canterbury), R J Boon (Taranaki), I N MacEwan (Wellington), C E Meads (King Country), P F Hilton-Jones (North Auckland), R H Horsley (Wellington), K R Tremain (Canterbury), E A R Pickering (Waikato), W D Gillespie (Otago), D J Graham (Canterbury), R J Conway (Otago), H C Burry (Canterbury)

124

TOUR RESULTS

Date	Venue	Opponents	Score
28 May	Potchefstroom	Transvaal Universities	45-6
31 May	Durban	Natal	6-6
4 June	Kimberley	Griqualand West	21-9
8 June	Windhoek	South West Africa	27-3
11 June	Wellington	Boland	16-0
15 June	Newlands	Western Province Universities	14-3
18 June	Pretoria	Northern Transvaal	27-3
25 June	Johannesburg	South Africa	0-13
29 June	Kitwe	Rhodesian XV	13-9
2 July	Salisbury	Rhodesia	29-14
6 July	Bloemfontein	Orange Free State	8-9
9 July	Durban	Junior Springboks	20-6
13 July	Port Elizabeth	Eastern Province	16-3
16 July	Newlands	Western Province	20-8
19 July	Oudtshoorn	South Western Districts	18-6
23 July	Newlands	South Africa	11-3
27 July	East London	Central Universities	21-12

DATE	VENUE	OPPONENTS	SCORE
30 July	Springs	Eastern Transvaal	11-6
3 August	Pretoria	Combined Services	3-8
6 August	Johannesburg	Transvaal	17-3
9 August	Potchefstroom	Western Transvaal	28-3
13 August	Bloemfontein	South Africa	11-11
17 August	Aliwal North	North Eastern Districts	15-6
20 August	East London	Border	30-3
27 August	Port Elizabeth	South Africa	3-8
3 September	Johannesburg	Transvaal XV	9-3

CHAPTER 12

Demonstrably Wrong

"RUGBY WAS THE winner."

This became the cliché of the tour. Kobus Louw, the beaming manager of the 1965 Springboks, used it over and over again. And his team was enormously popular. Teams are popular in New Zealand when they lose and mix.

There was a lot right with this tour, and rugby was at the heart of what was good and right. What was wrong was out of the hands of the players and even the rugby authorities. There was a battle on the field, but it was a wholesome one. Then came wrong, and when it came it came as a sudden bucket of cold water, but it was not a nasty prank. There was the grip of evil's cold fingers at the heart.

It was a series the Springboks were never going to win. They simply did not have the forward power, but their backs were clearly superior to the All Blacks and scored some marvellous tries. And they achieved one of the great turn-abouts of test rugby.

That year, 1965, was the *annus horribilis* of South African rugby. They went, grossly underprepared and out of season, to Ireland and Scotland and did not win any of their five matches. Avril Malan had let the SARFB know before the short tour that he was not available for Australia and New Zealand. The ship was without a captain.

They could have had Doug Hopwood. They should have had Doug Hopwood, the outstanding player in the team and the great Western Province captain. But Hopwood was *persona non grata* with the vice-president of the South African Rugby Football Board, Kobus Louw, who was also the manager of the 1965 Springboks. Louw had been instrumental in getting the SARFB's executive to veto the selectors' choice for Ireland and Scotland because they had chosen Hopwood as captain.

And so it came to pass that Dawie de Villiers, the fair-haired student prince, a theological student, captained the side to Australasia, but no fairy tale happened and no miracle either. The vice-captain was also a scrum half – Nelie Smith. The French did the same sort of thing with Jacques Fouroux and Richard Astre. It did not work for them either.

No captain should have had to endure the humiliation which Dawie de Villiers endured, and yet later he was to become part of the government that caused the humiliation, a cabinet minister no less.

The coach of the team was the great Hennie Muller, but more and more he was pushed aside by some elements in the team.

The Springboks lost both tests in Australia. They complained bitterly about the refereeing but the defeats remained. By the time they got to New Zealand the 1965 Springboks had played 11, won 3, drawn 1, and lost 7. It was not heartening.

Luckily they had a more gentle introduction than their 1956 predecessors. They started with the Poverty Bay-East Coast combination and won 32-3. But the reality of New Zealand was not long in coming. Down they went to Wellington and they went down to Wellington – 23-6, at the time the Springboks' biggest defeat ever. It did not matter that each side scored a try and that Wellington filled in with many kicks to lead 17-3 at half-time.

Manawatu and Horowhenua combined to play the Springboks in Palmerston North and got a hiding. The Springboks then went down to Dunedin and beat Otago, just. In Christchurch they beat the New Zealand Juniors before heading west to New Plymouth and tough Taranaki. From there they raced down to the bottom of South Island and then up to Christchurch for a 6-5 victory over Canterbury at Lancaster Park which was to prove their happiest venue, then to the west coast and then back to Wellington for the first test.

There is always something special about the first test of a series, so full of uncertainties, providing so many answers after it. For one thing, the side wanting to win the series really needed to win the first test, 1937 notwithstanding.

Nine players in that first test had played in 1960 – John Gainsford, Lionel Wilson, Keith Oxlee, Lofty Nel, Abe Malan, Wilson Whineray, who had played only club rugby the previous year, Dick Conway, who came in when Waka Nathan withdrew, Colin Meads and Kel Tremain. New Zealand won the first test 6-3. It was anybody's game in the cold, windy wet. The All Blacks were in for a try early when Bill Birtwistle, who had come into the side as a new cap when Malcolm Dick pulled out through injury, took a pass from Mick Williment on the blind side to score in the corner. Just before half-time, the All Blacks scored again, and the Springboks

The Sixth Division team at the end of World War II with Bombardier Boy Louw in uniform at the back left and the captain, Basil Kenyon, with the ball.

The Two Types _____ by Jon

THIS BAR was first discovered in A.D. 1944, and was once the scene of a terrific scrum, down between a party of Kiwis and a party of Springboks. It holds the record for having more jeeps stolen from outside than any other similar establishment in this ancient city.

GIN
COGNAC
STREGA
DEMIJ SING
GRAPPA

All over the Middle East South Africans and New Zealanders enjoyed their private war.

The players gaze into the distance during the exciting but controversial first test in 1949. On the extreme right is Eddie Hofmeyr, the referee of the day. The players are from the left: Felix du Plessis, Hansie Brewis, Bubbles Koch, Hennie Muller, John McNab, Larry Savage (on the ground), Louis Strydom, Charlie Willocks, Fiks van de Merwe, Ballie Wahl (on the ground), Lachie Grant and Floors Duvenage.

The great Bob Scott kicks at Newlands in 1949.

It was different long ago. The two captains, Felix du Plessis and Fred Allen, leave the field at the end of another tough encounter, the victor downcast, the vanquished wreathed in smiles.

The book according to the Kiwi.

Geffin (ringed below) reels away after kicking his record-breaking fifth penalty goal against the 1949 All Blacks. The ball (ringed above) sails high between the up-rights, to the delight of the spectators on the roof of the North Stand at Newlands.

Brewis scores one of the great tries as Bob Scott and Bill Meates try to stop him, Ceci Moss is filled with awe and Ryk van Schoor floats on the edge of ecstasy.

Tommy Gentles waits for the ball in the Lancaster Park test in 1956. Focus on the ball is intense. Those in close attendance are, from the left: Don McIntosh, Salty du Rand, Tiny White, Bob Duff, Frank McAtamney, Chris Koch, Johan Claassen, Theuns Briers, Bertus van der Merwe (face obscured), and Denis Young.

Ron Jarden, the 1956 star, kicks, and the Springboks flinch. From the left the Springboks are Salty du Rand, Daan Retief, Johan Claassen, Theuns Briers and Dawie Ackermann. On the right is the mighty Peter Jones.

Peter Jones scores the try that set the whole of New Zealand rejoicing.

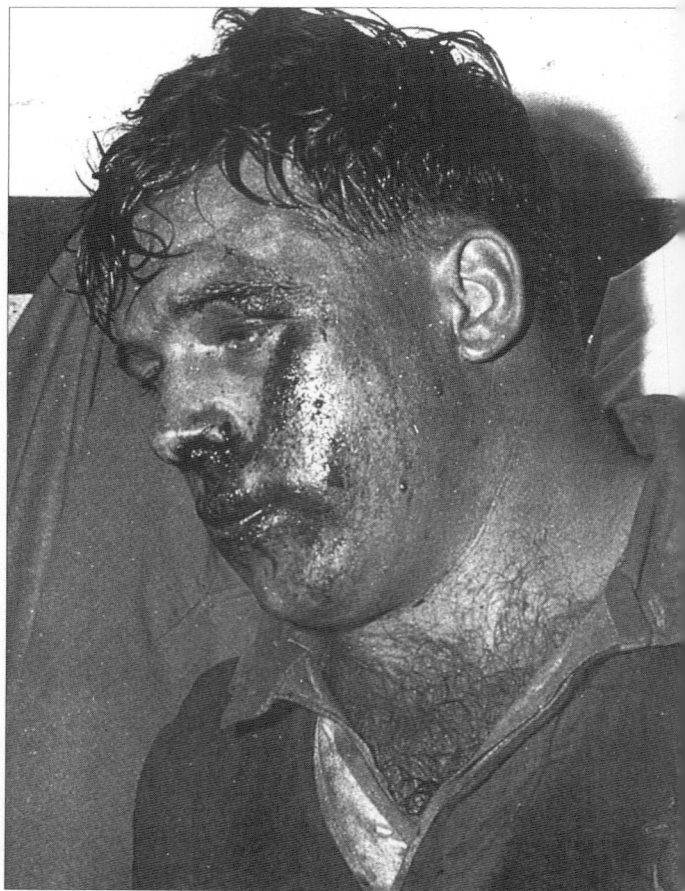

The ugly face of rugby football. Jaap Bekker gets attention after the third test in 1956.

"It's all yours, New Zealand." Craven broadcasts to a delighted Eden Park.

Pelser tackles Briscoe, part of a private war that endured throughout the 1960 series.

Don Clarke's powerful boot kept New Zealand in the hunt in 1960.

Hennie van Zyl beats Don Clarke to score a sensational try at Ellis Park.

would dispute Kel Tremain's try. Early in the second half Oxlee completed the scoring with a dropped goal.

There were three more victories including vengeance for the 1956 defeat at Hamilton, and then they got to Eden Park, Auckland, and the third defeat of the tour. Auckland won 15-14, scoring four tries to three. The best moment came when the Springboks counterattacked and Gert Brynard ran 90 yards to score at the posts.

The Springboks went down to South Island and the second test was played at Carisbrook in Dunedin. On the soggy ground the All Blacks were full value for their 13-0 victory. For one thing they scored three tries, through Kel Tremain, Bruce McLeod and Ron Rangi.

After that the Springboks reeled off seven victories in a row, including one that was staggering in its drama. One of those was a 9-3 (three tries to nil) win over the Maoris at Athletic Park in Wellington, a rare match for the time when kicks did not feature at all in the scoring.

On a slippery day in the sunshine at Lancaster Park in Christchurch, the All Blacks led 16-5 at half-time in the third test, mainly through tries by Tremain, Ray Moreton and Rangi. The Springboks replied with a dashing, crashing try by Gainsford.

The second half was charged with drama and in fact made the series.

Gainsford broke and gave to Mannetjies Roux who sent Gert Brynard over. Brynard did it again. Then Roux sent Gainsford through a gap and over in the corner and the score was 16-all.

Then Colin Meads went off-side and referee Alan Taylor penalised the All Blacks. Alan Taylor had been the touch judge but had replaced Pat Murphy, chosen again by the Springboks despite the defeats of the first two tests. Murphy had injured a knee.

It was not an easy kick. Tiny Naudé, tired lock forward, placed the ball at a slope on a mound in the mud. He plodded in straight and his toe struck the point of the ball nearest him. It rose, it travelled true and it was over. The Springboks won 19-16. It was the greatest turnaround in matches between Springboks and All Blacks, one of the greatest in test rugby. There was the possibility of a drawn series. The Springboks' surprise victory made the series.

It was the day of Springbok triumph. It was also the day of unutterable humiliation for the Springboks. On that day, 4 September 1965, H F Verwoerd, Prime Minister of the Republic of South Africa, talked to the Nationalist youth of the Transvaal at Loskop Dam northeast of Pretoria and assured them, to their approving relief, that there would be no Maoris in the All Black team when it toured South Africa in 1967.

Verwoerd, filled with righteous indignation, said: "In accordance with our basic principles and attitude, we say that when we are guests in another country we expect to behave according to their traditions . . . As we subject ourselves to their customs, we expect that when other countries visit us they will respect ours and they will adapt themselves to ours."

The Springboks woke from their celebrations to hear the suffocating political news.

The tour went on, and the results suggested that the Springboks were unaffected. They chalked up three big wins, over New Zealand Universities in Auckland, Hawke's Bay in Napier, and the combination of Bay of Plenty, Counties and Thames Valley in Rotorua.

Then they came to Eden Park for the fourth test. The backs did their best, but they were always trying to run out of trouble as the All Black pack took charge.

Initially things looked even. Red Conway's try was the only score in the first half and Tiny Naudé kicked the Springboks onto level terms early in the second half. Then the All Blacks stepped up the pace.

They scored another four tries through Bill Birtwistle, Ian Smith, who was called Spooky, Mac Herewini and the great Ken Gray. It was victory complete – 20-3, five tries to nil, at Eden Park where in 1937 the Springboks had won by five tries to nil. The All Black victory was the biggest ever over the Springboks. The 17-point margin equalled that of the Springboks in Durban in 1928.

The All Blacks were clearly the superior side. The only disaster on the tour was Verwoerd-made. For the rest it was a series devoid of controversy.

TOUR STATISTICS (NEW ZEALAND ONLY)

P	W	D	L	Pf	Pa	Tf	Ta
24	19	0	5	485	232	105	38

TESTS

4	1	0	3	25	55	4	13

The South African Touring Team of 1965:
L G Wilson (Western Province), C G Mulder (Eastern Transvaal), J P Engelbrecht (Western Province), J T Truter (Natal), C J C Cronjé (Eastern Transvaal), W J Mans (Western Province), G S Brynard (Western Province), S H Nomis (Transvaal), J L Gainsford (Western Province), F du T Roux (Griqualand West), E Olivier (Western Province), K Oxlee (Natal), J H Barnard (Transvaal), D J de Villiers (Western Province) (c), C M Smith (Orange Free State), J F K Marais (Eastern Province), A W MacDonald (Rhodesia), C G P van Zyl (Orange Free State), W H Parker (Eastern Province), G F Malan (Transvaal), D C Walton (Natal), P H Botha (Transvaal), C P Goosen (Orange Free State), F C H du Preez (Northern Transvaal), A Janson (Western Province), J A Nel (Western Transvaal), J H Ellis (South West Africa), J Schoeman (Western Province), D J Hopwood (Western Province), T P Bedford (Natal), L J Slabber (Orange Free State)

TOUR RESULTS

Date	Venue	Opponents	Score
30 June	Gisborne	Poverty Bay-East Coast	32-3
3 July	Wellington	Wellington	6-23
7 July	Palmerston	North Manawatu-Horowhenua	30-8
10 July	Dunedin	Otago	8-6
14 July	Christchurch	New Zealand Juniors	23-3
17 July	New Plymouth	Taranaki	11-3
21 July	Invercargill	Southland	19-6
24 July	Christchurch	Canterbury	6-5
27 July	Greymouth	West Coast-Buller	11-0

Date	Venue	Opponents	Score
31 July	Wellington	New Zealand	3-6
4 August	Wanganui	Wanganui-King Country	24-19
7 August	Hamilton	Waikato	26-13
11 August	Whangarei	North Auckland	14-11
14 August	Auckland	Auckland	14-15
17 August	Blenheim	Marlborough-Nelson-Golden Bay-Motueka	45-6
21 August	Dunedin	New Zealand	0-13
25 August	Timaru	Hanan Shield XV	28-13
28 August	Wellington	New Zealand Maoris	9-3
31 August	Masterton	Wairarapa-Bush	36-0
4 September	Christchurch	New Zealand	19-16
8 September	Auckland	New Zealand Universities	55-11
11 September	Napier	Hawke's Bay	30-12
14 September	Rotorua	Bay of Plenty-Counties-Thames Valley	33-17
18 September	Auckland	New Zealand	3-20

CHAPTER 13

Cometh the Maori

"Sheesinthair."

That was the beer-slurred message Craven got in a phone call from New Zealand in the early hours of a South African morning.

Craven did not understand.

"Danny, sheesinthair," the voice repeated.

He still did not understand.

Summoning great, concentrated deliberation, the voice said: "Danny, she's in the air – the greatest All Black team to leave New Zealand."

The triumph of the 1970 All Black tour of South Africa was that it happened. And even in its early stages, it became such a nonevent that one wondered what all the shattering fuss had been about.

The 1967 All Black tour was cancelled because Verwoerd's government had said No Maoris. This time the New Zealanders stood firm. No Maoris meant No Tour.

Verwoerd was assassinated in parliament and John Vorster took over – inauspiciously to start with when he stopped the MCC tour by telling them that they could not pick Basil D'Oliveira on a tour to South Africa.

John Vorster soon relented and the All Blacks were allowed to choose whomsoever they liked. They chose Buff Milner, Blair Furlong, who never actually played for the Maoris, and Sid Going, who had Maori blood, and Bryan Williams who had Samoan blood. The racial origins of these players became so unremarkable that no further mention need be made of it. The fact that 19-year-old Bryan Williams became the star of the tour had nothing to do with his Samoan blood and lots to do with his strength and skill.

New Zealand and rugby football heralded greater integration in South Africa, first sporting, then economic and social, and eventually over two decades later, complete. 1970 was halfway between the Nationalist takeover in 1948 and the release of Nelson Mandela in 1992. Ken Gray, the mighty All Black prop, did not tour. He was not a part of any group, just opposed to apartheid per se. Several demonstrators attended the All Black trials and saw the All Blacks off at Rongotai Airport in Wellington. They wanted apartheid dead.

Those two issues set aside, the 1970 All Black tour became a rugby tour, or at least as close to being one as was possible in the growing upheaval that was South Africa. There was naturally greater focus than ever on South Africa's apartheid system, which produced two distinct reactions amongst the All Blacks. Gerald Kember, Earl Kirton, who found the discrimination worse than he had imagined, and, especially, Chris Laidlaw took an intense interest in politics while most of the team decided to get on with rugby and entertainment. For Laidlaw rugby became his business.

He was the one player for whom the whole issue must have been absolutely clear. He had played against the 1965 Springboks when the lines were laid down clearly by Verwoerd at Loskop Dam. He had then gone off to Oxford as a Rhodes Scholar and captained Oxford in 1969 when the Springboks came to tour and Peter Hain and others organised demonstrations which bordered on rebellion. Knowing the situation clearly, he then hurried back to New Zealand to play in the trials to ensure his place on the tour to South Africa. Eventually Ron Burk read him the riot act and told him to keep out of political activities or be sent home. His interest did not then diminish but he became more circumspect.

At one level the All Blacks did astonishingly well, but that was at provincial level. In the tests they were mediocre, where they could have been great. They in fact had much in common with the 1965 Springboks. Like the 1965 Springboks they preferred the *dolce vita* of self-indulgence to the hard grind of victory, the flesh pots to the glory that was promised them if they became the first All Blacks to win a series in South Africa. They enjoyed touring. Late in the tour Ivan Vodanovich, the coach, beat Alistair Hopkinson and Alex Wyllie in a cross-country race, and was sorely aggrieved by their lack of fitness and dedication.

Like the 1965 Springboks, they rather pushed their coach aside, and as in 1965 the coach got scant support from the manager. As in 1965, the manager was an excellent diplomat but may not have been best for a successful team. As in 1965, they had a good player as captain who could not really focus his team on the task of being victorious tourists. In 1965 Kobus Louw had been the manager, Hennie Muller the coach and Dawie de Villiers the captain. In 1970 those positions were filled by Ron Burk, Ivan Vodanovich and Brian Lochore. Like the 1965 Springboks they suffered crucial injuries. For the Springboks it had been Doug Hopwood; for the All Blacks it was Colin Meads.

Unlike the Springboks they arrived in South Africa on a high. Before the Springbok tour to New Zealand in 1965, the Springboks had shared a series unconvincingly with the Wallabies at home, lost to France at home, and then played five matches in Ireland and Scotland without victory and then lost to New South Wales and twice to Australia *en route* to New Zealand. That was hideous.

The All Blacks of 1970 came trailing clouds of glory. They had just set a world record by winning seventeen tests in a row. In fact from the fourth test in 1965, the All Blacks had played a total of 46 matches. They had won 45 and drawn one. Their only defeat in 21 tests had been against South Africa in that astonishing come-back at Lancaster Park in 1965.

But the Springboks had been doing a bit of rehabilitation. At home they beat the French in 1967, the Lions in 1968 and the Wallabies in 1969. They beat France in France in 1968. The Lions had lost three and drawn one of the tests. The Wallabies had lost the lot. Just when things were looking better the Springboks went off to the Home Countries, wild demonstrations and not a single victory in four tests in 1969-70. They lost to Scotland and England and drew with Ireland and Wales. Two years before, the All Blacks had smashed England, Scotland, Wales and France on a trip that excluded Ireland. It was a tour arranged to replace the cancelled trip to South Africa. It was a tour that made Fred Allen, the failed captain of 1949, a guru. Ivan Vodanovich, the new coach, came to South Africa in Fred Allen's successful shadow.

Qantas brought the All Blacks to Johannesburg on the morning of Monday 15 June 1970, and there were thousands to welcome them. There was relief in the roar that greeted them. The tour was on. The relief did not stop several South Africans from boorish behaviour during the tour.

The All Blacks picked up their jerseys in South Africa. They had been stored in Nelie Smith's bank vault in Bloemfontein while the argument about the tour raged in New Zealand.

The rugby started in East London when the All Blacks scored seven tries for an easy win over Border. From there they travelled to Bethlehem in the Eastern Orange Free State to play the Paul Roos XV, chosen from the smaller unions in the north. It was a fun visit. There were floats and singing and an easy win, this time by nine tries. Two tries each went to Grahame Thorne and Bryan Williams, and Fergie McCormick, who would become increasingly prominent during the tour, also got one.

Griquas were next to be fed to the All Blacks on a day when the spectators got out of hand. Griquas, coached by Ian Kirkpatrick, were a strong side in those days and that very year beat Northern Transvaal in the

135

Currie Cup Final. The All Blacks won well, several coloured fans went onto the field to carry Bryan Williams off and several white yobbos belted into them.

Then the All Blacks went up to Upington and that narrow fertile strip along the Orange River. The All Blacks held a Court of Justice on the Sunday at which they were reputed to have drunk 50 dozen beers, practised hard in the heat on the Monday and the next day hunted springbok and gemsbok in the Kalahari. On Wednesday they had a comfortable but not satisfying win over a game North West Cape side who emerged from the encounter with lots of honour. Again there was unhappiness amongst spectators.

From Upington they hopped over the border to South West Africa and another mediocre victory over Jan Ellis's side.

They beat Eastern Transvaal 24-3, but it was almost a Pyrrhic victory. In those days Eastern Transvaal were strong. They had played with powerful destruction against touring teams and in 1972 they contested the Currie Cup Final. That afternoon at P A M Brink Stadium, the All Blacks scored four tries while the Red Devils became the sixth successive team to fail to score a try against them. But the great Colin Meads, playing his fifth match out of the first six, emerged from a maul with his left arm dangling. Brian Lochore told him to leave the field. Colin Meads was attended to and played on. Afterwards he and Alan Sutherland were taken to hospital. Meads's arm was fractured. Sutherland's nose was broken.

There was fighting in the next match when the All Blacks beat Transvaal 34-17, and Brian Lochore had his nose broken when he caught a high ball. His was not the only injury as a finger in the eye gave Bruce McLeod a nasty scare.

The All Blacks thought it a wonderful match, so much so that they swopped jerseys with the Transvaalers afterwards and Ron Burk said: "Punches are usually thrown in a game as tense and tough as this one was. We are not worried about it." Ivan Vodanovich agreed with him.

If rugby had suffered at Ellis Park, it was restored to honour at Olën Park in Potchefstroom when the All Blacks beat Western Transvaal 21-17.

There were two more simple victories, one over Orange Free State in Bloemfontein and one over a defensive Rhodesian team in Salisbury. In Bloemfontein thousands of people welcomed the All Blacks as they drove through the streets in vintage cars. Things happened there – Burk and Vodanovich had an argument about getting a replacement for Meads, which Vodanovich did not want to do, Burk went off in a Louis Luyt plane to Lourenço Marques, and the All Blacks let off a stinkbomb at a mayoral reception. Unlike their predecessors, the All Blacks flew to the Victoria Falls. They flew to Salisbury and on the Sunday after the match flew to Johannesburg to get ready for the first test in Pretoria.

South African rugby is at its worst when it is the favourite. Make it the underdog and you have a fight. Dawie de Villiers's team went into the first test as underdogs. The All Blacks had won 17 tests. They had won all ten of their matches on the tour without really being in trouble, not even against Western Transvaal. And the Springbok team looked so ordinary. There may have been many hoping for a Springbok victory, very few expecting it.

Piet Visagie kicked off and the Springbok forwards bashed in. Jan Ellis went on a weaving run of deceptive speed and the Springboks were close. The All Blacks won a scrum. Chris Laidlaw fumbled. Piet Greyling booted ahead and there was Dawie de Villiers diving on the ball for a try. Frik du Preez won a line-out and Visagie dropped for goal, and the Springboks were leading 6-0.

An essential part of New Zealand play was forcing the second phase. They invented it and brought a new concept into rugby. What it initially required was a centre to bash in to set up the second phase. Ian MacRae was good at it. Now Wayne Cottrell tried it.

From a maul he came round on the blind side. In came the find of the season, Joggie Jansen of the Orange Free State.

South African rugby is probably the most famed in the world for its tackling. There have been really great ones, like Jimmy White and Ryk van Schoor. Joggie Jansen is in that class.

Jansen dived at Cottrell, parallel to the ground, chest high. Cottrell snapped backwards, parallel with the ground under Jansen, head back, his body out of control. Jansen stood up, picked up the ball and South Africa launched an attack. Cottrell remained lying there.

It was the decisive tackle of the series. It put an abrupt end to second phase.

Ian McCallum kicked two penalty goals and South Africa led 12-0 at half-time.

In the second half Sid Going took Laidlaw's place and, as the Springboks lost three great opportunities to score tries, the All Blacks fought back. Fergie McCormick kicked a penalty goal. The Springboks threw away two more simple opportunities to score tries and then Sid Going slipped a pass to Bryan Williams on the blind side, 40 yards from the goal line. The powerful wing went round McCallum and away from Syd Nomis's despairing dive at a tackle and scored one of the great tries. And the score was 12-6.

137

The match seesawed. The All Blacks took a tapped kick, did a scissors and then Brian Lochore lobbed a pass towards Ian MacRae. In darted Syd Nomis and intercepted. Gerhard Viviers, the great Afrikaans commentator, was not quite lost for words as he shouted: "Siddie – Siddie – Siddie – Siddie!"

Syd Nomis scored, Ian McCallum converted and South Africa won 17-6 – to the astonishment of the whole of South Africa and the rest of the world. The invincibles had been beaten.

The All Blacks went off to the Kruger Park wondering what had gone wrong. And then they decided to get things right. They went down to Port Elizabeth and smashed Eastern Province. Then they went to Wellington and smashed Boland. Then they went to Newlands for the second test, and the series was all-square. In fact they were to win eight matches before they lost again.

That second test was no place for softies. The All Blacks brought in three tough men – Alex Wyllie, Neil Thimbleby, and Alan Sutherland, only to have Thimbleby withdraw with a septic thumb. Jazz Muller took his place.

The All Blacks won 9-8. They deserved a better result than that. For one thing they scored two tries to South Africa's one, nearly got a third through Bryan Williams and in the end had to rely on a controversial penalty goal.

This penalty goal was at odds with tradition. Myth has it that controversial penalty goals, especially those which win matches, go in favour of the home team.

The Springboks were up 8-6 in injury time, when the All Blacks attacked down the left-hand side of Newlands. They won a ruck. They moved right. Three All Blacks handled and then Mannetjies Roux, retreating, jumped on Bill Davis. Wynand Malan awarded a penalty in an easy position and Fergie McCormick goaled.

That could have made McCormick a hero, but he had already decided he was a villain, one of many on that combative, uncompromising afternoon.

Piston van Wyk, the small hooker from Northern Transvaal, was taken off the field streaming with blood. The villainy which summoned the headlines was perpetrated by Fergie McCormick. The Springboks counterattacked on their left, down in front of the Grand Stand when the All Blacks were on the attack. Faced by McCormick, Nomis kicked ahead to chase. He did not get past McCormick for the fullback swung a left elbow into his teeth.

Afterwards McCormick told Terry McLean that his act had been deliberate, but there was massive debate about it afterwards.

The All Blacks strode through the land after this, and ended up being misled by one bit of success. They had big wins over South Western Districts in George, Western Province, South African Country Districts in East London, Natal in Durban and Western Province Universities, who were made up of three from the University of Cape Town and twelve from Stellenbosch under the mature captaincy of Jannie Engelbrecht.

Two significant things happened in George. First of all Colin Meads, who had been in a slough of despond since the Western Transvaal match, played. He wore a leather casing on his left arm, and Dr Craven gave strict instructions that nobody was to dare to complain about it. Meads came back as captain and he told his team, at vast length, what he expected of them.

The other was a repeat of bottle throwing. It was not as bad as at Kimberley but the police again used riot sticks and a dog which at one stage carried a coat in its mouth.

At Newlands against Western Province, the All Blacks were misled. They moved Bryan Williams in to centre. Marking him was Nelson Babrow, Louis's son. Like his centre partner Johan Walters, the younger Babrow was a brilliant attacking player but not one given to tackling. Bryan Williams cut through him at will. The All Blacks believed that they had solved their centre problems and picked Williams there for the third test, thereby eliminating their best attacking force. In East London the All Blacks scored 10 tries in winning 45-8. In the five matches between the second and the third test, the All Blacks scored 33 tries. In the third test they scored none.

It was in Durban, where the All Blacks had too brief a stay, that Tommy Bedford said: "We are the last outpost of the British Empire", which has become part of South African rugby's folklore. And Basil Medway, president of the Natal RU, said afterwards of the All Blacks: "This is the greatest side ever to visit South Africa."

Playing fullback for Natal was a New Zealander, Terry Mehrtens. While he was in Natal, Terry's son Andrew was born, the All Black fly half in 1995.

Wars are fought by young men. The Springbok selectors brought back two ageing warriors to face the stern All Blacks in the third test – Mof Myburgh at prop at the age of 34 and Lofty Nel at number 8 at 35, the oldest Springbok until Deon Lötter played in 1993. The All Blacks thought the changes bizarre and decided that the game was in the bag.

The New Zealanders picked Colin Meads, who had now played five matches in a row, and off they went to Port Elizabeth.

Any violence in the match was controlled. In the first minute Piet Visagie kicked a high one for brave little Fergie McCormick whose stature seemed to shrink as the ball came down on him and the Springbok loose forwards homed in on him. McCormick knew this was a moment of retribution. The brave Canterburian caught the ball. Piet Greyling cut him in half and the rest of the pack piled in. McCormick was sore when he got up. Greyling and Jan Ellis then hunted Earl Kirton and destroyed him. Joggie Jansen homed in on Bryan Williams and destroyed him.

It was not a pretty match but Gert Müller scored two splendid tries and the Springboks won 14-3. New Zealand's only points were a penalty goal, scored, not by McCormick, but by Bryan Williams. McCormick would not play in the fourth test at all.

There was no shadow of doubt that the better side won.

The All Blacks took it out on North Eastern Cape whom they smashed 85-0 in Burgersdorp, scoring 17 tries, and then they had two toughies.

First they played Northern Transvaal and won 19-15, scoring three tries to two though people blamed Max Baise for allowing one of the three. They scored six tries to two against the Gazelles in Potchefstroom but won only 29-25. And the referee in that match was Gert Bezuidenhout whom they would meet again in 1976.

The victory over the Gazelles meant that Brian Lochore's All Blacks had won every nontest match on their tour of South Africa.

Thus came the fourth test at Ellis Park. Would the All Blacks emulate the 1928 team and square the series? That was the best they could hope for.

Ellis Park was packed. Gerald Kember, in for Fergie McCormick, kicked off and the All Blacks, with Keith Murdoch in the van, piled in. Colin Meads was more "aggressive" than he had been when sent off during the Scottish test in 1967. It did the All Blacks no good. They lost in the end only 20-17 but the score flattered them. At half-time the Springboks, who had played with the wind, led 14-3. Their scoring included an astonishing try. From a scrum nearly 40 yards out Piet Visagie, at fly half, broke. He scored a try. Not many fly halves in the history of international rugby can claim to have run 40 yards to score a try against the All Blacks, let alone from a scrum.

In the second half Sid Going broke blind when Ron Urlich won a tight head, and fed Bryan Williams who beat Syd Nomis and several other Springboks to score a spectacular try, but Gert Müller also got a try when

Joggie Jansen smashed into Kember and Mannetjies Roux picked up to send the big wing away in dramatic fashion. When Kember kicked the last All Black points on the tour there were only moments to go.

And so, astonishingly, the Springboks won the series nobody thought they could win.

Asked how it was possible, Danie Craven said simply: "We pushed them." His theory was that the Springboks had eliminated their loose forwards by shoving them back on to their heels whenever possible, but especially at set scrums.

Of the series Ian McCallum said: "The underdogs had pretty sharp teeth."

TOUR STATISTICS (SOUTH AFRICA ONLY)

P	W	D	L	Pf	Pa	Tf	Ta
24	21	0	3	687	228	135	23

TESTS

4	1	0	3	35	59	4	7

The New Zealand Touring Team of 1970:
W F McCormick (Canterbury), M J Dick (Auckland), B G Williams (Auckland), B A Hunter (Otago), G S Thorne (Auckland), W L Davis (Hawke's Bay), H P Milner (Wanganui), I R MacRae (Hawke's Bay), W D Cottrell (Canterbury), E W Kirton (Otago), B D M Furlong (Hawke's Bay), G F Kember (Wellington), C R Laidlaw (Otago), S M Going (North Auckland), B L Muller (Taranaki), K Murdoch (Otago), N W Thimbleby (Hawke's Bay), A E Hopkinson (Canterbury), B E McLeod (Counties), R A Urlich (Auckland), J F Burns (Canterbury), C E Meads (King Country), A E Smith (Taranaki), S C Strachan (Manawatu), B Holmes (North Auckland), T N Lister (South Canterbury), A J Wyllie (Canterbury), I A Kirkpatrick (Poverty Bay), A R Sutherland (Marlborough), B J Lochore (c) (Wairarapa)

TOUR RESULTS

Date	Venue	Opponents	Score
20 June	East London	Border	28-3
24 June	Bethlehem	Paul Roos XV	43-9
27 June	Kimberley	Griqualand West	27-3
1 July	Upington	North Western Cape	26-3
4 July	Windhoek	South West Africa	16-0
8 July	Springs	Eastern Transvaal	24-3
11 July	Johannesburg	Transvaal	34-17
13 July	Potchefstroom	Western Transvaal	21-17
18 July	Bloemfontein	Orange Free State	30-12
21 July	Salisbury	Rhodesia	27-14
25 July	Pretoria	South Africa	6-17
1 August	Port Elizabeth	Eastern Province	49-8
4 August	Wellington	Boland	35-9
8 August	Newlands	South Africa	9-8
12 August	George	South Western Districts	36-3
15 August	Newlands	Western Province	29-6
19 August	East London	South African Country Districts	45-8

DATE	VENUE	OPPONENTS	SCORE
22 August	Durban	Natal	29-8
25 August	Newlands	Western Province Universities	20-3
29 August	Port Elizabeth	South Africa	3-14
2 September	Burgersdorp	North Eastern Cape	85-0
5 September	Pretoria	Northern Transvaal	19-15
7 September	Potchefstroom	Gazelles	29-25
12 September	Johannesburg	South Africa	17-20

CHAPTER 14

Refereeing Rages

"WE OUTPLAYED SOUTH AFRICA. South Africa outkicked us. Goodbye, Rugby."

That was J J Stewart's summary of the 1976 All Black tour to South Africa, and he was the team's cantankerous coach.

Not even politics equalled the controversy about refereeing during this tour. Long after the revolution which broke out during this tour was forgotten by New Zealanders, the accusations against a referee persisted.

The year of this tour, 1976, was the beginning of the end of apartheid.

The Springboks were supposed to have gone to New Zealand in 1973. On 6 April 1973 Norman Kirk, Prime Minister of New Zealand, asked the NZRFU to postpone the tour till South Africa ran mixed trials. Jack Sullivan and his council saw the Prime Minister's request as a "requirement and a direction". The tour was off.

Instead of entertaining the Springboks, the All Blacks went on an internal tour, and then England, whose tour to Argentina had fallen through, came to visit. England lost to Taranaki, Wellington and Canterbury and then beat New Zealand. But then New Zealand's recovery from defeat in South Africa had been slow. The British Lions had come and won a series in New Zealand. New Zealand went to Europe and just beat Wales, Scotland and England, drew with Ireland and lost to France. This was not the New Zealand of the Sixties.

The Springboks, on the wobbly foundation of the hammering by the 1974 Lions, were further beset by uncertainty about their whole future in international rugby. It showed in selection and it showed in the caution with which they played. And even then they may just have been slightly more constructive than the All Blacks. It was not a thrilling series.

In 1976 the All Blacks decided South African rugby had made sufficient social changes. There were mixed trials and the All Blacks would play against the SA Rugby Football Federation's Proteas, and the SA Rug-

144

by Association's Leopards. South Africa, it seemed to relieved New Zealanders, had changed enough. Maoris were welcome. The trials were mixed. So the All Blacks went to South Africa in 1976. They wanted to go. Rugby football was not the same without the Springboks and that special battle for supremacy. And besides that the NZRFU would make quite a bit of money. Even the players made a bit of money through the sale of tickets and other enterprises – quite a bit of money for strictly amateur times.

The All Blacks had a warm-up against the visiting Irish and beat them 11-3. It was not a convincing performance. That night the selectors announced the 30 players to play 24 matches in South Africa. Bryan Williams, Sid Going, Alan Sutherland, who eventually settled in South Africa, and Ian Kirkpatrick were the only All Blacks who had been there in 1970. Even Colin Meads had retired!

It was not easy for the players to get to South Africa. Demonstrators threw paint at their bus as they drove off for Auckland's airport. There was the threat of trade union action against the team in Australia, and so they flew to Singapore, from there to Athens and from there to Johannesburg, not an enchanting journey. It took them 42 hours, but the warm welcome at Jan Smuts Airport made up for that.

It was not a great tour though it came close to being a successful one. The rugby played was not of the high standard expected of the two countries, there was too much arguing and an uprising started in South Africa with some of the All Blacks too closely involved for their own liking.

They started with a satisfactory win over combined Border and North Eastern Cape in East London. They had an exciting and enjoyable match with Eastern Province. Then they broke new ground.

They went to Cape Town, to vast Goodwood Showgrounds, and there in the wet they played the Proteas, the SA Rugby Football Federation's "coloured" team – a whole new experience for the All Blacks. It was not the Proteas' first contact with overseas teams as they had themselves toured overseas in 1971, and played England at Athlone Stadium in 1972 and the Lions at Goodwood Showgrounds in 1974. Nobody had found them easy opposition as they enjoyed their matches with a reckless commitment. The All Blacks did not find it easy either but won 25-3.

The star for the Proteas was their fullback Ronnie Louw. He was chosen for the next team as well – a President's XV, chosen by Danie Craven to play the All Blacks at Newlands. The year before, a similar, racially mixed team had beaten France at Newlands and changed the pattern of crowd behaviour because suddenly the whole of Newlands was supporting the home team against a touring team. It was no different in 1976, except that this time the visitors won.

Poor Ronnie Louw, the hero on Wednesday, lost his mother on Thursday, consulted the family and played on the Saturday as his mother would have wished and made mistakes which may have cost his team the game as the All Blacks won this, their hundredth match in South Africa, 31-24.

There were rain and mud as they beat Boland and then returned to Newlands for one of the most dramatic matches in years. The All Blacks had played 28 matches without defeat at this stage and it was Ian Kirkpatrick's hundredth match for the All Blacks. At half-time the All Blacks led 3-0 when Laurie Mains kicked a penalty goal. Then Western Province attacked with vigour, but Chris Pope dropped the ball and the All Blacks counterattacked with a try by Lyn Jaffray. They did the same again when cocky Grant Batty picked up a dropped ball and Duncan Robertson scored. The All Blacks led 11-0.

Western Province took a tapped kick, Divan Serfontein kicked ahead and Bossie Clarke scored. Robbie Blair, who missed eight kicks at goal that day, converted and the score was 11-6. Again the home side attacked. With two minutes to go Dawie Snyman, playing fullback, collected the ball on the halfway line on the Railway Stand side and counterattacked. He passed inside to rangy Morné du Plessis and he popped the ball to Chris Pope who surged across the line for a try in the corner. Robbie Blair converted from touch and Western Province won a famous victory, 12-11.

Back the All Blacks went to pleasant Port Elizabeth and a pleasant victory over the Gazelles. And so they went up the coast to Durban for the first test.

Durban is warm in winter and this was a warm day. The score was 3-all at half-time but the All Blacks kicked off the wrong way in the second half, as they did at the start of the World Cup semifinal against England in 1995, and scored a shock try to lead 7-3.

The try of the match was not long in coming. Ian Robertson came into the back line, Peter Whipp timed his pass to perfection as he missed out Johan Oosthuizen, and Gerrie Germishuys went striding down the touchline on tiptoe for a spectacular try which made the All Black defence look unusually brittle. It was the Springboks' 300th test try. Later Paul Bayvel broke and Edrich Krantz got over in the right-hand corner. The Springboks won 16-7, but already the first shots had been fired at a referee. Andy Leslie and all the other All Blacks were upset when Ian Gourlay penalised Leslie for being off-side at a maul near the Springbok posts when the All Blacks were doing particularly well in the maul.

The All Blacks are always shocked when they lose. They gave expression to their shock with a massive 42-3 win over Western Transvaal.

They beat Transvaal in a match of many, many stoppages. There were no fewer than 33 penalties, 17 to New Zealand. It was not a match to excite the crowd of 74 000 at the old Ellis Park. They went on to beat South African Universities, Eastern Transvaal and a humble combination of Northern Free State, Eastern Free State and Northern Natal without ever looking really convincing. There was none of the domination of the 1970 team. And then they had to go to Bloemfontein on the Highveld for the second test. Smart money was on the Springboks.

Smart money was lost. Joe Morgan swerved around a diving Morné du Plessis to score the only try of the match in the deserved 15-9 victory for the All Blacks. The series was even.

Next they played the Quagga Barbarians, who included Tom Grace and Fergus Slattery of Ireland, at Ellis Park. They may well have been hung over from the test but the Quagga Barbarians posted the highest score ever against the All Blacks when they scored 31 points. It is still a record. But the All Blacks scored 32 points and won the match. It was a match of dramatic turns. The home side was 31-9 ahead with twenty minutes to go, and the All Blacks are notoriously poor finishers. This time they gulped for pride in the thin Highveld air and came roaring back with a try from the kick-off.

In injury time Bill Davis kicked high and Alan Sutherland sent Lawrie Knight over for a try which Laurie Mains converted to make the score 31-28. This all happened in injury time.

Still the referee, Ian Gourlay, being more interested in the laws of the game than the score of the match, allowed time for the Quagga Barbarians to kick off and win a line-out. Recklessly they started a passing movement. Thankfully Andy Leslie intercepted and kicked ahead. The ball was caught by Ian Robertson of the Quagga Barbarians who was bowled over by Bruce Robertson of the All Blacks. The All Blacks piled into the ruck, won the ball and Terry Mitchell scored in the right-hand corner. 32-31. What a match!

From this happy carnival the All Blacks went down to Pretoria and Northern Transvaal at Loftus Versfeld. And there was more controversy.

The All Blacks scored three tries, Northern Transvaal four, though the All Black camp disputed three of them and claimed another for themselves. The All Blacks kicked three penalties, Northern Transvaal two. But one of those two was the cause of the controversy.

Northern Transvaal were to throw in to a line-out. Thys Lourens did not join in, thus making it a short line-out. He drew Piet Robbertse's attention to the fact that it was a short line-out and, in the manner of the polite Afrikaans player, he called the referee Oom. Robbertse penalised the All Blacks, Joos le Roux goaled the kick and Northern Transvaal won 29-27.

The All Blacks did not like the penalty and they did not like the fact that Lourens had called the referee Oom.

The hurt All Blacks beat the combination of South Eastern Transvaal, Rhodesia, and Far North 48-13, Natal 42-13, the Leopards 31-0 in East London, a first for the All Blacks to play against SARA's team who knelt before them in respect as they did the haka. Then they arrived at Newlands for the third test.

It was not a happy match. Ian Kirkpatrick and Bryan Williams tangled with a student uprising in Cape Town and were stung by tear gas. Perry Harris, who had been brought over as a replacement for Brad Johnstone, played instead of Billy Bush and was destroyed by Johan Strauss. Problems with the props really troubled the All Blacks. Brad Johnstone had damaged ribs, Kerry Tanner had blood poisoning, Kent Lambert hurt a thigh, Billy Bush had a bad ankle, and Perry Harris was not up to it.

Kit Fawcett failed to take a poor pass as the All Blacks, uncharacteristically ran the ball, and Johan Oosthuizen caught it for a free run at the posts. Gert Bezuidenhout stopped Sid Going from having a go at posts because the ball kept falling over. Dawie Snyman was credited with a dubious dropped goal. And the All Blacks lost 15-9. And they deserved to do so. It was a drab test, saved only by the tension of the occasion.

On Settlers Day holiday, the Monday after the test, the All Blacks beat a combination of South West Africa and North West Cape 34-17 in remote little Upington. There was a hunt in the Kalahari before the match during which the All Blacks shot 19 springbok. The hunting continued on the field of play. It was a disgraceful match, the worst of the tour. The worst of the culprits were Billy Bush, not for the first time, of New Zealand and Hennie Coetzee of South West Africa.

They did not play well against Orange Free State either and lost 15-10, the second All Black side to lose to the mealie farmers. That year Orange Free State won the Currie Cup for the first time. It was not a long journey to Kimberley to play Griqualand West/Stellaland at dusty De Beers Stadium. Again there was fighting. This time the referee, Tinkie Heyns from the Western Province, sent Jimmy Young of the combined side off the field in the first half and this time there was no clemency. He went

148

off. Afterwards J J Stewart and the owners of the hotel, Leon and Nathan Cohen, had a hefty argument which came close to blows.

The tour at this stage had a sour taste about it. But there was still worse to come.

Like their predecessors in 1928 and 1970, Andy Leslie's All Blacks had the opportunity to draw the series. Unlike the 1928 side but like that of 1970, they did not manage it. In the fourth test in Johannesburg they were undoubtedly the better side and scored two tries to one, but they lost the match 15-14 and with it the series and so there was no Elysian Field for them. History would consign them to the drab, featureless dwelling of the mediocre. And they blamed it on Gert Bezuidenhout, chosen by them to referee three consecutive tests in the series, though they believed he was not determined enough to put a stop to foul play. They believed that they should have been given a penalty try. They believed that the final penalty at the line-out was a hoax, but it gave the Springboks their one-point victory and the series.

It was not the best of series. The unsatisfactory ending to the fourth test was symptomatic of the whole tour. It was not a satisfying experience.

And at the end J J Stewart made some amends when he said: "I want to thank you all for putting up with the rudest bastard in New Zealand." He was referring to himself.

He undid his amends when he got back to New Zealand and had many disparaging things to say about South Africa, its people and its rugby. And Grant Batty said that the best thing about South Africa was leaving it. It was the spirit of 1949 all over again – New Zealand had been cheated by referees.

TOUR STATISTICS

P	W	D	L	Pf	Pa	Tf	Ta
24	18	0	6	610	291	89	27

TESTS

4	1	0	3	46	55	5	4

The New Zealand Touring Team of 1976:
L W Mains (Otago), C L Fawcett (Auckland), B G Williams (Auckland), G R Batty (Bay of Plenty), T W Mitchell (Canterbury), N A Purvis (Otago), B J Robertson (Counties), W M Osborne (Wanganui), J E Morgan (North Auckland), J L Jaffray (Otago), D J Robertson (Otago), O D Bruce (Canterbury), S M Going (North Auckland), L J Davis (Canterbury), A R Leslie (Wellington) (c), A R Sutherland (Marlborough), I A Kirkpatrick (Poverty Bay), L G Knight (Poverty Bay), K A Eveleigh (Manawatu), K W Stewart (Southland), H H Macdonald (North Auckland), F J Oliver (Southland), P J Whiting (Auckland), G A Seear (Otago), B R Johnstone (Auckland), K K Lambert (Manawatu), W K T Bush (Canterbury), K J Tanner (Canterbury), P C Harris (Manawatu), R W Norton (Canterbury), G M Crossman (Bay of Plenty)

TOUR RESULTS

DATE	VENUE	OPPONENTS	SCORE
30 June	East London	Border XV	24-0
3 July	Port Elizabeth	Eastern Province	28-15
7 July	Goodwood	South African Rugby Football Federation	25-3
10 July	Newlands	South African Invitation XV	31-24
14 July	Wellington	Boland XV	42-6
17 July	Newlands	Western Province	11-12
20 July	Port Elizabeth	Gazelles	21-15
24 July	Durban	South Africa	7-16
28 July	Potchefstroom	Western Transvaal	42-3
31 July	Johannesburg	Transvaal	12-10

DATE	VENUE	OPPONENTS	SCORE
4 August	Pretoria	South African Universities	21-9
7 August	Springs	Eastern Transvaal	26-12
10 August	Welkom	Orange Free State Country XV	31-6
14 August	Bloemfontein	South Africa	15-9
18 August	Johannesburg	Quagga-Barbarians	32-31
21 August	Pretoria	Northern Transvaal	27-29
24 August	Witbank	Transvaal Country XV	48-13
28 August	Durban	Natal	42-13
31 August	East London	South African African XV	31-0
4 September	Newlands	South Africa	10-15
6 September	Upington	North Western Cape XV	34-17
11 September	Bloemfontein	Orange Free State	10-15
14 September	Kimberley	Griqualand West XV	26-3
18 September	Johannesburg	South Africa	14-15

151

CHAPTER 15

Demonstrations

THERE WERE SOUTH AFRICANS who hated demonstrators, and some who loved them and saw them as a hope for the future.

Those who hated them were amongst the Springboks' biggest fans. They saw the demonstrators as a lot of long-haired, ne'er-do-well, hippies, communists, out-of-works, won't-works, queers, professional do-gooders, mercenaries.

Tales abounded – of the man shouting "Free Nelson Mandela" who admitted he had no idea who Nelson Mandela was; of the placards with Down with Apartheid only thinly disguising Save the Whale; of people paid £5 to march round and round a field till it was time to go back to Bristol.

There were those who accused them of all sorts of things, above all dragging politics into sport at a time when it was a clichéd slogan amongst some South Africans that one should "Keep politics out of religion or sport".

To many South Africans the passion of the demonstrators came as a shock, but then they were fed limited information. The view of John Carlisle, the British Member of Parliament, received more publicity in South Africa than the views of Peter Hain, the South African who breathed so much spirit into the demonstrations and would later also be a British Member of Parliament. The belief was that the demonstrators were just a crazed minority. This was not the case, certainly not in New Zealand.

In view of the vehemence of the demonstrations, it is astonishing that South Africa kept staggering on in international rugby. There is no doubt that the man who made it possible was Danie Craven. He would later claim that he had not been influenced by the demonstrations and boycotts in bringing changes into South African rugby, but it is stretching credibility not to accept that they played an important rôle.

The demonstrations started quietly and went largely unreported in South Africa. Nobody noticed them particularly when the 1960 All Blacks left New Zealand or the 1965 Springboks arrived there. And in any case most people in New Zealand loved rugby and cheered the Springboks. But some 500 people went to the inaugural meeting of CABTA (Citizens' All Black Tour Association) in Wellington in 1959, ten years after the first, small protest against the exclusion of Maoris. CABTA took off quickly. Soon it had over twenty branches and 153 000 signing a petition to stop the 1960 tour. And they began to invade rugby fields when All Black trials were held. Marches started, with two thousand parading down Queen Street in Auckland at the urging of the Mayor of Auckland. That was news that simply did not get through to South Africa, most of South Africa. It did get through to some, and Dennis Brutus, a founder and the first secretary of the SA Sports Association from which the SA Non-Racial Olympic Committee and the SA Council of Sport sprang, also organised a petition in South Africa asking the New Zealanders to cancel unless all South Africans could play, a change of emphasis from the days when concern was with the composition of New Zealand teams, a change which is relevant to the cataclysm of 1981.

When the 1960 All Blacks left from Whenuapai Airport, their baggage was searched because of a bomb threat. Demonstrators, risking their lives and those of others, ran across at the Electra aircraft as it took off and actually got close to it. From the very start the anti-apartheid protest in peaceful New Zealand was an aggressive one. South Africans were shaken by the Springbok tour to Britain in 1969-70 when Peter Hain made a political name for himself, when clashes with spectators were at times violent, as in Swansea, when demonstrators were reckless in spreading glass and tacks on fields and hijacking the Springboks' bus. But still they were led to believe that it was a hooligan, communist-prodded minority.

The 1967 All Black tour was cancelled because the South African government would not allow Maoris in the New Zealand team. The South African government changed its stance and the tour happened in 1970, with Maoris in the team. There were active demonstrations then, too. ATAC (Anti-Tour Action Committee) burnt the Papakura Rugby Club's grandstand, for example. New Zealand cancelled the 1973 Springbok tour because there were no mixed trials in South Africa to give all South Africans a chance to play for the Springboks.

When the 1970 All Blacks, Maoris and all, were about to leave, demonstrators let off a fire bomb at the Auckland RFU offices and rugby fields were vandalised.

Protests along the lines of Britain in 1969-70 continued in Australia in 1971, but nowhere did they reach the heights of fever that they did in New Zealand in 1981.

In Britain and Australia the governments let the tours take their course and provided protection for both sides – those who wanted to watch rugby and those who wanted to demonstrate their disapproval of apartheid by attacking white South African rugby which was seen by many to be the Nationalist Party at play. The New Zealand government adopted the same policy in 1981.

The All Blacks had a taste of protest action themselves when they toured South Africa in 1976. They were due to play at Newlands when rioting started in central Cape Town at that time. Bryan Williams and Ian Kirkpatrick were in Cape Town. The police fired stinging tear gas. The All Blacks in the midst of turmoil had a whiff of teargas. Coming from quiet New Zealand, they found it an unnerving experience. This was the start of the Student Uprising. The spark was the language policy in black schools whereby some subjects had to be taught in Afrikaans. It was, as retrospection teaches us, the beginning of the end of apartheid.

In 1976 twenty-six African nations stayed away from the Montreal Olympics because the All Blacks toured South Africa.

In June 1977 the Commonwealth Heads of Government issued the Gleneagles Agreement, stating that it was the "urgent duty of each of their Governments vigorously to combat the evil of apartheid by withholding any form of support for and, by taking every practical step, to discourage contact or competition by their nationals with sporting organisations, teams or sportsmen from South Africa".

In 1977 the first mixed trials took place in South Africa. In 1980 Errol Tobias became the first coloured man to play rugby for South Africa. That year South American countries, the Lions and France toured South Africa and the Springboks went to South America. The Springboks were playing more tests than the All Blacks, and playing them really well. It was time for the battle for the rugby crown to begin again.

As far as the NZRFU and the New Zealand government were concerned South African rugby had fulfilled the criteria which would enable it to tour. And so the government of the Prime Minister, Robert Muldoon, who had won the 1976 election and gave the impression of being a man reluctant to be pushed around, allowed the tour to happen. And as in Britain and Australia he provided the opportunity for the rugby to be played and the demonstrations to be made. As in Britain and Australia, there were conservative governments in power at the time of the

154

Springbok tours. As in Britain and Australia, opposition to the tours would come largely from socialists, educationalists and church groups. The media were also opposed to the tour, increasingly stridently as the tour approached.

Muldoon himself was against the tour, keen as he was on rugby, fond as he was of South Africa and conservative as he was by nature. Afterwards he said: "A disaster. I said it would be a disaster, and it was." But he resented lectures on apartheid by Malcolm Fraser of Australia especially in view of Australia's discriminatory immigration policies and domestic practices. Muldoon refused even to discuss the tour at a Commonwealth Heads of Government meeting in Melbourne in October 1981. He believed it was not the duty of the meeting to discuss the sporting activities of member nations. And anyway he had a plane to catch!

The estimated cost of policing the 1981 tour was given as $NZ2 million. That would come from tax payers. The protestors protested at this. Ben Couch, the Minister of Police, found it a strange view that people could say: "We are going to break the law to prevent you from doing what you think is right, and we expect you to pay the costs of our law-breaking."

For two months New Zealand was in turmoil, a homogeneous nation rent asunder. Even families were split. And the feelings were expressed with increasing violence. New Zealander battled with New Zealander, spat on him and vilified him.

The contrast with the normal New Zealand was stark – the pastoral country, restful and compliant, accepting wind and rain, geyser and volcano, snow and sunshine, life and death, success and failure with laconic equanimity. Now suddenly storms of passion raged out of control. And the catalyst was a rugby tour, normally New Zealand's most unifying invasion.

People believed, horror of horrors, that this was the death knell of rugby in New Zealand, the rattling last gasp of New Zealand's rugby achievement. And yet it was not long before New Zealand's rugby was sitting proud on top of the world. The storm seemed to pass, as storms do, the people shook themselves, stroked their feathers, and flew higher than ever. But at the time it was hideous.

There were people who perversely believed that it was good for New Zealand, a sort of puberty of the nation. There were people who believed it was good for the police force, equipping them and giving them a status they had not had because they stood firm and proved their worth in the performance of their duty regardless of their personal convictions. They did their duty calmly, preserved dignity and even cheerfulness, and so they came out of it stronger – so some say.

155

One man stood quiet and firm – Ces Blazey, the chairman of the NZRFU. He and his committee had taken a decision. They were entitled to do so, and he went ahead. In 1985 when the court stopped the All Blacks from going to South Africa, Ces Blazey accepted that too. He did not accept the duplicity of the Cavaliers' tour in 1986. Then he lost his cool.

They say, they do, that the New Zealand Labour Party's decision to postpone the 1973 tour by the Springboks brought about their fall from government. They also say that the New Zealand's National Party's decision to allow the 1981 tour by the Springboks brought about their fall from government. The mood of the people had changed that much in half a dozen years.

In 1976 there had been the Student Uprising in South Africa with another brutal response from government agencies. In 1977 there had been the Gleneagles Agreement. All the rest of the Commonwealth, the old Empire, had decided against sporting links with South Africa, even the fractious Australians. And here was New Zealand girding itself to welcome the Springboks.

Muldoon, who had said of Gleneagles: "In the application of the Gleneagles Declaration, the cap will have to fit each nation", was not all that clear on the tour. He was busy hedging his bets, which annoyed many New Zealanders even more. They took the fight from his hands and attacked. The attack was met by their own people, the police who were left to serve "law and order". The anti-Springbok movement was not just a spontaneous national feeling. It was organised. There were people behind the anti-apartheid movement in New Zealand – Rolland O'Regan, John Minto, Pauline Mackay, Dick Cuthbert, Michael Law, and Trevor Richards of HART (Halt All Racist Tours), Tom Newnham of CARE (Citizens' Association of Racial Equity), John Denny of CAT (Citizens Against the Tour), Alexander Shaw and Tom Poata of COST (Citizens Opposed to the Springbok Tour), Penelope Bright, Bill Andersen, Donna Awatere and Rebecca Evans who were Maori activists, Tim Shadbolt, Marx Jones, who was the flour bomber, Roger Fowler, and university people like Bruce Hucker, Ruth Butterworth, Andrew Beyer, the chairman of MOST (Mobilisation to Stop the Tour) and Dave Tolich, who above all was dedicated to peaceful protest. There were other acronyms – ATAC (Anti-Tour Action Committee), four of whose members were found guilty of daubing the Canterbury RFU offices in Christchurch with their own blood and then went on a hunger strike in Addington gaol, AAA (Artists against Apartheid), CEDRIC (Campaign

156

for the Disruption of Racism's International Collaborators), BATT (Bay Against The Tour), CAST (Citizens Against the Springbok Tour), MAST (Manawatu Against the Springbok Tour), PRISM (Passive but Resolute Invasion of Springbok Matches) and SCAR (School Children Against Racism). Police claimed that there were also gang members involved, and that many were paid to protest.

Oddly enough the working man did not object to the tour and there was little trade union activity to make the tour uncomfortable.

Many of the protestors were idealists, many were not. Many conducted themselves with dignity and consideration, many behaved like thugs. Many wanted peaceful protest, many went for physical confrontation and sheer violence. The latter brought the protest against apartheid into disrepute.

The protests started well before the arrival of the Springboks in New Zealand, because the demonstrators' first objective was the cancellation of the tour. Some believe that that would have saved New Zealand much money and heartache. Others believe it would have been capitulating to a tyranny of the left and a possible drift towards anarchy.

The Springboks flew to New Zealand via the USA where they met their first taste of demonstrations even though they were not then playing there. They played in the USA on the way back when a rugby club was blown up, a court order saved their match in Albany and such cat-and-mouse was played on the way to the test that the non-playing Springboks did not even get to the match and most of the 38 spectators were state troopers.

The visit to the USA served two purposes. It enabled them to fly to New Zealand without stopping in Australia or using an Australian airline. Secondly it took some of the heat off New Zealand if the big USA also took the South African tourists in, not because they had any truck with apartheid but because they protected the freedom of choice of their own citizens.

From Los Angeles they flew Air New Zealand to Auckland via Honolulu. And on the plane an elderly woman shouted her protest till the crew shushed her. There was vigorous protest at Whenuapai Airport in Auckland. Protestors tore down security fences in their attempt to get onto the tarmac. And already the police were being abused.

At this stage, too, the chants that accompanied the tour began:
1,2,3,4 We don't want your racist tour.
Amandla Awethu
Free Nelson Mandela.
Boere gaan huis toe.

157

From there the Springboks transferred to their charter plane, an Air New Zealand Fokker Friendship, without leaving the tarmac, flew to Gisborne where a crowd of some 100 people were gathered, roughly half for and half against the tour. Three protestors jumped the security fence and ran out onto the tarmac. The first three arrests of the tour were made. Dick Cuthbert was an early arrest.

The Sandown Hotel in Gisborne had been fortified and throughout the tour, hotel security would be tight, not that that stopped noisy protesting outside the hotel. There were some 40 noisy demonstrators outside the Gisborne ground when the Springboks practised and then photographed the demonstrators whom they did not take seriously. After all, they had been told that such people were a minority in New Zealand. This attitude had a rude awakening in Hamilton.

The opening press conference, attended by some 70 journalists, did not go well for the Springboks. The questions were hostile and obviously political. Professor Claassen, the Springbok manager, insisted that he was there to talk rugby and not politics. With him at the media conference were Abe Williams, the assistant manager, who was coloured, Nelie Smith the coach, and the captain, Wynand Claassen.

On the day before the match a man and three women crashed through the fence at the ground and drove round scattering glass and metal objects onto the field. During the match the demonstrators kept their noise going and after the match enjoyed police protection on their march back into town.

Four days after arriving in New Zealand the Springboks beat Poverty Bay as Edrich Krantz scored a hat trick of tries and Errol Tobias got the fourth as police and demonstrators clashed, especially on the golf course adjacent to the ground.

In Hamilton, the demonstrators had their biggest victory, which, in a sense, turned into defeat for them.

They stopped the match between the Springboks and Waikato. Waikato, the land of Mooloo, is rugby country. It is also farming country, and the farmers wanted their rugby. They parked their trucks along the back of the Grand Stand at Rugby Park, a big area, forming a protective wall.

The Minister of Police Ben Couch, who – irony of ironies – had been barred from going to South Africa as a player because of his Maori blood, came from Wellington for the match. He was to see that the tour went ahead. The Police Commissioner, Bob Walton, was there.

For the demonstrators Hamilton was seen as an important battle, claiming even beforehand that they were being provoked. Pauline Mac-

158

kay said: "We have organised a couple of general gatherings, but, unlike the police, we are not billing this as the Gunfight at the OK Corral." At times the New Zealand police seemed a bigger target for the protestors than the apartheid system in South Africa.

So the two sides went to rugby, two groups of homogeneous people who were poles apart.

The teams spun and Waikato won the toss.

Suddenly from the far corner, a charging group of some 250 demonstrators came hurtling onto the field, screaming in triumph, heads down, many wearing crash helmets, one carrying a large wooden cross. Smoke flares were fired, whistles blown, and the group gathered in the middle of the field.

Over the intercom the rugby authorities asked the pro-tour spectators not to use violence. The police jogged about, discussions were held, the demonstrators remained.

The police started carrying protestors from the field, frogmarching others. They had teargas but were reluctant to use it because there were so many people at the ground.

Pat McQuarrie had stolen an aircraft from Taupo, west of Hamilton, where there was an air force base. He took off and threatened to crash his plane into the Grand Stand if the match went ahead. He was later gaoled for three months.

Just after three o'clock that afternoon, Frank O'Connor, chairman of the Waikato RFU, announced: "The game has been officially cancelled."

The 28 000 people who had come to watch rugby, were angry and it was the turn of the protestors to have police protection. Beer cans rained on the demonstrators and the pressmen. The media took much of the fans' ire because they were seen as anti-tour. A Maori woman attacked the demonstrators with her brolly and was led away. Later some people broke into John Minto's house. He called the police for help. He called them three times. They did not come. Generally throughout the tour the rugby people showed restraint, certainly far greater self-control than the protestors did. The only real occasions of retaliation by rugby fans were at the second and the third tests.

Eventually the ground at Waikato was abandoned. The tour looked ended. And then, humiliated, the New Zealand police decided that they could not afford to capitulate. They would make sure the tour worked.

Robert Muldoon was in London at the time for the wedding of the Prince of Wales to Lady Diana Spencer, but the government then decided that equipment would be got from the army to improve police effec-

159

tiveness. The NZRFU decided that the tour would proceed. The police were better equipped and utterly determined after what they saw as a humiliating defeat. The barbed wire and the jumbo bins came out to stop the protestors. Rugby was on a war footing – literally.

The Springboks swopped the Mooloo of Waikato for the Ferdinand of Taranaki. They went to New Plymouth, still in farming country and a relatively quiet time before more storms.

There were two demonstrations planned for Dunedin when the Springboks played Otago – a gathering at the Boer War Memorial and a march to Carisbrook.

The first test would be crucial. Before it the police and the demonstrators fought in the streets. Some demonstrators got to the broad street in front of the ground and let off smoke bombs. There was a brief invasion of the field by some 150 protestors five minutes before kick-off, while the rugby spectators shouted their disapproval. The Red Squad arrived and the protestors fled from the field. After this litter was removed, which included broken glass, tacks and fish-hooks, which did nothing to endear the demonstrators to the rugby men. One of those removing hurtful objects was Alex Wyllie, later the coach of the All Blacks. The match went ahead as scheduled. Even in gentle Nelson, the police found offensive weapons – knuckledusters, thunder flashes, tennis balls filled with fish-hooks, steel spikes, knives, and a bomb. Bullets were fired at the home of Ron Don, president of the Auckland RFU and the most strongly pro-tour of all influential New Zealanders.

The demonstrators were not losing easily. In the early hours of Sunday morning after the test protestors tried to storm the Linwood Rugby Club because the Springboks were billeted there, but the police fought them off. The Wellington City Council proposed blocking off the roads to Athletic Park to make the second test impossible. Demonstrators picketed Air New Zealand offices and actually invaded a plane.

In Wellington the police manned the streets from early in the morning. The protestors, whose numbers reached about two thousand, tried to stop spectators getting to the ground. Inevitably there were ugly scenes. Shop windows were broken. Some protestors were injured as the police defended their barricades, visors down, batons drawn. The protestors wore padded clothing and hard hats. Several were armed in various ways and carried shields. Five or six times, the protestors charged the outnumbered police and, provocatively, stopped fractionally short of their ranks.

Just before kick-off the protestors attacked the police with a variety of

Tiny Naudé wheels away and Lofty Nel shows delight after the kick that gave South Africa a stunning victory in the third test in 1956.

ohn Gainsford rubs Colin Meads's face in it in 1956. Despite this act of consummate oolhardiness, they stayed good friends.

Meads leaves Pam Brink Stadium in distress in 1970.

No place for sissies. Frik du Preez tackles Chris Laidlaw at Loftus Versfeld.

Gert Müller on the run in 1970 with Joggie Jansen on his inside, two of the most significant players of the 1970 series.

Syd Nomis gasps to find his teeth after Fergie McCormick had stopped him. Dawie de Villiers is concerned.

Brian Lochore in 1970 – a great captain of
great team.

That's how high he was lifted. Leslie in con
versation with Gert Bezuidenhout.

Bryan Williams on the run, as he did gloriously on successive tours of South Africa.

It was not even a South African make! Demonstrators overturn a car in 1981.

There is anger in men's eyes. Fred Woodman attacks and Naas Botha, Danie Gerber and Divan Serfontein defend in 1981.

Try time! Ray Mordt scores one of a hat trick of tries at Eden Park.

A fateful moment at Eden Park in 1981, as Clive Norling signals and Alan Hewson prepares to kick the last goal of the series.

Controversy knows no bound
as Andy Dalton leads the
Cavaliers out at Loftus Vers
feld.

Below: A hero's heroic try
Uli Schmidt on the way to a
famous try against the Cava
liers, and he did it at Loftu
Versfeld.

More than ever the haka, performed here at Ellis Park by the Cavaliers, was a challenge – to the whole rugby world this time.

weapons, including bottles, knives, acid bombs and iron bars. Some 60 police put nearly a thousand protestors to flight. In their activities that afternoon, the demonstrators caused much damage to private property.

After the match, returning rugby fans laid into protestors who then sought police protection.

In Nelson the rugby union allowed a demonstrator time to speak to the crowd on condition he was moderate. He soon started getting emotional, the speakers were silenced and the band struck up.

There was a clever demonstrator in Auckland – the Reverend Geoff Walpole, who dressed up as a referee, white jersey and all, and stole the match ball and kicked it away. The match started a bit late as a result.

The protest was not all crude and violent. On the evening of 11 September, the eve of the third test, between ten and twelve thousand protestors marched in an orderly fashion down Queen Street in Auckland to register their protest. It was a dignified action, but the importance of their message did not get through to South Africa because it was obfuscated by the actions of reckless and violent people. The next day there were some 60 000 out in the Auckland streets to demonstrate against the tour, and many of them were unfriendly. Some 37 police needed medical attention after the demonstrations that day.

Auckland was to be the scene of the most bizarre demonstration of the lot, and gave ample proof of the recklessness of the anti-tour feeling. Two men set it up – Marx Jones, a 32-year-old truck driver with Shell Oil and a Drivers' Union delegate to the Auckland Trades Council, who had had a pilot's licence for 13 years, and Grant Cole, a 19-year-old railwayman. They had hired a Cessna 172, called Dixie. They loaded the Cessna at the North Shore Aero Club at Dairy Flat airfield with pamphlets and flour bombs and took off for Eden Park. On the way they radioed Auckland Information: "This is Radio Anti-Apartheid. Please, inform the police and the Rugby Union they've got just ten minutes to stop the third test."

In conversation with Chief Superintendent Graham Perry, Jones was told that much damage could be done to the protestors if the test were stopped and the rugby supporters left the ground in a bad mood, but he did not find that acceptable.

In all the Cessna flew 67 times over Eden Park, staying for the whole of the match as Cole dropped pamphlets, smoke bombs, which did not work, and flour bombs out of a window at the back. Most runs were lower than 200 feet above the ground. One of the bombs floored Gary Knight. The referee, Clive Norling, asked the two captains if they would like to stop the match. Both wanted to play on.

At one stage the announcer at Eden Park said to the crowd: "Please, refrain from throwing missiles at the plane overhead."

Eventually the Cessna flew back to Dairy Flat airfield with two helicopters and another aircraft as company.

Marx was later gaoled for eight months.

On the ground, too, there was violence as the frustrated demonstrators vented their spleen on the police.

Church or no church, intellectuals or no intellectuals, liberals or no liberals, the anti-tour movement in New Zealand had degenerated into brutal tyranny.

Several incendiary devices were found at various times on the tour, but most before the third test. The protestors created barricades of their own in Auckland but the police had a specially constructed vehicle with a battering ram to cope with them.

This time the protestors were even better armed and protected. Two hours before kick-off they moved against the police. Pitched battles were fought in the streets of Auckland. Nonriot police were injured in large numbers but again the discipline of those trained in riot activities triumphed and the mob was put to flight.

One policeman, Constable Dennis Rastovich, received a broken collar bone, a dislocated shoulder, a cracked pelvis, cracked ribs, a ruptured ear drum and a large cut on the side of his face. He was one of several severely injured. In some squads of police, every one sustained some form of injury.

Bob Howitt wrote afterwards in an editorial of *Rugby News* after the third test: "Incidents around Auckland on Saturday, and particularly in the immediate vicinity of Eden Park, illustrated pretty plainly that the issues that supposedly sparked the anti-tour movement had been long forgotten.

"Some 270 protestors received medical treatment and 32 police. There were 91 arrests.

"Those front-line policemen who at times on Saturday were fighting for their very lives against unbelievable aggression were defending more than a simple game of rugby. They were defending this country's democracy."

The demonstrators were back at Whenuapai Airport to see the Springboks off. Some 200 invaded the airport terminal where the police surrounded them and flung them out of the terminal.

During the tour 1 944 demonstrators were arrested and there were further arrests after the tour. In all over two thousand charges were laid, the

162

commonest being obstruction of roads and trespass. Most arrests happened in Christchurch, followed by Wellington, followed by Auckland. It was estimated that 35% of those charged escaped conviction.

Apart from McQuarrie and Marx, John Minto was sentenced to six weeks in gaol, later reduced to periodic detention, two were sentenced to nine months in gaol for damage to the microwave station on Moirs Hill which housed the earth satellite station and where they cut the microwave link which meant there was no Afrikaans commentary, and five Patu (from the Maori word to hit) members to a year in gaol for rioting in Auckland. They had formed a "human tank" to charge the police.

The Springbok tour grossed some $NZ2 million for the NZRFU but the costs of the tour were so high that their nett profit was only $NZ190 000. The cost to the New Zealand government, as given in 1982, was $NZ7,2 million.

Ross Meurant, a member of Red Squad and later a member of parliament, said: "When the Springboks left New Zealand soil at 20.30 hours on Sunday, September 13, 1981, much of the country breathed a sigh of relief. It had been a long, hard and shattering experience for police, protestors, Springboks and general public alike."

The Springboks have the custom, dating back to Billy Millar's team in 1912, of giving a Springbok head to the first team to beat them in a match outside the tests. No side did that in 1981, but the Springboks gave away the head anyway – to the police.

Afterwards there were court cases and enquiries into police activities after protestors submitted 362 complaints, 211 of which were found unjustified. In 48 cases an apology was deemed fitting. In 65 cases there was insufficient evidence. In 30 cases there were justified complaints but no positive identification. Six policemen were prosecuted – unsuccessfully. Only two of the six got to court, where the cases were dismissed.

At the end of the tour John Minto of HART said: "We didn't stop the tour, but the cost has been so high that it should ensure that this is the last by a racist South African team."

CHAPTER 16

The Divided Team in the Divided Country

INASMUCH AS IT can be considered a rugby tour, that of 1981 was a remarkable one. For the only time between 1921 and 1994, save only 1937, the Springboks could be considered a better side than New Zealand. It was a series they would have deserved to have won, should have drawn and did not deserve to lose.

The best rugby in the world was being played in the Southern Hemisphere at the time. South Africa had just come off convincing victories over the Lions and France and a series win over Ireland. They were in the process of forming one of the fastest and most potent back lines of all time. The All Blacks had wobbled against the Wallabies and then walloped Wales in Cardiff.

Despite the conditions under which the teams played, it was a remarkably tense and well-contested series.

The Springboks, as had suddenly become the wont with touring teams, were too strong for provincial combinations. This is possibly because international teams had come to play so many matches that the provincial unions' advantage of cohesiveness no longer applied.

Four days after their long journey via New York, Los Angeles and Honolulu, they played their first match in Gisborne, in Maori country, where Sir Graham Latimer, the President of the Maori Council, welcomed them at the Pho-o-Rawiri marae.

On July 22 the Springboks and Poverty Bay ran out onto the heavy, clinging mud of Rugby Park. Two demonstrators ran onto the field and were removed, the Springboks kicked off and the tour started. Edrich Krantz scored the first try, Errol Tobias the second. The Springboks won 24-6. The strangest thing about that first match, and a sign of things to come, was the omission of the captain Wynand Claassen. Normally the captain leads his team out to start the tour. This time Eben Jansen led the Springboks into the tour.

Sadly, it was a divided tour. Not only were there divisions in New Zealand rugby and society over the tour as an issue, but there were also divisions within the Springbok team, specifically between the captain Wynand Claassen and the coach Nelie Smith. Claassen believed that Smith did not want him and worked against him. In fact Claassen claimed that Smith had refused to coach the team when there was the suggestion that Claassen captains the team. The selectors, instead of yielding, had then told Smith he should resign, which he did not do. But he did phone the selectors to try to persuade them to change their minds before the team was finally announced. Claassen got in on a 3-2 vote – Daan Swiegers, Dougie Dyers, and Brian Irvine against Smith and Butch Lochner who was then the convener of the selection committee. There were other accusations levelled by Claassen against his coach. The gap between the coach and the captain would grow as the tour progressed.

From Gisborne the Springboks went west to the farming town of Hamilton, in the province called Waikato, the Waterloo of the 1956 Springboks, a place with an awesome reputation in South African minds – Mooloo and mud and Don Clarke. There was worse on this day – a bigger defeat than in 1956. Waikato were the holders of the Ranfurly Shield in 1981, but that was not the essence of the defeat.

Demonstrators broke onto the field and despite requests to withdraw did not do so. As a result the match was called off, 28 000 irate fans went home and the Springboks went on to New Plymouth, wondering about the future of the tour.

If anything the Waikato team were more disappointed than the Springboks. That was their only chance of playing against the Springboks destroyed.

On the bus down to New Plymouth, they went through farming land, King Country. Their bus stopped and onto it got the massive frame and impassive face of Colin Meads. He assured the Springboks that he was glad to see them and that they were in fact welcome in New Zealand and on they went to play Taranaki.

The cancellation of the Waikato match threw a spanner in the Springboks' works. They had picked a powerful side for Waikato. Now that match was off, but they still needed to give their top players a match, and soon after that they were to play Manawatu, at that time a powerful side. The later cancellation of the match in Timaru also reduced the number of matches available. Then they themselves made positional switches here and there. It became harder and harder to give players enough matches and in their right positions. Opportunities to experiment were limited.

They beat Taranaki easily, Manawatu well, and Wanganui easily when Errol Tobias scored two tries. Then they headed down to Invercargill where they won again.

Up they went in the cold rain to Dunedin for the Otago match. They scored three tries to one but won only 17-13. And then came the first test in Christchurch.

The Springboks left out their captain, as they had done in 1921, 1937 and 1956 (and were to do in 1994, and they lost the first test, as they had done in 1921, 1937, 1956 and 1994), but also as they did in 1965 when Dawie de Villiers was the only Springbok captain on a tour of New Zealand to play in the first test.

Theuns Stofberg captained the side from flank, but it soon became clear in the other tests that, as in 1937, the Springboks did better with their captain on the field. And they played Darius Botha on the wing instead of flying Gerrie Germishuys. That, too, was a mistake which would be put right.

On the eve of the first test the Springbok team and the reserves – which meant that Wynand Claassen was not even with his team – moved into the draughty squash courts at Linwood Club where they would be quieter than in a hotel in the city and have easier access to the ground. The rest of the team were billeted out.

There were 39 000 spectators at Athletic Park to watch the test.

New Zealand scored three tries to one but won only 14-9. Though the Springboks started off well and Naas Botha got a drop, the All Blacks deserved better than their five-point victory margin. For them Doug Rollerson on the blind side from a five-metre scrum, Stu Wilson in a spectacularly scything break, and Mark Shaw from a plunging surge scored tries. Hennie Bekker took a reverse pass from Ray Mordt and scored for South Africa a couple of minutes from the end. That is what gave the final score its respectability.

Afterwards, Andy Dalton, who was the All Black captain because Graham Mourie refused to play against the Springboks, said: "We sympathise with you because of all the carrying on, but we don't feel sorry for you. We still want to beat you."

There was a break after the test because the South Canterbury match at Timaru was cancelled to give the police a rest. The Springboks headed for Greymouth and rest and recreation. The next match was up in Nelson, where the game is supposed to have started in New Zealand, and the Springboks made their own bit of history. The local names, associated with a famous victory were no omen, for at Trafalgar Park the Springboks beat

166

Nelson Bays 83-0. They scored 14 tries of which Naas Botha converted 12. He scored a try himself and added a penalty for 31 points. There were records – the total, the number of tries and Naas Botha's tally.

There was also an interesting bit of evasion. The Nelson Bays coach, Merv Jaffray, who had played for Otago and New Zealand, coached his team for the match but refused to watch in protest against apartheid.

There was drama in Napier when the Springboks played the Maoris and more police guarded the Maori hotel than that of the Springboks lest somebody attack Billy Bush's men for being sell-outs.

After the match on slippery McLean Park Bush announced: "We won 16-all!" He had a point. But he also professed gratitude. He claimed he had deliberately collapsed the final scrum and feared a penalty try. Neither penalty nor penalty try happened.

The Maoris were magnificent. They did not score a try but deserved their 9-0 lead at half-time as they attacked again and again.

The Springboks got back with a try and Colin Beck kicked a penalty goal. With time virtually up, the Maoris led 12-9.

Germishuys may well have scored when he chased a kick-ahead by Divan Serfontein, the captain of the day, but the referee Brian Duffy of Taranaki, who had refereed a test in 1977 when the Lions were on tour, awarded a scrum to the Maoris. The Springboks heeled against the head and drove for the line. They were stopped and there was another scrum to South Africa. From 10 m away Colin Beck slammed his boot into a high, hard drop at goal. Duffy did not signal whether it was over or not and there was confusion as the Springboks jogged back to their own half and the Maoris drifted towards their 22 m-line and Duffy drifted somewhere between the two till he blew his whistle for no-side. Later he said that he had no doubts that the kick was over.

Colin Beck had no doubts at all about the kick. "No, it wasn't over," he says with a chuckle in 1996.

The surprise of Springbok selection for the second test was the exclusion of charismatic Rob Louw, a great Springbok loose forward, a friendly man. In fact he was gregarious and, in the surmise that followed his shock omission, it was thought that the management had a charge against him and equally friendly Hempies du Toit of fraternising with the enemy. They had both gone out late with Andy Haden and others after the first test and crept back in the wee hours. But then most of the team had gone out on the town, preferring what it had to offer to what the Linwood Club had to offer. The reason for the omission of Louw is one of the mysteries of South African rugby. The solution may simply be that he was dropped because of a change of game plan and to accommodate Wynand Claassen.

Before the second test the Springboks stayed in the changing rooms at Wellington's Athletic Park, the Grandstand Hotel, as they called it. The changing rooms at Athletic Park are notoriously poky, not places of comfort or beauty. But the New Zealanders did their best to brighten things up for the Springboks. There were beds this time, a pool table, a television set and a music player. The Springboks found the arrangement passable. In fact the All Blacks afterwards claimed that the Springboks, by staying at the ground, had actually had the advantage whereas they had to get up early and travel to the ground four hours before kick-off.

Philip Nel, captain of the 1937 Springboks sent Wynand Claassen a telegram before the test: "Fight for the survival of South African rugby. Tackle hard. Run hard."

The wind blew, the rain fell in cold showers, and the Springboks won convincingly before 31 000 people.

Andy Dalton won the toss and played against the wind. The Springboks nearly scored right at the start and then did so through a Botha penalty. Gerrie Germishuys, back in place of Darius Botha, raced a way in splendour to score the only try of the match and Naas kicked the rest to which Alan Hewson replied with four penalties for New Zealand. Naas Botha, a genius in the wet, won the day. At half-time the Springboks were already leading 18-3. The final score was 24-12. The series was very much alive.

The Springboks were delighted. It did not matter that the showers were cold. A protestor had got into the dressing room and run the hot taps for the duration of the test, thus ensuring cold comfort for the players after the match. The whole Springbok team stayed out to the wee hours of the morning after the match, and there were no managerial complaints!

From Wellington the Springboks moved to sulphurous Rotorua to play Bay of Plenty. What a game! There were 25 000 spectators to see the Springboks, down 18-13 at half-time, win 29-24, and the referee, Bill Adlam of Wanganui, was unpopular. He was the only New Zealand referee that the Springboks had a complaint about on the tour. In his speech after the match, the Bay of Plenty captain, Craig Ross, reported that a Springbok had said to the referee: "Gaan kak in die mielies." (Roughly and politely translated as: Contribute to the fertilising of the maize field.) The referee had not understood.

Now it was back to the protestors' den – to Auckland. This is New Zealand's biggest city. There would be more of everything there, includ-

168

ing demonstrators. And in addition the Springboks would have to play the great province of Auckland.

They moved into very comfortable quarters at Eden Park, dubbed the Ron Don Grandstand Hotel, made as comfortable as possible by New Zealand rugby men who are able to get things right more often than other rugby nations.

Before the Auckland match Ron Don, the chairman of the Auckland RFU, said: "Naas Botha is the best five-eighth in the world." Naas Botha proved that with an astonishing display against Auckland, perhaps his best-ever performance.

The Springboks won 39-12. Naas Botha scored 19 points – two tries, four conversions and a solitary penalty goal. But it was the way he played. Suddenly on the firmer surface he set the Springboks running. They scored seven tries that day – seven against Auckland! And one of Botha's tries started not far from his goal line.

After Auckland the Springboks went up in happy sunshine to Going territory, to play North Auckland, now Northlands, in Whangarei. They won on a windy day 19-10, and came back, carrying many critical injuries, to Auckland for the third test, the most dramatic test the history of rugby football has ever known.

Forget about all the sideshows – the fighting in the street and the lunatic bomber flying in the air. Concentrate on the rugby – and it was a match packed with drama. Recalling the match, Andy Dalton, captain of New Zealand, son of 1949 vice-captain Ray Dalton, said: "We all knew how important this game was going to be, probably the most important game we'd ever play."

Just as a rugby match it had that aura about it – another decider in matches between South Africa and New Zealand. It was a match to grip the throat and freeze the heart.

The Springboks spent the night under the Grandstand at Eden Park. Four players who played in the test were not there, as there were no fewer than two last-minute withdrawals, as Div Visser and Theuns Stofberg had to be replaced by Hennie Bekker, who was himself carrying a groin injury, and Rob Louw, and Johan Heunis and Colin Beck had to come on for Gysie Pienaar and Willie du Plessis, who went into the test injured.

Wynand Claassen won the toss and opted to play against the breeze. In fact playing into the flight path of the flour-bombing pilot would have a greater effect on the players than the weather. Clive Norling blew his whistle to get the match under way and New Zealand soon built up a lead that looked unassailable. After Naas Botha and Alan Hewson had swopped penalties, Stu Wilson scored a great try when Hewson came into the line and cut through. Then Gary Knight powered over for a try after Frank Shelford had knocked on. At half-time the All Blacks led 16-3. Shades of 1965 and Lancaster Park?

In the history of tests, the All Blacks have only once beaten the Springboks after trailing at half-time and that was way back in the first test in 1921 when the Springboks led 5-0 at the break and the All Blacks won 13-5. By way of contrast the Springboks have won six times after trailing at half-time. The most notable of these occasions was at Lancaster Park in 1965.

Seven minutes into the second half, in a half in which time was to become a crucial factor, Colin Beck chipped ahead and Ray Mordt beat Hewson to the try, which Naas Botha converted and the score was 16-9. The game was on.

New Zealand got into South African territory, which it did rarely in that half, and Hewson kicked a penalty to make the score 19-9.

Ray Mordt got a run down the left, lobbed the ball over Hewson's head, won the race for the ball and scored. Botha converted. 19-15.

Murray Mexted was penalised at a ruck after Gerrie Germishuys had a dab down the left, and Botha made the score 19-18. Imagine the tension as the game slipped into its last, long quarter.

Danie Gerber tried to run deep in Springbok territory and was tackled. The Springboks lost the ball and Doug Rollerson potted a goal. 22-18. This came after thirty-nine and a half minutes. There was half a minute of playing time plus injury time left. Injury time was a long, fatal time.

Colin Beck was moving right from the scrum which Norling had announced would be the "last scrum" of the match. As Beck was tackled he shovelled the ball towards Mordt. As it bounced Naas Botha came round and footed it ahead. He gathered the bouncing ball, swerved infield to take three All Blacks out of the game and fed Ray Mordt who drove through Dave Loveridge and beyond Frank Shelford to score. Naas Botha missed the conversion and after 47 minutes of the second half the score was 22-all.

The All Blacks kicked off. South Africa had the ball to put into a scrum. Norling awarded New Zealand a free kick before the ball was put in. The free kick became a penalty, and, with preternatural calm, Alan Hewson, who had had to leave the field in the North-South trial because he was suffering from exposure at Carisbrook in Dunedin, kicked the winning points. 25-22.

After some 52 minutes of the second half Clive Norling blew the final whistle.

It was possibly the bitterest result in all matches between South Africa

170

and New Zealand, save only the whole result of 1949. Even the New Zealanders felt for the Springboks, as South Africans had done for the 1976 All Blacks.

Bob Howitt of *Rugby News* wrote: "It takes more than a crazed pilot flour-bombing his target for 90 minutes to stop the two greatest rugby countries in the world from producing a game of the finest quality." Despite the sideshows, the players' concentration had been absolute.

After the 56 sometimes tense, often enjoyable, occasionally frustrating days in New Zealand the Springboks flew to the USA and the rest of their bizarre tour. In 1991, the 1981 Springboks had a reunion. They were all there except Edrich Krantz. All those present voted that, if they had to undertake the same tour under the same conditions, they would certainly go. Whether, with the wisdom of hindsight, New Zealand would have allowed them in is a moot point.

TOUR STATISTICS (NEW ZEALAND ONLY)

P	W	D	L	Pf	Pa	Tf	Ta
14	11	1	2	410	171	59	14

TESTS

3	1	0	2	55	51	5	5

The South African Touring Team of 1981:

Z M J Pienaar (Orange Free State), J W Heunis (Northern Transvaal), J S Germishuys (Transvaal), D S Botha (Northern Transvaal), E F W Krantz (Orange Free State), R H Mordt (Transvaal), C J du Plessis (Western Province), W du Plessis (Western Province), D M Gerber (Eastern Province), E G Tobias (South African Rugby Football Federation), H E Botha (Northern Transvaal), J J Beck (Western Province), D J Serfontein (Western Province), B J Wolmarans (Orange Free State), G P Visagie (Natal), H J van Aswegen (Western Province), P R van der Merwe (South Western Districts), O W Oosthuizen (Northern Transvaal), P G du Toit (Western Province), W J H Kahts (Northern Transvaal), R J Cockrell (Western Province), S A Povey (Western Province), H J Bekker (Western Province), L C Moolman (Northern Transvaal), J de V Visser (Western Province), M T S Stofberg (Northern Transvaal), E Jansen (Orange Free State), S B Geldenhuys (Northern Transvaal), R J Louw (Western Province), M B Burger (Northern Transvaal), W Claassen (Natal) (c), J H Marais (Northern Transvaal)

TOUR RESULTS

DATE	VENUE	OPPONENTS	SCORE
22 July	Gisborne	Poverty Bay	24-6
25 July	Hamilton	Waikato	Cancelled
29 July	New Plymouth	Taranaki	34-9
1 August	Palmerston	North Manawatu	31-19
5 August	Wanganui	Wanganui	45-9
8 August	Invercargill	Southland	22-6
11 August	Dunedin	Otago	17-13
15 August	Christchurch	New Zealand	9-14
19 August	Timaru	South Canterbury	Cancelled
22 August	Nelson	Nelson Bays	83-0
25 August	Napier	New Zealand Maoris	12-12
29 August	Wellington	New Zealand	24-12
2 September	Rotorua	Bay of Plenty	29-24
5 September	Auckland	Auckland	39-12
8 September	Whangarei	Northland Auckland	19-10
12 September	Auckland	New Zealand	25-22

CHAPTER 17

The Judgement of Casey

At the eleventh hour, Judge Casey handed down his judgement and the All Blacks, who were due to tour South Africa in 1985, were stopped from going. This led to much upset.

Because the NZRFU, moans and groans notwithstanding, stuck to its principled belief that the people should be free to decide and because the rugby people decided that the All Blacks should tour South Africa, the NZRFU did all the normal things to organise a tour.

Not that voting was unanimous. Auckland and North Harbour were against the tour, as were Ray Harper of Southland and Peter Wild of Nelson Bays. They believed that going ahead with the tour would harm rugby football in New Zealand, especially because the game could be lost in the schools. In 1981 the vote had been unanimous and in 1985 it was still substantially in favour of the tour.

They held trials, at New Plymouth and Invercargill, picked a team, booked the seats, assembled the team and equipped it. And as is usual in New Zealand they fostered the enormous hope that at last they had a side capable of beating the Springboks on their own fields. And this time unattached referees had been appointed for the series of three tests – Alan Hosie of Scotland for the first two and Fred Howard of England for the third.

In South Africa, too, there were trials at Newlands, to sort out the Springboks to face the invasion.

Rugby excitement in both countries was great.

Political excitement amongst those opposed to such tours was also great.

South Africa's international rugby had had a bit of a shot in the arm in the early Eighties when the Jaguars, Lions, Irish, French and English came to tour, and the Springboks went off to South America, New Zealand and the USA. But the promise of that needed sustained impetus.

The All Black tour to South Africa could provide that. Both those in favour of the tour and those opposed to it realised this. Massive demonstrations did not stop the tour, nor did the New Zealand government, nor did the NZRFU have a sudden, bright revelation. Two legal men set the ball in motion, Judge J P Casey gave his judgement, and the NZRFU abided by it, as was their constant principle in allowing or disallowing tours to and from South Africa.

The government, a Labour government this time under Prime Minister David Lange, tried to dissuade the NZRFU councillors from approving the tour. Amongst other things Lange said: "The Government is totally opposed to sporting contacts with South Africans outside New Zealand. All New Zealanders are however entitled to the freedom to leave and return to New Zealand, and no New Zealand Government could or would interfere with that right . . . My view is that a rugby tour of South Africa would do New Zealand great damage, and that for that reason the tour must not proceed." By a "substantial majority" the eighteen councillors of the NZRFU voted for the tour to proceed. On the day of the meeting the anti-tour group took a full advertisement in the newspaper, signed by over two thousand opponents of the tour. And it was all the talk of the newspapers and the radio. The itinerary was approved. The first match was scheduled for 24 July in Welkom, the last for 24 September in Durban, the third test. There were to be 16 matches, three of them tests.

On Saturday 13 July in New Zealand's High Court in Wellington, Justice Casey of Auckland ruled on the application of Patrick Thomas Finnigan, a barrister of Auckland, and Philip James Recordan, a barrister and solicitor of Auckland, to have the All Black tour to South Africa stopped.

The defendants in the case were, first, the New Zealand Rugby Football Union (Incorporated) and, second, Cecil Blazey and 17 others, in other words the Council of the NZRFU.

Finnigan was a member of the University RFC and Recordan of Teachers Eastern RFC. That was an important point, even though they played seldom. Their clubs were affiliated to the Auckland Rugby Union which was affiliated to the NZRFU.

Their point was that the NZRFU was bound by its constitution which stated as one of its objects:

(a) To control, promote, foster and develop the game of amateur rugby union football throughout New Zealand. The proposed tour, according to the plaintiffs, would harm rugby football. They also

174

found reasons within the Rules of the Union for questioning the procedures which had been followed in agreeing to the tour.

They wanted the decision to tour declared "invalid and unlawful" and an injunction brought to restrain the defendants from proceeding with the tour.

Finnigan claimed that he did not want to stop the players from touring, only challenge the Union's right to accept South Africa's invitation in the way that it had done.

It was all a costly process, beyond the normal procedures of rugby football.

The statement of claim was filed by the plaintiffs' solicitor, Rodney Harold Hansen of Wellington. And the rugby establishment probably did not take the whole thing seriously enough and so did not organise as well as they should have.

Finnigan and Recordan had first applied to the High Court of New Zealand where Sir Ronald Davison had dismissed their application on the grounds that their membership of rugby clubs did not give them the right to challenge the NZRFU. The lawyers then took the matter to the appeal court which ordered the high court to hear the case, as a matter of national importance. A single judge, Maurice Casey, later Sir Maurice, began hearing the case on 8 July, six days before the All Blacks were due to assemble for their trip to South Africa, and on Saturday 13 July 1985 brought an injunction against the tour. He said: "In the responsible exercise of my discretion I consider the only order I can make is one which will preserve the position existing at the date of the NZRFU's decision."

That meant that the NZRFU's decision was frozen. They could take no further steps to promote the tour due to start on 24 July 1985.

The tour was off because there was no time to fight the injunction. If the NZRFU had gone ahead with the tour they could have been held in contempt, and there would then have been a case for impounding passports and air tickets. The NZRFU opposed the court decision and it cost them $NZ159 thousand – five times their profit for the season.

The matter was taken to the Privy Council in London, which supported Judge Casey's decision on the grounds that that particular period, between 24 July and 14 September 1985, was not the only time when an All Black tour could occur. In any case by the time the matter got to the Privy Council it was no longer a real case, and so was dismissed.

The day of that case and the subsequent injunction against the players who had decided to go anyway was the birthday of the Cavaliers' tour which, whatever it may have been intended to achieve, achieved one thing – it turned the council of the NZRFU against the South African Rugby Board. There would be no more contact till 1992.

Instead of going to problematic South Africa, the All Blacks, captained by Jock Hobbs, went to Argentina which was then in the throes of a state of emergency. They played two tests, winning the first 33-20 and – big shock – drawing the second 21-all when Hugo Porta kicked the last penalty goal after Mark Shaw had punched him.

At the end of 1985 Danie Craven announced the postponement of the Lions' tour to South Africa scheduled for 1986. It has not happened yet.

CHAPTER 18

Cavalier Rebellion

THE 1985 ALL BLACKS were ninety minutes away from a rebellion. On Tuesday 23 July 1985 25 All Blacks were about to leave for Auckland's airport to board a Continental Airlines flight, leaving at 8 p.m. for Los Angeles, when a telex arrived from Ted Thomas, QC, who had represented Pat Finnigan and Phil Recordan in the High Court proceedings concerning the 1985 tour.

Thomas claimed that Brian Lochore, the coach, Andy Dalton, the captain and Andy Haden would, as agents of the NZRFU, be in contempt of court if they went on an unofficial tour.

An unofficial tour had been planned. Twenty-five players would resign from their New Zealand clubs, fly to South Africa via Los Angeles and New York, form a Barbarians XV and take over the abandoned All Black itinerary. Four more players would join them in South Africa, and Brian Lochore was to be the coach.

They had assembled in Wellington on 16 July. On that very day the Prime Minister, David Lange, stated in an interview that the players were free to go as individuals, as Andy Haden had suggested to the NZRFU before it had even taken its April decision to accept the South African invitation. They could, said Lange, even call themselves the All Blacks.

The players and the NZRFU met in adjoining rooms in Wellington but communicated only through the Union's lawyer Kit Toogood for fear of being held in contempt of court. At lunch some of the councillors did manage to indicate to the players that they should go and where they could get their jerseys in South Africa.

The players decided to go as individuals and gathered in Auckland a week later. They had tickets. Their passports had already been handed in to immigration for processing, and their baggage was already loaded into an airline container. They had arranged to board in such a way that demonstrators could not find them. The man behind the arrangements, as he would again be a year later, was Andy Haden.

Then came Thomas's telex. He claimed to have a tip-off from somebody who had "the good of rugby at heart". Thomas, strongly opposed to ties with South Africa, warned the players about the possibility of their being in contempt of court and lectured them on contacts with South Africa. The tour was off.

Ted Thomas invited Haden to a victory celebration. Haden did not go.

The tour was postponed for a year. It was planned during the replacement tour to Argentina in 1985. Murray Mexted did a lot of talking on that tour but Andy Haden would be the active agent and go-between.

Just before Christmas 1985 Haden, Andy Dalton, Ian Kirkpatrick and Winston McDonald flew up to Hong Kong to meet Louis Luyt, the millionaire businessman who was President of the Transvaal RU, Robert Denton, and two South African businessmen, Johan Claasen of Volkskas and Mervyn Key, who would also act as the attorney representing Ellis Park (Pty) Ltd. The driving force in South Africa was Robert Denton, who at the time was the managing director of Ellis Park (Pty) Ltd. When the Transvaal Rugby Union got into financial difficulties and was virtually bankrupt in 1984 towards the end of the Jannie le Roux regime, Volkskas were obliged to repossess Ellis Park. The estimated cost of building the new Ellis Park had been R27 million. The actual cost had been much higher, and the Transvaal Rugby Union asked Volkskas for a loan of R37 million. To look after its loan Volkskas took over Ellis Park in March 1984.

Johan Claasen became the chairman of Ellis Park (Pty) Ltd, Robert Denton ran the business. But things actually got worse, and in August 1984 Volkskas froze the TRU's bank account and asked the Union for R42 million by 4 September 1984, and Volkskas threatened to sequestrate the TRU. Volkskas refused to deal with Jannie le Roux, then still the president of the TRU and soon a palace revolution occurred, ousting Le Roux and replacing him with Louis Luyt. It was all a complicated situation but ended with an agreement that the Transvaal Rugby Union would rent the ground for matches. Ellis Park needed activities. Rugby was the activity to which it was best suited. At the same time the All Blacks, who had a great team, had made it known after the cancellation of their 1985 tour, that they felt it their right to play in South Africa. They were top sportsmen wanting to compete with the best.

The Cavaliers tour was Denton's idea. According to Haden, he was the South African link. He had to get the rugby authorities in South Africa to go along with the tour while Andy Haden got the players in New Zealand and Winston McDonald, a travel man but acting in his personal capacity after a long association with South Africa dating back to the tour by the Auckland club Ponsonby, saw to the logistics.

At the Hong Kong meeting, Johan Claassen was in the chair. Andy Dalton and Louis Luyt were not present. They stayed in their rooms, but that evening the group got together for a dinner.

Forty-eight hours after leaving Auckland, the Cavaliers' tour was in place for the following April, four months later. It's a long time to keep a secret, but it seems to have been kept, even though Mervyn Key, the South African attorney at the Hong Kong meeting, travelled through New Zealand contacting players and their families and girlfriends. He drew up tight contracts with the players.

And, if any money was made by the Cavaliers as individuals, it remained a secret – a remarkable feat. And Haden claimed the tour was "undertaken because the country's top players wanted to play rugby in South Africa – and that was all there was to it".

In 1986, suddenly, the team left for South Africa and called itself the New Zealand Cavaliers. Time and again they said they were not the All Blacks. Over and over, they were referred to in South Africa as the All Blacks.

There was some justification for this. After all, it was the team chosen to tour South Africa in 1985, except that David Kirk was not with them. He was about to go to Oxford as a Rhodes Scholar and withdrew from the Cavaliers a week before departure. His place was taken by All Black Andy Donald. John Kirwan, playing in Italy, also did not tour. His father was stricken with a severe heart attack. His place was taken by veteran Bernie Fraser, one of the great wings of New Zealand's history.

Brian Lochore was not available this time and the management of the team was made up of Colin Meads and Ian Kirkpatrick, as respected a rugby duo as the world could have produced.

The Cavaliers did not have the same itinerary as the All Blacks would have had in 1985. They had the fiercest itinerary any tour team ever had, but then money was playing an important rôle in the tour which was sponsored by Yellow Pages, who put in R2½ million, while SABC put in R1½ million. Toyota sponsored the Springboks to the tune of R75 000 and for that their logo appeared on the Springbok jersey, the first time a logo had been used on the jersey, causing much upset amongst traditionalists.

In fact the tour did much to change the face of sports sponsorship in South Africa. Robert Denton got *Yellow Pages* as the sponsors, and Robin Binckes Promotions, previously involved in cricket, did the promotion. In a brilliant merchandising coup, *Yellow Pages* were prominent as they had never been before, as no company had ever been before, even in a game as conservative as rugby football. At the prominence given to *Yellow Pages*, many other sponsoring companies and promotion companies sat up, took notice, and began to realise the vast possibilities in sports sponsorship. And the sporting bodies began to realise the extent of the financial rewards to be gained.

Influential *Rugby News* of New Zealand ran a poll on the tour and its readers were well over 80% in favour of the Cavaliers tour and opposed to sanctions against them on their return. In fact had they returned successful they would have been heroes.

The tour was organised by Robert Denton and Winston McDonald with Transvaal Rugby Union as the front. The tour started while Danie Craven and Fritz Eloff were attending an IRB meeting in London. The news caused ructions. Ronnie Dawson of Ireland led the attack on the SARB. Ces Blazey, ever the man of principle, refused to shake Craven's hand. Craven denied knowledge of the tour and said that it was not an SARB tour. That said, the SARB gave the team an official welcome and the Springboks were awarded caps for the tests. That there should have been as much ignorance in official rugby circles in South Africa as there was in New Zealand seems unlikely.

It was simply not possible that the SARB did not know of the tour before the Cavaliers arrived, any more than it was possible that nobody in rugby authority in New Zealand knew of the tour before the Cavaliers left.

The IRB passed a resolution disapproving of the tour and urging the SARB to send the players home, which did not happen. Craven said when he got home: "To stop this trip would be such a deep disgrace that no man in his right mind would ever do such an injustice to South Africa." Craven never again attended an IRB meeting.

Ces Blazey ended his period as chairman of the NZRFU and was replaced by Russ Thomas, who said, while the tour was in its infancy: "I am not against the rugby tour by the New Zealand Cavaliers in South Africa. It is, however, the manner in which the players and the officials went there that is a disappointment. Most of them are my friends and it's very hard to condemn a friend."

It was essentially a players' tour with Andy Dalton and Andy Haden in real control. This had its weaknesses as the players were harder to discipline and some of what happened at the end of the tour was not really worthy of top New Zealand rugby.

180

In their first match of the tour, they beat the Junior Springboks 22-21 at Ellis Park. They scored two tries to one but it took a dropped goal by Grant Fox a minute before the end to give them the narrow victory. It was not going to be an easy tour for the Cavaliers.

Scoring the only try of the match, the Cavaliers beat Northern Transvaal 10-9. Burger Geldenhuys punched Andy Dalton from behind just before half-time and ended the Cavaliers' captain's tour. Danie Craven, president of the SA Rugby Board, decreed that Geldenhuys would not play for South Africa that year. There was anger and upset in Pretoria over this decision and there is no doubt that the tough flanker would have been a first-choice player in his position, but he did not play. He played again in 1989 against the World XV.

Craig Green, one of the Cavalier successes on the tour, scored a hat trick of tries in a fine victory over Orange Free State in an evening match in Bloemfontein. That was a great display. Their display at Ellis Park before a small crowd of 22 000 was poor. They lost to Jannie Breedt's Transvaal although Green scored two tries and Deon Coetzee Transvaal's only try. That day they did not like Wynand Mans, the referee, at all.

The Cavaliers were magnificent against Western Province at Newlands. They won only 26-15, but the truth was that they were, with the ruthless driving of their forwards, light years better than the home side. Not for the first time, the New Zealand team looked invincible ahead of the first test.

It rained at Newlands, and Naas Botha was magnificent. There was a moment of genius from him to win the match.

The scores were level at 15-all after Grant Fox had kicked three penalty goals and converted the first-ever penalty try given against the Springboks and Naas Botha had kicked three penalty goals and two dropped goals.

Louis Moolman won a line-out on the Grand Stand side of the field, on the Springboks' right. The ball skidded to Botha on the soggy turf, but he gathered it in and kicked wide across the field where the Cavaliers had expected a drop at goal.

Carel du Plessis, on the left wing for the Springbok, set off smooth and upright after the ball as it skidded towards the junction of touch-in-goal and the dead-ball line. In desperation Mike Clamp raced back. Du Plessis dived, got the ball and skidded in the wet. He rose and lifted an arm in triumph. In the wet, from the touchline Naas Botha converted and the Springboks won a thriller 22-15.

With a test each Saturday for four Saturdays, the Cavaliers had only the bare-fisted fight with Natal in Durban before their next test. They won the match/fight 37-24 when they scored seven tries to two. Bryce Robins, a surprise choice in 1985, scored three of the tries.

The second test was also at King's Park, and the Springboks gave the Cavaliers a present of a 19-18 victory. It was the day when Naas Botha played in Durban and left his kicking boots in Pretoria. He missed no fewer than seven kicks at goal and missed four attempts at drops, one from right under the bar in the dying moments of the game. Like the great Don Clarke, he flopped at King's Park. His failure meant that the series was alive. It was the first Springbok defeat at King's Park. Naas's boot notwithstanding, the Cavaliers scored two tries to one. Warwick Taylor got one when he charged down a Botha clearance. And Murray Mexted got another from a scrum close to the Springbok line. At one stage the Cavaliers led 19-9 and they were putting enormous pressure on Christo Ferreira at scrum half.

The Springbok try was a great one as Naas Botha picked up and counterattacked for Danie Gerber to set Jaco Reinach away. The Cavaliers survived the last twelve minutes.

Jock Hobbs had been brought into the side and captained the team. It was a must-win match for Cavaliers, and at the end of it Jock Hobbs wept as he walked from the field.

The Cavaliers and the Barbarians had an amiable romp at Ellis Park with Frank McMullen, the former All Black, as the referee. The Cavaliers that day were, inevitably, their dirt-trackers. Their captain was Wayne Shelford, which is significant for he would become one of the great All Blacks and one of their great captains. Shelford celebrated with two tries.

The Springboks selected Garth Wright at scrum half for the third test at Loftus Versfeld. They scored four tries to a great one by Kieran Crowley, the Cavaliers' fullback, after his team had won five powerful rucks. That try put the Cavaliers ahead 15-12. In the next ten minutes the Springboks destroyed them. Naas Botha counterattacked, chipped, collected his own kick and scored. Carel du Plessis cut past Fox and picked his moment to send Danie Gerber racing in for a try of enormous grace. Then Jaco Reinach ran 50 m down the blind side for a great try.

But the try of the match had happened in the first half. It may just be the greatest try scored by a hooker in a test match. The Springboks won a scrum on their left, moved right to Jaco Reinach on the right wing. The ball came back to the left where Carel du Plessis flipped the ball inside to Uli Schmidt about 40 m from the Cavaliers' goal line. Schmidt swerved inside Gary Knight and Michael Clamp and dived over for a popular try as Kieran Crowley attempted to tackle him.

The Springboks were full value for their victory, 33-18.

The Cavaliers' filler match was against Western Transvaal at Olën Park in Potchefstroom. They led 26-3 with half an hour to go and ended winning 26-18, scoring three tries to two.

Before the fourth test the Cavaliers performed a haka, to the delight of the whole of a packed Ellis Park.

For the last test the Cavaliers replaced Grant Fox with Wayne Smith. Both scrum halves scored a try each, Naas Botha kicked better than Robbie Deans and Michael du Plessis kicked a dropped goal, but the most remarkable feature of the match was the disintegration of the Cavaliers' discipline as the tour ran towards a series defeat.

The Cavaliers' tour angered the New Zealand government and the NZRFU. The government retaliated by not having the matches broadcast over state-owned radio or television. But New Zealanders were able to hear the matches on a private radio network.

When they got back, the Cavaliers were charged by the NZRFU with misconduct and incurred legal expenses in defending themselves.

Louis Luyt and Jan Pickard attended the IRB meeting when the possibility of infractions of the amateur code were discussed. The two millionaire businessmen produced statements of the tour, audited by a company which the IRB found acceptable. They could find no evidence of the payment of players.

Then there was an investigation into the financial implications of the tour and rugby football's amateur principle. The rumours were that they received a lot of money, R110 000 per player according to one rumour. They admitted receiving plenty from tour funds, such as auctioning the wire from Andy Dalton's jaw and the stitches from Gary Knight's eye, and personal appearances. There was talk of a fund administered by Andy Haden and banked in Hong Kong in the name of his firm Sporting Contacts, which he founded in 1984. There it stayed for a while, accumulating interest. Presumably all that is possibly true, but what is certainly true is that it must be rugby's best kept secret if it is true. Rugby loves gossip. There was no gossip about any moneys paid to the Cavaliers. It was *omertà* as would have made even the mafia proud! Investigative journalists from many parts of the world did their best to find the money and failed.

One charge levelled at the Cavaliers proved palpably untrue. They stood accused of ruining New Zealand rugby.

The All Blacks had been a goodly lot during the previous few years, but by no means a dominant force in world rugby. They had lost tests to Australia and England and drawn with Argentina and Scotland.

Then they suspended the Cavaliers, and chose the "Baby All Blacks". The tour of the Cavaliers and the premature introduction of the Babies bridged the ageing process which all teams endure, even the All Blacks. New talents came through – Wayne Shelford, Grant Fox, Alan Whetton, Scott McDowell, Sean Fitzpatrick, Michael Jones, Smoking Joe Stanley and Frano Botica. And, lo and behold, one of the world's greatest teams was born in New Zealand in 1987 – the team which won the first Rugby World Cup and did it more decisively than Australia did in 1991 or South Africa did in 1995. The comprehensiveness of New Zealand's victory changed the shape of rugby football throughout the world.

Danie Craven claimed that the Cavaliers' tour saved South African rugby. It certainly brought an injection of enthusiasm.

And in the end, the TRU was able at the end of 1987, to resume control of Ellis Park, list it on the stock exchange and by mid-July 1988 have a ground free of debts and in fact have R15 million in the bank. Louis Luyt had done it.

TOUR STATISTICS

P	W	D	L	Pf	Pa	Tf	Ta
12	8	0	4	275	229	33	16

TESTS

4	1	0	3	62	96	5	7

The Cavalier Touring Team of 1986:
K J Crowley (Taranaki), R M Deans (Canterbury), C I Green (Canterbury), M Clamp (Wellington), B G Robins (Taranaki), B G Fraser (Wellington), S T Pokere (Auckland), V L J Simpson (Canterbury), W M Osborne (Waikato), W T Taylor (Canterbury), G J Fox (Auckland), W R Smith (Canterbury), D S Loveridge (Taranaki), A J Donald (Wanganui), J C Ashworth (Hawke's Bay), G A Knight (Manawatu), S C McDowell (Auckland), A G Dalton (Counties) (c), H R Reid (Bay of Plenty), J G Mills (Auckland), G H Whetton (Auckland), A M Haden (Auckland), M J Pierce (Wellington), A Anderson (Canterbury), M J B Hobbs (Canter-

bury), M W Shaw (Manawatu), F N K Shelford (Bay of Plenty), A J Whetton (Auckland), M G Mexted (Wellington), W T Shelford (North Harbour).

TOUR RESULTS

Date	Venue	Opponents	Score
23 April	Johannesburg	Junior Springboks	22-21
26 April	Pretoria	Northern Transvaal	10-9
30 April	Bloemfontein	Orange Free State	31-9
3 May	Johannesburg	Transvaal	19-24
6 May	Newlands	Western Province	26-15
10 May	Newlands	South Africa	15-21
13 May	Durban	Natal	37-24
17 May	Durban	South Africa	19-18
20 May	Johannesburg	South African Barbarians	42-13
24 May	Pretoria	South Africa	18-33
27 May	Potchefstroom	Western Transvaal	26-18
31 May	Johannesburg	South Africa	10-24

CHAPTER 19

The Return of the Springboks

THE DIVIDING WALLS of apartheid came tumbling down, and the world trumpeted approval. In no time rugby football welcomed back the Springboks whose competitive edge it had so missed.

First to welcome them back were the old foemen – New Zealand. In no time the All Blacks were beating at the door. It was, when one thinks of it a reckless decision to start off at the top like that. Perhaps the reckless-ness was born of arrogance – the belief that if you took any group of dis-jointed mortals and pulled Springbok jerseys over their heads, they would instantly acquire preternatural powers which could beat the world.

The All Blacks came to South Africa in 1992 well prepared. They had played a series in Australia, the land of the Rugby World Cup champions and lost 2-1. But they were battle-hardened. The Springboks had only the Currie Cup to boost their capabilities and egos.

More than that, the All Blacks had four warm-up matches before the one-off test. The Springboks picked a team, practised and played. In ret-rospect that they were only three points behind at the final whistle was probably an achievement. But then the truth was that the All Blacks were much better than that.

En route to the test the All Blacks smashed Natal in the fullness of their Currie Cup powers, Orange Free State, the Junior Springboks, captained by Tiaan Strauss, and Central Provinces. The warning bells were ringing. Only a miracle could bring a Springbok victory. But then a miracle had happened many, many times before.

In 1992 it did not happen. The Springboks took the field with their tiny bundle of 62 test caps and faced the All Black haka which had more than 300. They also suffered an unsympathetic referee.

The All Blacks led 20-3 at one stage and later 27-10. Zinzan Brooke was alert and scored a try from a penalty close to the Springbok line, and then John Kirwan scored a great try when the All Blacks counterattacked.

Danie Gerber scored the sort of strong, bursting try that was so much a hallmark of his greatness. He got two tries and Pieter Müller stretched an arm to score the third. Each side scored three tries. The Springboks could have had two more. Danie Gerber may well have scored in the corner in the first half when he was ruled to be just short of the line, and James Small had the ball in his hands and an open line ahead of him when he lost the ball – inexplicably. The Springbok fight-back had been impressive. As in 1986, the Springbok backs were better their New Zealand counterparts. At 34 years of age, Danie Gerber was the best attacking back on the field.

For the first time in the history of matches between the two countries the visiting team had won the first match. But it was not a series as there was only one test match on the tour.

Of course, it was not a match without controversy, for contrary to the prematch agreement, Louis Luyt had both anthems played before the match – God Defend New Zealand and Die Stem. This produced much political upset.

Pierre Berbizier, the French coach, who watched the match as the Springboks would later be touring his country, said of the Springbok performance: "The Springboks played with such panache. They will quickly return to the highest level. They are brave."

Berbizier's prophecy was wrong, as events soon proved, for the Springboks staggered to several depressing defeats before soaring up to the heights of victory in the World Cup of 1995.

TOUR STATISTICS

P	W	D	L	Pf	Pa	Tf	Ta
5	5	0	0	167	79	20	6

TESTS

1	1	0	0	27	24	3	3

The New Zealand Touring Team in 1992 (South Africa only):
T J Wright (Auckland), M J A Cooper (Waikato), J J Kirwan (Auckland), V L Tuigamala (Auckland), J K R Timu (Otago), E J Rush (North Har-

bour), W K Little (North Harbour), F E Bunce (North Harbour), M C G Ellis (Otago), G J Fox (Auckland), S J Bachop (Otago), A D Strachan (Auckland), J P Preston (Canterbury), S B T Fitzpatrick (Auckland) (c), G W Dowd (North Harbour), R W Loe (Waikato), S C McDowell (Auckland), O M Brown (Auckland), G H Purvis (Waikato), I D Jones (North Harbour), R M Brooke (Auckland), M S B Cooksley (Counties), B P Larsen (North Harbour), M N Jones (Auckland), J W Joseph (Otago), D J Seymour (Canterbury), A T Earl (Canterbury), Z V Brooke (Auckland), A R B Pene (Otago)

TOUR RESULTS

Date	Venue	Opponents	Score
1 August	Durban	Natal	43-25
5 August	Bloemfontein	Orange Free State	33-14
8 August	Pretoria	Junior Springboks	25-10
10 August	Witbank	Central Provinces	39-6
15 August	Johannesburg	South Africa	27-24

CHAPTER 20

The One that Got Away

If ever New Zealand was ripe for the picking it was when the Springboks arrived in 1994.

A mere six days before the first test against the Springboks, while the South Africans were already in the country, the All Blacks lost a home series to France. After the Springboks had left, New Zealand lost the Bledisloe Cup to Australia. In between that pair of disasters, the All Blacks beat the Springboks 2-0 in a three-test series. The 1994 Springboks, well heeled and well housed, chests out in the warmth of the welcome, became the only Springbok team not to win a test in New Zealand. For that, and other reasons, they were flops, part of South Africa's downward plunge to ignominy when the game in South Africa seemed to stagger from scandal to scandal in a headlong rush to its own destruction. There were political infighting, drug scandals, money scandals, violence on the field of play and undiplomatic and arrogant behaviour off it, and much of the rugby world rejoiced at South African discomfort.

They were a curate's egg side – good in parts. The parts where they were not good – onfield manners and discipline – were very bad, the worst by a Springbok team ever. They were good on public relations – walking in parades, visiting schools and hospitals. And in this the team's leadership gave the lead. But they too paid heavily and bitterly for failure.

In contrast to 1981 the Springboks of 1994 were warmly welcomed. The tour was eagerly awaited by the rugby-besotted country.

They started off in style, running freely and scoring tries, confident on the field and friendly off it. Jannie Engelbrecht, the manager, was much in demand everywhere and he did well.

In Taupo they played the King Country of the mighty Pinetree Meads, though now long Meads-less, and won 46-10 on an afternoon near the lake and in sight of three volcanic peaks capped with snow. The eccentricity of the match was the award, by Dave Bishop, of two penalty tries, one to each

189

side. At Pukekohe, both sides ran when the Springboks, captained by Wahl Bartmann, beat Counties 37-26. A young man called Jonah Lomu could not get a game for Counties. It was Bartmann's only match on the tour as he was injured and replaced by Ruben Kruger who had initially been unavailable – "for business reasons".

Down they went to New Zealand's capital and a thrilling match with Wellington who led 19-8 at half-time. The Springboks roared back with great spirit and won 36-26. It was a superb match, probably the best of the tour. But it cost the Springboks dearly. They used four replacements. One of the players replaced was the captain, Francois Pienaar, who was taken off on wobbly legs because there was inadequate first aid to allow him to leave the field with dignity. It ruled him out of several matches, including the first test. Pieter Müller injured his neck and he, too, had to be replaced on the tour, by Japie Mulder.

They flew down past Mt Cook to Invercargill. It had been intended that they should go via quaint Queenstown but snow prevented them from landing. They came back by coach through magnificent country, and that evening the lights failed. Lovely Queenstown was a holiday. The weather degenerated in Invercargill where Ruben Kruger joined the team and was soon as sodden as the rest on the practice field. The climate was cold, the welcome warm, and there were Bluff oysters as usual. And there was an easy victory over Southland the day before the French won a famous and drama-charged victory over New Zealand at Eden Park in Auckland with one of the greatest test tries of all time.

Kruger came and Kobus Wiese left, hurt against Southland. The next to leave would be Pieter Müller, injured in the first test. Theo van Rensburg would follow after the second test. And Balie Swart's concussion, like Pienaar's, would rule him out for three weeks.

In all their matches up till now the Springboks had been more penalised than the local teams, but not dramatically so. That changed in friendly Timaru by the sea. The Springboks had an easy victory over the Hanan Shield XV (South Canterbury, North Otago and Mid-Canterbury). But that afternoon at Fraser Park Dick Ross of North Harbour penalised the Springboks 22 times and the composite fifteen four times. Some of the Springbok behaviour in the face of this hammering was not good, and Johan le Roux, a powerful prop, may have been lucky to be still playing at the end of the match.

It was in Timaru that Jannie Engelbrecht, the manager of the team, and Louis Luyt, the executive president of SARFU, had their first acrimonious conversation. Luyt was feeling neglected by the NZRFU who made no special arrangements for him, which meant he booked into a hotel room inferior to those enjoyed by the players. Luyt had moved in with the team. He was in the changing room and at practices. Engelbrecht objected, and there in Timaru the first showdown occurred, one of those either-you-go-or-I-do discussions. Luyt left the team after that.

The positive side of the Hanan Shield match was the reappearance on the field of Chester Williams. He had been heavily concussed in the England test at Newlands and therefore forced to stay away from the game for a month. This led to much speculation in suspicious quarters in New Zealand that he was being sidelined by the closet racists that made up South African rugby or that he was just a token selection. It did not take long for such words to be swallowed.

From cheerful Timaru the Springboks plunged down via the Moeraki boulders, which look like Bushman huts, into the freezing cold of Scottish Dunedin. New Zealanders were entirely apprehensive. After losing to the French they expected a walloping by the mighty Springboks. The All Black team was unsure of itself and angry at the opprobrium heaped on it.

Throughout that first test they were ripe for the picking, though they firmed up as the game went on and the Springboks failed to take their chances. The All Blacks sniffed victory and became more resolute.

There was a significant moment in the match when things swung New Zealand's way. Brian Stirling, the Irish referee, penalised the All Blacks and André Joubert came to kick at goal, a kick that was not difficult even by his standards. But the Australian touch judge had his flag out. Johan le Roux, who had earlier given away three points with a monstrous offside under his goal posts, had been guilty of foul play – against Sean Fitzpatrick, as it turned out, though this was not yet the infamous incident which would occur in the second test and for which Le Roux was not penalised during the match. The penalty was reversed. The All Blacks found touch, won the line-out and moved the ball. The next time the Springboks touched the ball was to kick off after Shane Howarth's conversion of John Kirwan's try – ten points as a result of one act of ill-discipline. Add to that his earlier indiscretion and the wrongful penalising of Tiaan Strauss when he carried out the law to perfection in staying on his feet and picking the ball up after an opponent had been tackled before any ruck could be formed. The decision cost South Africa three points. The score of 22-14 looks a comfortable victory for New Zealand. It was not a match they deserved to win, except that they were better behaved. That was virtue enough for victory.

It was at this stage that the wheels started to come off the Springbok wagon as it lumbered around New Zealand. In the meantime the New Zealanders suddenly sniffed victory over the invading enemy. Newspapers carried many pages of rugby. Rugby dominated the television and the wireless. Phone-in programmes were devoted to rugby. Shops had displays. The enemy was within but could be sent home with his tail between his legs.

The Taranaki match in beautiful New Plymouth was a drab affair which the spluttering Springboks won 16-12. Theo van Rensburg scored all their points and in all four possible ways. Veteran fullback Kieran Crowley, who was already a life member of the Taranaki RFU, scored all Taranaki's points with four penalties in a match of 35 penalties, eleven in favour of South Africa. The mascot of Taranaki is Ferdinand the Bull, and playing for Taranaki was one of the most charismatic of rugby players in New Zealand, the prop Bull Allen, who was married not long afterwards. It is no surprise that the ground, with its high bank in front of Mt Egmont is referred to as The Bullring.

Things looked much better in Hamilton when the Springboks played good, constructive rugby to give Waikato a hiding, 38-17. The matches at Hamilton and Timaru were regarded as having historical significance, as they were venues of cancelled matches in 1981. History of an unpleasant nature was made as all the glory of the Waikato game was sloughed off. After the Springboks had left for Palmerston North, the news came that James Small had been cited for some form of foul play when, in the open, his action of leaping for a bouncing ball caused Steve Gordon of Waikato to be knocked out. He was not suspended, but again there was about the whole affair a feeling of war psychosis. The South Africans felt as angered and bemused as the All Blacks had been in Australia in 1992 when the press had a go at them and the New South Wales Rugby Union went in for citings – of All Blacks, not Australians, of course.

This was accentuated in the bad-tempered match at the Showgrounds in Palmerston North when the Springboks were too fast and smooth for Manawatu, winning 47-21, six tries to two. But in the midst of many unpleasant things the referee decided to send Adri Geldenhuys off. He is a player of no great repute when it comes to onfield innocence but on that day he was certainly considerably less guilty than several opponents who finished the match.

Playing for Manawatu was Bruce Hansen. He had been playing for several seasons for Wanganui but changed provinces when Wanganui were not given a match with the Springboks, and it was an ambition of Hansen's

Robert du Preez looks to break with Pieter Müller on his outside. Watching from the ground are Michael Jones and Ian MacDonald.

John Kirwan sweeps through for a try at Ellis Park in 1992 with support from Walter Little.

Pressure on the All Blacks – for a change – as Shane Howarth passes back to Frank
Bunce while Graham Bachop, Chester Williams and Brendan Venter watch.

Dirty game! Tiaan Strauss
and Fritz van Heerden in
the Rotorua mud in 1994.

Demonstrators, but not hostile. A pre-match welcoming party for the Springboks.

Horror movie. This is what New Zealand television showed over and over again – Johan le Roux making his attack on Sean Fitzpatrick's ear.

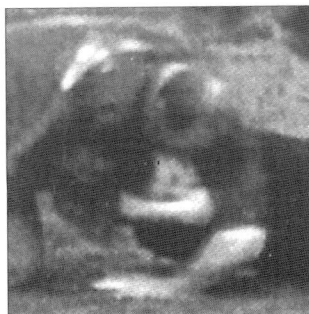

The Springboks attack at Athletic Park in 1994. Theo van Rensburg has the ball with Chester Williams striding on his outside as John Timu covers.

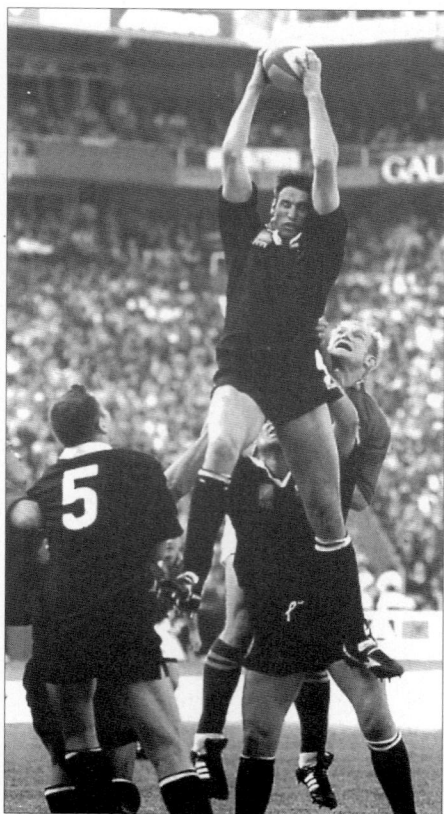

Above: No, you don't. James Small grits his teeth at fearsome Jonah Lomu in the World Cup Final. *Photo: Action Shots*

Left: Up and up he goes – and there was, they say, no lifting in these days! Ian Jones wins *another* line-out in the World Cup Final. *Photo: Action Shots*

The greatest dropped goal rugby football has ever known. Joel Stransky kicks it in extra time in the 1995 Rugby World Cup Final. *Photo: Action Shots*

Joel Stransky floats back as André Joubert shows dignified approval. *Photo: Action Shots*

The Final's final whistle – the moment of joy, disappointment and gratitude. *Photo: Action Shots*

Joy unbounded in the Springboks' dressing room after the World Cup Final – and throughout South Africa. *Photo: Action Shots*

Number 6 to Number 6, President to Captain, Nelson Mandela to Francois Pienaar, with smiles and the William Webb Ellis Trophy. *Photo: Action Shots*

It's hard to beat New Zealand even if you score more points than they do. *Rugby News* of New Zealand carried this advert for Mike Brewer's book. The superscription perpetuates Kiwi belief in foul food before the World Cup Final.

This is it! Francois Pienaar shows the cup of joy to the nation and the world.
Photo: Action Shots

to play against the Springboks. He had a great match, but it was not a satisfactory affair.

It was cold, wet and windy in Wellington for the second test. This time the All Blacks were full value for their 13-9 victory and deserved it by quite a bit more than the four-point margin.

There was honour in the manner of the Springboks' acceptance of defeat, but what happened afterwards plunged the tour into the depths of disgrace as over and over again, on television, in slow motion, with the miscreant ringed, there was the sight of Johan le Roux plunging downwards to bite Sean Fitzpatrick's ear just after half-time.

Springbok reaction was swift and Johan le Roux was sent home. He was later cited and suspended until 1 March 1996.

They went back down to Carisbrook which was a lake, and they lost to Otago. The Springboks played highveld rugby, Otago played lakeside rugby. The Springboks scored two tries to one but lost, leaving a Springbok head in proud Otago.

The tour was at its nadir. It says much for the leadership that after this it started to climb.

In the rain and the cold they convincingly beat Canterbury at Lancaster Park in English Christchurch, and then in churned-up mud they beat the Bay of Plenty in Rotorua 33-12, a happy match.

The rain went away and Eden Park was a classy venue for the third test, and the Springboks ended their tour with a classy display, scoring the only tries of the match and settling for a draw with the All Blacks, a match which they deserved to have won. Sadly their discipline let them down, they succumbed to the wiles of Sean Fitzpatrick, who engineered two penalties for his side, and they did not have a goal kicker of Shane Howarth's class.

But then selection was one of the team's problems. Joel Stransky for a totally inexplicable reason had been left at home. This meant that the Springboks had no serious option at fly half and no reasonable kicker. On the tour, the test kickers, André Joubert and Theo van Rensburg, barely managed a 50% success rate.

This series was the one that got away.

The tour was barely over when Louis Luyt was weighing into the management. The coach, Ian McIntosh, was sacked. Jannie Engelbrecht was sacked, then allowed back, and eventually fired as well. It was all a thoroughly undignified period for South African rugby – a period of tawdry fighting and ill-manners on and off the field.

Nobody would have imagined that a phoenix could rise out of this cold ash.

TOUR STATISTICS

P	W	D	L	Pf	Pa	Tf	Ta
14	10	1	3	445	241	54	22

TESTS

3	0	1	2	41	53	3	3

The South African Touring Team in 1994:
A J Joubert (Natal), J T Janse van Rensburg (Transvaal), G K Johnson (Transvaal), C Badenhorst (Orange Free State), C M Williams (Western Province), J F van der Westhuizen (Natal), J T Small (Natal), P G Müller (Natal), B J Venter (Orange Free State), J P Claassens (Northern Transvaal), F A Meiring (Northern Transvaal), J C Mulder (Transvaal), H P le Roux (Transvaal), L R Sherrell (Natal), J P Roux (Transvaal), J H van der Westhuizen (Northern Transvaal), I S Swart (Transvaal), G R Kebble (Natal), K S Andrews (Western Province), J H S le Roux (Transvaal), A-H le Roux (Orange Free State), J Allan (Natal), J Dalton (Transvaal), M G Andrews (Natal), S Atherton (Natal), J J Wiese (Transvaal), K Otto (Northern Transvaal), A Geldenhuys (Eastern Province), G N Wegner (Western Province), I MacDonald (Transvaal), R J Kruger (Northern Transvaal), F J van Heerden (Western Province), J F Pienaar (Transvaal) (c), W J Bartmann (Natal), C P Strauss (Western Province), R A W Straeuli (Transvaal), A H Richter (Northern Transvaal). Mulder, Johnson, A-H le Roux, Geldenhuys, Kruger and Wegner were the respective replacements for Müller, Janse van Rensburg, J H S le Roux, MacDonald, Bartmann, and Wiese

TOUR RESULTS

Date	Venue	Opponents	Score
23 June	Taupo	King Country	46-10
25 June	Pukekohe	Counties	37-26
28 June	Wellington	Wellington	36-26

194

DATE	VENUE	OPPONENTS	SCORE
2 July	Invercargill	Southland	51-15
5 July	Timaru	Hanan Shield	67-19
9 July	Dunedin	New Zealand	14-22
13 July	New Plymouth	Taranaki	16-12
16 July	Hamilton	Waikato	38-17
19 July	Palmerston	North Manawatu	47-21
23 July	Wellington	New Zealand	9-14
27 July	Dunedin	Otago	12-19
30 July	Christchurch	Canterbury	21-11
2 August	Rotorua	Bay of Plenty	33-12
6 August	Auckland	New Zealand	18-18

CHAPTER 21

The Case of the Poisoned Hamburger

FOOD POISONING FLATTENS BLACKS

That is the headline which appeared in *Rugby News* of New Zealand, not in 1995, but in 1980. It was a report on the test between New Zealand and Australia, played in Sydney on 12 July. Australia had, surprisingly, won 26-10. The victory gave the Wallabies the Bledisloe Cup, for the first time since 1949 when they had beaten a New Zealand team made up of those not on tour in South Africa.

The article reads:

> "Yet an air of optimism persisted and spirits were high. It lasted till the eve of the match. That's when the food poisoning began to grip the players. "No one knew for sure the source of the con- tamination. The most likely cause was a pork dish served at the New Zealand High Commissioner's function on the Thursday, although fresh fruit placed in the players' rooms could have borne a poisonous spray (although the fact no other guests at the hotel reported sick makes this unlikely)."

After the All Blacks had lost the World Cup final in 1995, much was again made of food poisoning. Initially the implication was that it had been deliberate, because the All Blacks were the only people in the hotel to suffer from food poisoning.

The following is a quote from Internet in the week following the World Cup Final. It seemed to sum up New Zeeland feeling:

Bill Taylor of Canterbury (wft@math.canterbury.ac.nz):
   Congratulations to South Africa for a gritty, committed, even

196

magnificent defensive effort. But it wouldn't have done against a non-food-poisoned team . . . SA scrape past France on a non-French (soggy) ground; then scrape past (at second chance) a NZ suffering from food poisoning. What a pathetic effort . . . So that leaves them "champions" in 1995; unquestionably the least-deserving ever. The "only-just-champions". Just managing to beat a poisoned team. And the food poisoning; was it deliberate? A sneaky secret service attack? (Who knows what subtle chemical weapons they've discovered?) A bit of bribe-backed Luytery? Some private enterprise by the hotel staff? . . . Home ground advantage is expected, but surely guests can expect better than this Borgia treatment! A New Zealand source close to the team reported as follows:

"On the Thursday before the final the team sat down in a private room at our hotel to a meal of chicken burgers, hamburgers and pasta. It was the food ordered by the team doctor and prepared in the hotel, the Sandton Holiday Inn. Later that evening several members of the squad complained of being unwell with bouts of dysentery and vomiting. Whether that meal was responsible no one can say for sure but given the fact that it was the common factor in all those who became sick it appears the most likely cause. As the evening progressed several more members of the team reported to the doctor with the final count being 27 out of 35 members of the tour party suffering some degree of food poisoning. Medical advice sought subsequently said that is an exceptionally high percentage. Amongst the worst were Andrew Mehrtens and Jeff Wilson and on Friday afternoon there was serious doubt whether either would play. We made a conscious effort not to say anything publicly about the state of the team. However the *Sunday News* here in New Zealand soon worked out something was wrong. On Friday they interviewed a number of people and several times interviews had to be punctuated with trips to the toilet. They then made a number of calls to players and soon discovered a large number were ill. So on the day of the final they ran a speculative piece on the food poisoning written before the game was played but with no comment from the team. It was a couple of days after the match that the questions started to be asked in light of the team's sub par performance. We stated a number of times that while we did suffer a bout of food poisoning we were not seeking any excuses for losing the game. There have of course been a wide number of theories put forward to us as to how we came to suffer food poisoning from someone putting something in our drinks to a plot by British bookies. As far as the team is concerned all we know is that unfortunately two days out from the World Cup final a large number of our party became ill as a consequence of something we ate or drank. The team still took the field confident of doing well and were beaten in the dying moments by a dramatic Joel Stransky drop goal. As far as the All Blacks are concerned any other theories about the food poisoning being the deliberate work of some sinister force remain unproven theories. As far as the matter still being an issue, it only remains that way because we are asked questions about the matter fairly regularly. These comments hopefully will give you some background information. However in my role I am not able to be directly quoted. The cause of the food poisoning is unknown. It clearly was not staphylococcal food poisoning, the commonest cause of gastro-enteritis, which causes abdominal cramps, diarrhoea and vomiting and may occur from eating foods such as cream-filled pastries, custard pies, processed meats, and potato salad and which could take violent effect in two to four hours but would have meant that the All Blacks would not have played and some would have been in hospital. Bacterial or viral food poisoning usually develops 10 to 16 hours after ingestion of contaminated food, which would have meant that the All Blacks would have had the poisoned food some time during the Wednesday evening or during that night.

No effort, apparently, was made to establish the nature of the food poisoning or its cause."

The hotel believed firmly that there was nothing wrong with their food, that the All Blacks had the same chef for the duration of their stay of roughly six weeks and that the All Blacks frequently ate away from the hotel, once eating prawns at Mare Sol at the Waterfront in Randburg. There was talk that the All Blacks wanted the chef that they had had in Cape Town to accompany to them to their Johannesburg hotel because his food was more palatable. It is not clear to whom the request was made and therefore who turned it down. The implication, presumably, was that the Johannesburg chef struck back!

There were also complaints about the water used at practice on the

198

Thursday. The story went that the water bottles had always been prepared "from within the team" but that on that fatal Thursday the water bottles were prepared "from outside" and that at the time the players complained of an "unusual, unpleasant taste". That really is a far-fetched one – that the All Blacks decided to let somebody else put water into their water bottles and that some secret agent saw his opening and slipped in a germ.

For their 1996 visit to South Africa, the All Blacks opted to stay again in the Sandton Holiday Inn.

The betting firm, William Hill of London, called the story of untoward involvement by British bookmakers "unsubstantiated nonsense" and had the following to say:

> "There was betting on the World Cup Final, for which New Zealand were 1/4 favourites with South Africa at 11/4. The biggest bet we struck was one of £8 000 on New Zealand. Although New Zealand to win would have been a worse result than a South African victory, in terms of the tournament as a whole we made a profit regardless of which of the two won."

I asked about the possibility of deliberate interference by bookmakers and received the following angry riposte:

> "I will not dignify your question number two with a reply as I regard it as an unwarranted slur on our business that you should even contemplate asking it of an established company with an unblemished world-wide reputation.

I asked Laurie Mains to comment, but received no reply. I asked Colin Meads, the manager of the All Blacks during the 1995 World Cup who was subsequently replaced as All Black manager by Mike Banks, and the captain, Sean Fitzpatrick, but got no reply. I asked the All Black team doctor, Mike Bowen of Hamilton, but got no reply.

I could not establish which of the All Blacks did not suffer from food poisoning and how severely the players were affected.

It's a miserable affair as nobody can get to the bottom of it. New Zealanders will believe more fervently that they were robbed of the 1995 Rugby World Cup by food poisoning, almost certainly deliberate, than South Africans and others will continue to believe that the All Blacks are cry-babies.

CHAPTER 22

World Cup

SOUTH AFRICA DID IT!

They said South Africa could not do it. They believed South Africa could not organise the World Cup.

South Africa organised a splendid World Cup, the first held in only one country. It produced the best spectacle of the three World Cups and the biggest profit from the World Cup. It even managed to publish accounts, audited by Coopers & Lybrand, within two months of the end of the World Cup, as did not happen in 1987 and 1991!

They said South Africa could not win it! It did not have the players, the coaching, the discipline.

South Africa did it!

The 1995 World Cup produced the romantic final – South Africa and New Zealand. For over seventy years they had been battling with rare intensity to see who would wear the mythical world crown as champions of the world. Here was their chance to win a real one.

South Africa licked the gloomy prophets on two days in particular. The first was the 25 May 1995 at Newlands in the Cape, a beautiful day, a day charged with emotion, when for the first time there was felt a burgeoning force which Morné du Plessis, the manager of the Springboks, would later call "the surge of the nation".

The crowd was joyous and there was no doubting their loyalty. The opening ceremony was spectacular and national pride surged to the heavens. Into this singing, cheering, flag-waving atmosphere the Springboks emerged to play the Wallabies – the host nation against the holders, the underdogs against the world champions.

Australia started out on top but eventually the Springbok victory was more comprehensive than the score.

If they had lost that match, the Springboks would have met New Zealand in the semifinal. The romance would have flown out of the window.

The Springboks followed this with a tawdry performance at Newlands when they played rugby-sumo against Romania, and then they plunged into the depths of disgrace at Boet Erasmus on a night when the lights failed and then the players betrayed rugby football, themselves and their countries in a disgraceful outburst of ill temper that ended the World Cup for three Canadians as well as Pieter Hendriks and James Dalton for their involvement in the warfare.

At that stage it looked as if all the worst predictions about South Africa and the World Cup were going to be true.

In the meantime the New Zealanders were playing glorious rugby. Their way to the final was a triumphant march through accolades along an easy road adorned with records. They were the rugby sensation of the World Cup, as they had been in 1987, and they had produced the greatest star the World Cup had known – the shy but mighty Tongan Jonah Lomu. In their three pool matches the All Blacks scored 222 points. They waltzed through their quarter final, scoring 48 points against the brave Scots. And then they scored 45 against England in an awesome display. Everything the All Blacks were doing was so very, very proper and so very successful. They were the glory of the World Cup.

Down the other side of the draw, the Springboks contended with a bruising lot of Western Samoans who did their image no good, and then they played that quarter-final in the bucketing rain in Durban and some mysterious force stopped Abdelatif Benazzi from scoring a try which would have won the match for France.

And lo and behold, there was the romantic final – South Africa vs New Zealand at Ellis Park on a day for South Africans to remember, recall, cherish for ever and ever.

Whatever glories South Africa had achieved on the rugby field, there was none to compare with this as a whole nation unified behind its team – ONE TEAM, ONE COUNTRY.

The State President, Nelson Mandela, stood before the country that loved him, a Springbok jersey with a number 6 on his back and a Springbok cap on his head, the most venerated and admired man in the world at home with his people, his team, "my Springboks".

The display was dignified and lively and then just above the stadium there flew an SAA Jumbo and across the bottom of its wings was written: GOOD LUCK BOKKE. The nation surged. As never before it became one, with one president, one flag and even content with its two anthems. The match was a seesaw affair, as befitted a final between these two countries. The Springboks did what they did best throughout the tournament

201

– tackled and scrummed. The All Blacks dominated the line-outs and tried to keep the ball alive. In the end aggressive defence triumphed and the Springboks ended with better scoring opportunities than the All Blacks had had. They will die believing Ruben Kruger scored a try. They found it hard to believe that the pass to Joel Stransky was forward. And then Chester Williams, James Small and André Joubert got in close.

Jonah Lomu, the massive spectre that haunted South Africa for the week leading up to the World Cup, was held in check – only just. His best moment was a dash for the corner only for Japie Mulder to bundle the giant of a man into touch.

In the end it came down to kicking. Joel Stransky got one more over than Andrew Mehrtens did and so the Springboks won, but it could hardly have been closer.

Mehrtens kicked a penalty goal. 3-0 to New Zealand. Stransky kicked a penalty goal. 3-3. Mehrtens kicked a penalty goal. 6-3 to New Zealand. Stransky kicked a penalty goal. 6-6. Stransky kicked a dropped goal. 9-6 to South Africa. And then it was half-time. Mehrtens kicked a dropped goal. 9-9. And then it was full-time.

For the first time in the history of the World Cup, extra time would be played, a cruel ten minutes each way.

Mehrtens kicked a penalty goal. 12-9 to New Zealand Stransky kicked a penalty goal. 12-12.

The Springboks attacked on the right. Scrum to them. They won the scrum. Joost van der Westhuizen passed deep to Joel Stransky and he dropped for goal. The ball soared and the hopes of the nation soared with it. High between the uprights it soared. 15-12 to South Africa.

The All Blacks, noble and determined, attacked but the Springboks drove them back deep into their territory and there the referee blew the whistle that said the World Cup 1995 was over and won.

It was a moment of utter division – the elation of the Springboks who leapt in the air and then sank to the turf in prayer, and the dismay and disappointment of the noble team from New Zealand. There was ecstasy in that final result, it is true, and there was also acute sorrow for the defeated New Zealanders who had meant so much to the 1995 World Cup.

Nelson Mandela presented the William Webb Ellis Trophy to Francois Pienaar and thanked his captain, and the captain thanked his president for all he had done for the nation.

"There were not 65 thousand people supporting us today," Francois Pienaar said. "There were 43 million."

It was an enormous victory, as nearly destined as one could be.

The New Zealand Team at the World Cup in South Africa in 1995:
G M Osborne (North Harbour), J T Lomu (Counties), E J Rush (North Harbour), J W Wilson (Otago), M C G Ellis (Otago), F E Bunce (North Harbour), A I Ieremia (Wellington), W K Little (North Harbour), S D Culhane (Southland), A P Mehrtens (Canterbury), G T M Bachop (Canterbury), A D Strachan (North Harbour), N J Hewitt (Southland), S B T Fitzpatrick (Auckland) (c), O M Brown (Auckland), C W Dowd (Auckland), R W Loe (Canterbury), R M Brooke (Auckland), I D Jones (North Harbour), B P Larsen (North Harbour), M R Brewer (Canterbury), P W Henderson (Southland), J W Joseph (Otago), J A Kronfeld (Otago), K J Schuler (North Harbour), Z V Brooke (Auckland)

The South African Team at the World Cup in South Africa in 1995:
A J Joubert (Natal), G K Johnson (Transvaal), P Hendriks (Transvaal), C M Williams (Western Province), J T Small (Natal), B J Venter (Orange Free State), J C Mulder (Transvaal), H P le Roux (Transvaal), C P Scholtz (Transvaal), J P Roux (Transvaal), J H van der Westhuizen (Northern Transvaal), I S Swart (Transvaal), J P du Randt (Orange Free State), M H Hurter (Northern Transvaal), G L Pagel (Western Province), J Dalton (Transvaal), C L C Rossouw (Transvaal), A E Drotské (Orange Free State), M G Andrews (Natal), J J Wiese (Transvaal), K Otto (Northern Transvaal), J J Strydom (Transvaal), R J Kruger (Northern Transvaal), J F Pienaar (Transvaal) (c), R A W Straeuli (Transvaal), A H Richter (Northern Transvaal), R Brink (Western Province)
   Williams replaced Hendriks, Drotské Dalton.

World Cup Performances

ALL BLACKS

DATE	VENUE	OPPONENTS	SCORE
27 May	Johannesburg	Ireland	43-19
31 May	Johannesburg	Wales	34-9
4 June	Bloemfontein	Japan	145-17
11 June	Pretoria	Scotland	48-23
18 June	Newlands	England	45-29
24 June	Johannesburg	South Africa	12-15

WORLD CUP STATISTICS

P	W	D	L	Pf	Pa	Tf	Ta
6	5	0	1	327	119	41	12

SOUTH AFRICA

DATE	VENUE	OPPONENTS	SCORE
25 May	Newlands	Australia	27-18
30 May	Newlands	Romania	21-8
3 June	Port Elizabeth	Canada	20-0
10 June	Johannesburg	Western Samoa	42-14
17 June	Durban	France	19-15
24 June	Johannesburg	New Zealand	15-12

WORLD CUP STATISTICS

P	W	D	L	Pf	Pa	Tf	Ta
6	6	0	0	144	67	13	5

It was not quite perfect. At the dinner afterwards Louis Luyt made a speech which angered many, but especially the All Blacks. First of all he suggested that South Africa might well have won the previous two World Cups as well, had they taken part. This drew an angry response from Mike Brewer in particular and the All Blacks left the proceedings prematurely. Secondly he made a fuss of Derek Bevan, the referee who had been in charge of the semifinal clash between South Africa and France. Luyt gave him an expensive watch for being the "best referee at the tournament". This angered the other referees and made Bevan suspect, especially to the French.

Luyt said afterwards that he was only joking, which he may well have been. Most people present missed the punch line.

The Captains

1921

1. The first Springbok captain to take a team to New Zealand did not play a single test in the whole of his rugby career, and it was a long one.

He was a good man, and yet his tour started the greatest of controversies in relations between South Africa and New Zealand, the controversy based on race.

Theodorus Barend Pienaar, known as Theo, was born in Barrydale on 23 November 1888, the son of a dominee. He went to school at Somerset West and then to the University of Stellenbosch. He became a schoolmaster and retired from teaching as the principal of Caledon High School. He died in the Johannesburg General Hospital on 14 November 1960, the father of five children.

He played his rugby at Stellenbosch, Malmesbury and Caledon, at a time when the latter two clubs were still a part of the Western Province. He played for Western Province from 1914 to 1922 as a forward. He suffered severe concussion in Australia on the 1921 tour.

After his playing days he was a referee, a selector and the manager of the 1931-32 Springboks in Britain and Ireland. Theo Pienaar was a highly respected man.

Because he was such a respected man he was made captain of the 1921 Springboks, at 33 years of age and not really good enough to command a place in the test side but certainly good enough to get on with people.

When the Maori chief Karaitiana Tetupe gave a welcome to the Springboks in Maori and had it translated by Dr Penara, Theo Pienaar replied in Afrikaans with a translation by Nic du Plessis. And on that tour, forgotten in the midst of controversy, a Maori boy Buster Parata accompanied the Springboks throughout.

2. The All Black captain for the first two tests was a surprise choice. After all, **George Aitken** was not even the captain of Wellington, though he

was a centre capable of creating opportunities for those outside him.

George Gothard Aitken was born in Westport on 2 July 1898 and died in Wellington on 8 July 1952.

He played provincial rugby, first for Buller and then for Wellington, from 1914 to 1922. He won a Rhodes Scholarship. While at Oxford he played for the Barbarians and eight times for Scotland. His only tests for New Zealand were as captain in 1921. Fred Allen, Pat Vincent and Andy Leslie were also captains of New Zealand in all the tests in which they played.

3. **Boy Morkel**, the aged but powerful forward, was the Springboks' playing captain in 1921.

William Herman Morkel, known universally as Boy, was farming in the Western Transvaal and not particularly interested in rugby football when he got the call-up to be a member of the Springbok team. He left the ploughs and the mealie fields and off he went to New Zealand, at 36 years of age, a powerful and much respected forward, regarded as the best forward of his time.

In all he played 9 tests for South Africa between 1910 and 1921.

He was born in Somerset West, the Morkel home town, on 2 January 1885. Unmarried, he came back to the Cape and died on 6 February 1995 at the Goudini High School where he was a caretaker.

4. **Teddy Roberts** was brought in as the All Black captain for the third test in 1921. Like his predecessor George Aitken, he was from Wellington and was in fact the Wellington captain at the time though he battled to get into the All Black side as scrum half ahead of Ginger Nicholls.

Edward James Roberts was born in Wellington on 10 May 1891 and died there on 27 February 1972. He played for New Zealand from 1913 to 1921 and for Wellington from 1910 to 1923. In all he played in five tests.

1928

1. **Maurice Brownlie** was a martinet, not a lovable captain but one who could get the job done.

Maurice John Brownlie was born in Wanganui on 10 August 1897 and died in Gisborne on 21 January 1957. He played for Hawke's Bay from 1921 to 1930. He played in eight tests for New Zealand.

Two of his brothers, Cyril and Laurence, were also All Blacks. Cyril, a huge forward, has the ghastly distinction of being the first player ever

207

sent off in an international match. This inspired Maurice to his greatest performance which included a stunning try of great determination.

Maurice reached the final of the New Zealand amateur heavyweight championship – shades of Kevin Skinner.

2. **Phil Mostert's** mother did not want him to play rugby at all, but he started playing when the family moved back down to the Cape from the Transvaal and he went to Stellenbosch Boys' High, as Paul Roos Gymnasium was then known.

Phillipus Jacobus Mostert was born in Krugersdorp on 30 October 1898. A year later his father was killed in the Battle of Colenso, and Phil and his mother spent much of the war in miserable circumstances in a concentration camp.

When he gave up rugby at the age of 34, he was full of honours. He had captained his club, Somerset West, (for nine years in a row), his province (Western Province) and his country. He was then the most capped Springbok of all time with 14 tests to his name, four more than the Springboks played in 1995!

It was said of him that there was no man who would not want to play under his captaincy and that he never balled a fist on a rugby field, saying: "I'm strong enough to take a punch or two."

He was on a visit to his son in Harare when he died on 3 October 1972. He is buried in the Strand.

1937

1. **Danie Craven** and rugby football were synonyms for six decades. He first played for South Africa in 1931, before he had even played for Western Province, and when he died in 1993 he was the executive president of the South African Rugby Football Union. In between there was no facet of the game that had not benefited from him.

Daniel Hartman Craven was born at Lindley in the Eastern Orange Free State on 11 October 1910. He went from Lindley to Stellenbosch with a far greater reputation for his rugby potential than for academic ability, though he later gained three doctorates and was awarded an honorary one. He fell in love with Stellenbosch, where he died on 4 January 1993.

He played for South Africa in four different positions in test matches and one more in a provincial match. He was best known as a scrum half. He captained South Africa in the first test in 1937 as well as in 1938 against the Lions. After he had stopped playing he became a national selector, the Springbok coach, the manager of the Springbok team and in 1956 the president of the SARB.

2. **Ronald Russell King**, a powerful lock forward, was born in Waiuta on 19 August 1909. He played for New Zealand from 1934 to 1938, playing for West Coast from 1928 to 1945, first as a wing. He became a forward in 1931. He later was a national selector.

Although he was the captain in the three tests in 1937, he was one of nine New Zealand captains during the uncertain Thirties, and was not captain in 1938.

He had a hotel, suitably named King's Hotel, in Greymouth.

3. **Philip Nel**, a powerful forward in the front row, at lock or number 8, played for South Africa in 16 tests between 1928 and 1937, in eight of them as captain, including the second and third tests in 1937.

On the long sea voyage back to a heroes' welcome after the 1937 tour, Philip Nel threw his boots overboard. From then on he was to be a farmer in the midlands of Natal.

Philip Jacobus Nel was born on the farm Elandskop in the Kranskop District of Natal's Midlands on 17 June 1906. He was educated at Maritzburg College, played for Natal when still at school and then farmed at Elandskop. He died in Pietermaritzburg on 12 February 1984.

1949

1. **Fred Allen**, the captain of the most unsuccessful All Blacks of all time, the captain who dropped himself, became one of New Zealand's most successful coaches.

He came to South Africa as a powerful inside centre, struggled against injuries and did not really do himself justice as a player and he did not play the last two tests of the series, the worst in New Zealand's rugby history.

Allen played his provincial rugby for Canterbury, Marlborough, Waikato and Auckland, and there were those who thought that he played his best rugby for the Kiwis during wartime.

He would have coached the 1967 All Blacks in South Africa, instead of which he did so in Canada, England, Wales, France and Scotland. His team was unbeaten in 17 matches and were great in the style of rugby they played. Allen then got out of coaching, a revered figure in New Zealand rugby.

209

Frederick Richard Allen was born in Oamaru on 9 February 1920 and was educated at Phillipstown School.

2. **Felix du Plessis**, like Fred Allen, was dropped during the series. He on the other hand was dropped after achieving unprecedented success, a third successive victory over New Zealand.

When he captained South Africa in the first test, his wife Pat, who had captained South Africa at hockey, was heavily pregnant with their son Morné.

Transvaal played against the All Blacks twice. Felix du Plessis played in the second match but was not the captain. Jan Lotz captained Transvaal in that match.

He was born in Steynsburg on 24 November 1918 and died watching rugby at the club in Stilfontein on 29 April 1978.

3. There was a special power in **Dr Ron Elvidge**, who was presented with the tough job of trying to save a series for New Zealand after the Springboks had won the first two tests in 1949, taking South Africa's run to four in a row. That they extended it to six in a row was no fault of Ron Elvidge's in the third and fourth tests of 1949.

Ronald Rutherford Elvidge played in nine tests (five as captain) for New Zealand between 1946 and 1950, a rugged, clever centre who could punch holes in any defence.

He was born in Timaru on 2 March 1923. He specialised in England as a gynaecologist and obstetrician. When the train with the All Blacks on board crashed on the way from Salisbury, Elvidge attended to the injured passengers.

4. **Basil Kenyon** was the Springbok captain in the only test he played and captained the 1951-52 Springboks on their tour to the UK, Ireland and France till an injured eye ended his rugby career. Danie Craven regarded him as the greatest captain ever. He certainly was an inspiring leader of men. He led Transkei and they became Border champions. He led Border twice against the All Blacks, once in victory and once in a drawn match.

Basil James Kenyon was born in Umtata on 19 May 1918, which meant that he was a senior player by the time the war ended and a veteran by the time he came to play his first test.

After his playing days he was a national selector, a man Craven would have liked more involved in South African rugby.

He died on 9 May 1996 in Plettenberg Bay.

1956

1. **Basie Viviers** (later Vivier) came in as an emergency choice for captaincy after Salty du Rand and Jan Pickard had come to blows during trials in Cape Town in 1956.

He had toured with Basil Kenyon's Springboks in 1951-52 without playing a test, a particularly popular tourist. He was a versatile back, playing for South Africa at centre, fly half, and fullback. He led South Africa in the second, third and fourth tests in 1956.

He played his provincial rugby for Orange Free State, Northern Transvaal and Western Transvaal.

Stefanus Sebastian Viviers was born in Pietersburg on 1 March 1927.

2. **Salty du Rand** captained South Africa in the first test in New Zealand in 1956.

He was the first Rhodesian player chosen to play for South Africa, a tough forward at flank, lock or number 8. When he retired he was South Africa's most capped player ever.

He went to Rhodesia after playing for Western Province and ended his playing career with Northern Transvaal. He captained South Africa in only one test.

Jacobus Abraham du Rand was born on 16 January 1926 in Hofmeyr, where his father farmed sheep. He died in Pretoria on 27 February 1979.

3. **Pat Vincent** of Canterbury did not survive the All Black defeat in the second test in 1956. In fact his only two tests were as captain, a tough scrum half. He eventually emigrated to California where he coached. Eventually he coached the Grizzlies and became first the president of the North California RFU and then a governor of the USA RFU.

Patrick Bernard Vincent was born in Wataroa on 6 January 1926 and died suddenly of an asthma attack in Pittsburgh on 10 April 1983.

4. **Bob Duff** of Canterbury took over the captaincy of the All Blacks from Pat Vincent for the last two tests of 1956. He had retired from rugby in 1954 and had made a comeback against Australia in 1955. He was a tough lock, big for those times. He was later a national selector and coach.

Robert Hamilton Duff was born at Lyttelton on 5 August 1925 and educated at Christchurch Boys' High.

1960

1. The New Zealanders held **Wilson Whineray** in awe long after he had stopped playing. He played for New Zealand in 32 tests, 30 as captain. He was on the losing side in only five tests. He was only 23 when he first captained his country, the same age as Avril Malan when he became captain. He became instantly a dignified but gregarious leader of men. He, it was believed, had the right values for a rugby man.

Initially he battled as the captain, against the Wallabies and the Lions at home and then was on the losing end in South Africa in 1960. Then came the triumphant series against France, triumph in England, Ireland, France and Canada and then, the great prize, the undisputed victory over South Africa in 1965. He ended his rugby on a high note.

Wilson James Whineray, OBE, was born in Auckland on 10 July 1935.

2. Before the All Black tour had started, **Roy Dryburgh** bet Peter Taylor, who had captained Natal till the end of 1959, a case of whisky to a case of beer that he would captain South Africa, which he did. He was an astonishing player, an attacking fullback before his time. He was an excellent utility back, playing for South Africa at fullback, wing, centre and fly half. His six tries against Queensland are a record for a Springbok in a single match. He captained South Africa in the first two tests in 1960.

Roy Gladstone Dryburgh was born in Cape Town on 1 November 1929. He played his provincial rugby for Western Province and Natal.

3. There was something sterling about **Avril Malan** that made him a leader of men. There was nothing flashy about him, just a quiet determination and constancy – the sort of man the Romans would have liked. He was pitched into captaincy for the third and fourth tests in 1960, young and inexperienced, and he made a success of it. His players rallied to him, strong and quiet as he was, probably because of his example of dedication and courage. He would have made an ideal flank in modern rugby. He captained the Springboks on their successful tour in 1960-61, but would strangely be dropped from time to time. Eventually he retired, prematurely, after the disastrous tour of Ireland and Scotland in 1965.

After his retirement from the game he was quiet for a long time and then became a development officer with the Transvaal RFU.

Avril Stéfan Malan was born in Pretoria on 9 April 1937.

1965

1. **Dawie de Villiers** was the charismatic leader – the perky, boyish-looking, blond scrum half from Stellenbosch, the student prince, who played for South Africa after just one match for Western Province; the courageous leader who came back from a horrifying knee injury to captain his country in a record number of tests, for when he retired in 1970 he had captained South Africa 22 times, a figure passed only by Francois Pienaar in 1995. He had the ability to inspire men.

He played in two series against the Lions and two against New Zealand. In both series against New Zealand he was the Springbok captain.

Dawid Jacobus de Villiers was born in Burgersdorp on 10 July 1940 and educated at Bellville High School. From Stellenbosch he became a minister in the Dutch Reformed Church, then a university lecturer, then a politician. He was the South African ambassador at the court of St James and a cabinet minister, surviving as one in the government of national unity under President Nelson Mandela.

2. **Nelie Smith**, as a scrum half and a captain, played in the shadow of Dawie de Villiers. Nonetheless he played in seven tests and was captain in four of them. On the tour to New Zealand in 1965 he was vice-captain to Dawie de Villiers, leading the Springboks in the second test.

After his playing days were over he became a shrewd coach famed as a tactician, a national selector and the coach of the Springboks, including their tour to New Zealand in 1981. He was also the national director of coaching and then a coach of Rovigo in Italy and of his home province, the Free State.

Cornelius Michael Smith was born in Bloemfontein on 8 May 1934.

3. **Wilson Whineray**

1970

1. **Brian Lochore** is one of the gurus of New Zealand rugby – the great and successful player, the great and successful captain. And then his involvement in New Zealand rugby continued. It is surprising in retrospect to think that he was a surprise choice as Whineray's successor. Certainly he continued where Whineray left off, showing the good and successful face of New Zealand rugby.

He coached New Zealand and was regarded as the architect of their victory in the inaugural Rugby World Cup. In 1995 he was the All Blacks' campaign manager at the Rugby World Cup.

There is still a move in certain clubs in the South Africa which involves the number 8, called a Lochore. It still works!

Brian James Lochore, OBE, was born in Masterton on 3 September 1940. He played provincial rugby for Wairarapa from 1959 to 1971. He captained New Zealand in 18 tests.

2. **Dawie de Villiers**

1976

1. **Andy Leslie** was neither large nor noisy, nor was he necessarily the star player, but he was effective and inspiring. And he was appointed captain when everybody expected national hero Ian Kirkpatrick to be. In fact he took over from Kirkpatrick and was greatly supported by the great player, a better loose forward than Leslie was.

Andy Leslie was named captain of New Zealand at his first selection. He played in ten tests and captained New Zealand in them all.

He played softball for New Zealand and, at colts level, waterpolo. His son captained Otago.

Andrew Roy Leslie was born in Lower Hutt on 10 November 1944, was educated at Hutt Valley Memorial Technical College and played for Wellington from 1964 to 1977.

2. If ever a man was born to lead, it was **Morné du Plessis**. His father Felix captained South Africa against New Zealand in 1949. His mother Pat captained South Africa at hockey. His uncle Horace Smethurst captained South Africa at soccer. And all of them were successful captains, as Morné was. And there was a born-to-lead air about his captaincy. His players followed him, and when he stopped playing people still held him in high regard and hung on his words, making his wishes commands.

He played for South Africa in 22 tests, fifteen as captain. Four of those were against Andy Leslie's side, and Danie Craven believed firmly that if he had gone to New Zealand in 1981, South Africa would have won the series. The tall number 8 captained Western Province in 103 of the 112 matches he played for them.

People listened to him off the field as well. He played a leading rôle in establishing the Chris Burger Fund for injured players and many hoped that he would be more involved in the administration of rugby. There is no doubt that the part he played as manager of the Springbok team at the Rugby World Cup was crucial. His is the acceptable face of South African rugby.

Morné du Plessis was born in Vereeniging on 21 October 1949 and educated at that great rugby school, Grey College in Bloemfontein. From there he went to that great rugby university, Stellenbosch. When he got there he was not much known as a rugby player. In a short time he was famous.

1981

1. **Wynand Claassen** was a captain who arrived at greatness in the twilight of his career, and he had the toughest assignment of them all – captaining the Springboks in New Zealand in the tumult of anti-apartheid demonstration. As if that were not enough, he was also the captain of a team and the coach did not want him. To his eternal credit he got it right. He led his men on the field to the brink of success and he kept them so cheerful off the field as well that his team a decade later all voted that they would do it again. In New Zealand he led South Africa in the second and third tests.

Wynand Claassen was born at Schweizer-Reneke in the Western Transvaal on 16 January 1951. He represented a different face of rugby – long haired, bespectacled, an architect and an artist, and a rugby captain with ideals for the game, creative and willing to take a chance. When he played for Northern Transvaal, one of his great fans was the classic actress and academic Anna Neethling-Pohl. Then he went off to Natal and captained them, from the B Section of the Currie Cup, to the Currie Cup Final.

After his playing career he coached and became a national selector – but only for a year. His autobiography, *More Than Just Rugby*, was the most significant rugby biography written in South Africa. But it caused upset in certain positions of power and he was voted out, though he did make a comeback as the manager of the Springbok Sevens to Hong Kong in 1994. He also edits a magazine, *Rugby XV*.

2. **Marthinus Theunis Steyn Stofberg**, who played in winning Currie Cup teams for Orange Free State, Northern Transvaal and Western Province, was one of the great forwards of his era, whether as a flank or a lock – big, mobile, thoughtful, dedicated and immensely strong. He played in 21 tests. Despite a severe speech impediment, he captained South Africa in

215

four tests, including the first in 1981. Named after President Steyn of the Orange Free State, he was born in Villiers on 6 June 1955, the son of Dominee Koos Stofberg, who had played rugby for Western Province.

3. **Andy Dalton** got to captain the All Blacks because Graham Mourie would not play against the Springboks in 1981. He went on to become a great and charismatic captain, retaining the captaincy despite leading the Cavaliers to South Africa in 1986. He was appointed captain of the 1987 All Blacks who won the inaugural World Cup, He did not play a single match, because of injury. In his place David Kirk captained the team and Sean Fitzpatrick hooked.

Apart from 1981, when the All Blacks won a tight and tumultuous series, his other chance to captain his team against the Springboks came with the Cavaliers' tour of 1986. He was the captain. On the field he captained the Cavaliers for 37 minutes of the first match when a brutal blow from behind cut his tour short.

There was about his leadership the calm thoughtfulness which is a characteristic of so many All Black captains.

Andrew Grant Dalton was born in Dunedin on 16 November 1951, the son of Ray Dalton who had been the vice-captain of the 1949 All Blacks.

1986

1. **Andy Haden** was always uncommonly outspoken, for a New Zealander and for a lock forward. He was an early proponent of financial rewards for players, articulating what many believed and were too chary of saying anything. He was also an outstanding line-out forward, the tallest up to his time to represent New Zealand.

Andrew Maxwell Haden was born in Wanganui on 26 September 1950. He captained the Cavaliers in one test after the injury to Andy Dalton. He was one of the prime movers behind the Cavaliers' tour.

He had in his time many occupations, including salesman, journalist and rugby player.

2. **Naas Botha** was a rugby genius. He had insight into the game and the ability to make up his mind in an instant and with utter confidence in his judgement. There is no doubt that he would have been universally acknowledged as one of the greatest players of all time had South Africa not been staggering over the rocks of isolation at the time.

As a youngster in 1981, he was brilliant, never more so than against Auckland and in the last two tests. In 1986 he was the Springbok captain when the Cavaliers came to South Africa, He had a shaky match – for him – in the second test and the Springboks lost by a point. Otherwise he was the man in charge and the Springboks deserved their series victory.

Hendrik Egnatius Botha was born in Breyten on 27 February 1958. He was educated at Hendrik Verwoerd High School, the Police College and the University of Pretoria. But really rugby football became his livelihood, through the generosity of businessmen in Pretoria who desired to keep him there, by playing rugby for Rovigo in Italy, and by several promotions, including television work and newspaper columns.

He was possibly the most high-profile Springbok of all time. Whatever he said or did became instant news.

In all he played for South Africa in 28 tests, captain in nine. He scored 312 test points. He was nineteen when he first played for Northern Transvaal and 22 when he captained them for the first time. He was four times voted South Africa's player of the year.

3. One of the great sights of the 1995 World Cup was that of **Jock Hobbs** waving a large New Zealand flag with fervour.

He took over as captain of the Cavaliers from Andy Haden who found the experience too emotional. Hobbs led the Cavaliers in three tests. In all he played in 21 tests for New Zealand. He played his provincial rugby for Canterbury.

The son of a judge, he was himself a lawyer.

Michael James Bowie Hobbs was born in Christchurch on 15 February 1960. Oddly he is the only All Black captain born in Christchurch. He married Robbie Deans's sister.

1992

1. **Sean Brian Thomas Fitzpatrick** became New Zealand's most capped hooker, player and captain. He certainly has been a player of the greatest resilience. From the time when he took over from Andy Dalton for the 1987 World Cup till the end of 1995 the only other hooker to appear for New Zealand was Norm Hewitt who played against Japan in 1995, the only other captain Paul Henderson when Fitzpatrick sat out the match with Japan during the 1995 World Cup.

Sean Fitzpatrick was born in Auckland on 4 June 1963.

2. **Naas Botha**

1994

1. By the end of 1995, **Francois Pienaar** had played 24 tests and captained South Africa in all of them – a South African record. He was the charismatic captain who received the World Cup from President Mandela. The captain and the president both wore a number 6 jersey. Kitch Christie, the Springbok coach, forecast that he would be the greatest Springbok captain of all time. Certainly he was successful, leading the Springboks to nine victories in nine tests in 1995 alone.

He was originally a flank but moved to number 8 when it suited the team, a brave player who put his body on the line in every match he played.

Jacobus Francois Pienaar was born in Vereeniging on 2 January 1967 and played his provincial rugby for Transvaal.

2. **Sean Fitzpatrick**

3. True to the traditions of Springbok tests in New Zealand, the tour captain did not play the first test. Instead **Tiaan Strauss** captained the team at Carisbrook in Dunedin in place of Francois Pienaar who was recovering from concussion.

Strauss with 157 caps became the most capped Western Province player of all time. He captained his province 92 times, before deciding to play rugby league in Australia.

In 1993 he was Naas Botha's vice-captain when the Springboks toured France and England. In 1994 he was chosen as a number 8 but played flank in the first two tests before being dropped for the third. A powerful forward, his play was noted for his strong tackling and driving and his relentless courage. Christiaan Petrus Strauss was born in Upington on 28 June 1965.

1995

1. **Sean Fitzpatrick**

2. **Francois Pienaar**

The Tests

SETTING THE PLAYERS out in teams according to positions is an impossible exercise. The numbering, or even lettering, has changed from time to time. The New Zealand fashion is to separate the three-quarters from the second five-eighth. Then there was a time when forwards were listed simply as forwards.

1.   NEW ZEALAND 13   SOUTH AFRICA 5
Carisbrook, Dunedin, 13 August 1921.
Crowd: 25 000
Referee: E McKenzie (Wairarapa, New Zealand)

NEW ZEALAND: C N Kingstone, J Steel, G G Aitken (c), P W Storey, M F Nicholls, C E O Bladely, H E Nicholls, J G Donald, R Fogarty, E A Belliss, J Richardson, J E Moffitt, A White, W D Duncan, E Hughes

SOUTH AFRICA: P G Morkel, A J van Heerden, C du P Meyer, W A Clarkson, H W Morkel, J P Michau, WH Townsend, W H Morkel (c), A P Walker, J M Michau, H J Morkel, H H Scholtz, F W Mellish, T L Krüger, P J Mostert

For New Zealand: tries by Belliss, Steel, Storey; two conversions by Nicholls
For South Africa: try by Van Heerden, converted by P G Morkel

2.   SOUTH AFRICA 9   NEW ZEALAND 5
Eden Park, Auckland, 27 August 1921.
Crowd: 40 000
Referee: A E Neilson (Wellington)

219

NEW ZEALAND: C N Kingstone, J Steel, M F Nicholls, P W Storey, G G Aitken (c), C E O Badeley, E J Roberts, E A Belliss, A H West, E Hughes, J Richardson, J E Moffitt, A L McLean, W D Duncan, J G Donald

SOUTH AFRICA: P G Morkel, A J van Heerden, S S F Strauss, C du P Meyer, W C Zeller, J S de Kock, J P Michau, W H Morkel (c), A P Walker, G W van Rooyen, J A Morkel, M C Ellis, N J du Plessis, P J Mostert, F W Mellish

For South Africa: try by Sendin; conversion, dropped goal P G Morkel
For New Zealand: try by McLean, converted by Nicholls

3. **New Zealand 0**   **South Africa 0**
    Athletic Park, Wellington, 17 September 1921
    Crowd: 35 000
    Referee: A E Neilson (Wellington)

NEW ZEALAND: C N Kingstone, J Steel, M F Nicholls, S K Siddels, K D Ifwersen, W R Fea, E J Roberts (c), E A Belliss, A H West, C J C Fletcher, J Richardson, J E Moffitt, A L McLean, W D Duncan, R Fogarty

SOUTH AFRICA: P G Morkel, A J van Heerden, S S F Strauss, C du P Meyer, W C Zeller, J S de Kock, J P Michau, W H Morkel (c), A P Walker, G W van Rooyen, J A Morkel, M C Ellis, N J du Plessis, P J Mostert, F W Mellish

4. **South Africa 17**   **New Zealand 0**
    Kingsmead, Durban, 30 June 1928
    Crowd: 10 000
    Referee: V H Neser (Transvaal)

NEW ZEALAND: D F Lindsay, B A Grenside, S H Carleton, W A Strang, A C C Robilliard, L M Johnson, W C Dalley, G Scrimshaw, S Hadley, J P Swain, G T Alley, M J Brownlie (c), I H Finlayson, W E Hazlett, R T Stewart

SOUTH AFRICA: J C Tindall, J P Prinsloo, S Osler, B A A Duffy, J Slater, B L Osler, P du P de Villiers, P J Mostert (c), T L Krüger , N J V van Druten, S P van Wyk, G M Daneel, N F Pretorius, P J Nel, H J Potgieter

For South Africa: try by Slater; 2 dropped goals, 2 penalty goals by B L Osler

5. **South Africa 6**   **New Zealand 7**
Ellis Park, Johannesburg, 17 July 1928
Crowd: 38 000
Referee: V H Neser (Transvaal)

NEW ZEALAND: D F Lindsay, B A Grenside, S H Carleton, W A Strang, A C C Robilliard, L M Johnson, W C Dalley, R G McWilliams, S Hadley, J P Swain, G T Alley, M J Brownlie (c), I H Finlayson, W E Hazlett, R T Stewart

SOUTH AFRICA: J C Tindall, G H Brand, J A R Doble, J C van der Westhuizen, N S Tod, B L Osler, D Devine, P J Mostert (c), T L Krüger, N J V van Druten, S P van Wyk, G M Daneel, N F Pretorius, P J Nel, H J Potgieter

For South Africa: penalty by Osler, goal from a mark by Mostert
For New Zealand: penalty by Lindsay, dropped goal by Strang

6. **South Africa 11**   **New Zealand 6**
Crusader Ground, Port Elizabeth, 18 August 1928
Crowd: 18 500
Referee: V H Neser (Transvaal)

NEW ZEALAND: D F Lindsay, B A Grenside, S H Carleton, L M Johnson, A C C Robilliard, H T Lilburne, W C Dalley, R G McWilliams, S Hadley, J P Swain, G T Alley, M J Brownlie (c), I H Finlayson, W E Hazlett, R T Stewart

SOUTH AFRICA: J C Tindall, G H Brand, W P Rousseau, J C van der Westhuizen, H P K de Jongh, B L Osler, P du P de Villiers, J F Oliver, P J Mostert (c), A F du Toit, N J V van Druten, M M Louw, G M Daneel, N F Pretorius, P J Nel

For South Africa: tries by De Jongh, Nel, Daneel, conversion by Osler
For New Zealand: tries by Grenside, Stewart

7. **South Africa 5**   **New Zealand 13**
Newlands, 1 September 1928
Crowd: 23 000
Referee: V H Neser (Transvaal)

NEW ZEALAND: H T Lilburne, B A Grenside, F W Lucas, M F Nicholls, A C C Robilliard, L M Johnson, W C Dalley, R G McWilliams, S Hadley, J P Swain, I H Harvey, M J Brownlie (c), I H Finlayson, W E Hazlett, R T Stewart

SOUTH AFRICA: J C Tindall, J A van Niekerk, W P Rousseau, J C van der Westhuizen, P K Morkel, B L Osler, P du P de Villiers, J F Oliver, P J Mostert (c), M M Louw, N J V van Druten, P J Nel, A F du Toit, G M Daneel, N F Pretorius

For South Africa: try by Van der Westhuizen, conversion by Osler
For New Zealand: try by Swain, 2 penalty goals, a dropped goal by Nicholls.

8. **South Africa 7   New Zealand 13**
   Athletic Park, Wellington, 14 August 1937
   Crowd: 42 000
   Referee: L E Macassey (Otago)

NEW ZEALAND: J M Taylor, D G Cobden, J L Sullivan, J A Hooper, J Dick, D Trevathan, H J Simon, E S Jackson, A Lambourn, D Dalton, R Mc C McKenzie, S T Reid, R R King (c), R H Ward, A A Parkhill

SOUTH AFRICA: F G Turner, P J Lyster, J White, L Babrow, D O Williams, D H Craven (c), P du P de Villiers, S C Louw, J W Lotz, C B Jennings, L C Strachan, M A van den Bergh, W F v R v O Bergh, W E Bastard, G L van Reenen

For South Africa: try by Williams; dropped goal by White
For New Zealand: try by Dick; dropped goal and 2 penalty goals by Trevathan

9. **South Africa 13   New Zealand 6**
   Lancaster Park, Christchurch, 4 September 1937
   Crowd: 45 000
   Referee: J S King (Wellington)

NEW ZEALAND: J M Taylor, W J Phillips, J L Sullivan, J A Hooper, J Dick, D Trevathan, H J Simon, E S Jackson, A Lambourn, D Dalton, R Mc C McKenzie, S T Reid, R R King (c), J G Rankin, A A Parkhill

SOUTH AFRICA: G H Brand, F G Turner, J White, L Babrow, D O Williams, T A Harris, D H Craven, S C Louw, J W Lotz, M M Louw, L C Strachan, M A van den Bergh, P J Nel (c), W E Bastard, W F v R v O Bergh

For South Africa: tries by Turner, Bastard; 2 conversions, a penalty goal by Brand
For New Zealand: 2 tries by Sullivan

10. South Africa 17   New Zealand 6
Eden Park, Auckland, 25 September 1937
Crowd: 55 000
Referee: J S King (Wellington)

NEW ZEALAND: J M Taylor, T H C Caughey, N A Mitchell, J A Hooper, J L Sullivan, D Trevathan, H J Simon, E S Jackson, A Lambourn, D Dalton, R Mc C McKenzie, S T Reid, R R King (c), R H Ward, A A Parkhill

SOUTH AFRICA: G H Brand, F G Turner, G P Lochner, L Babrow, D O Williams, T A Harris, D H Craven, S C Louw, J W Lotz, M M Louw, L C Strachan, M A van den Bergh, P J Nel (c), W E Bastard, W F v R v O Bergh

For South Africa: tries by Babrow (2), Bergh, Williams, Turner; conversion by Brand
For New Zealand: 2 penalty goals by Trevathan

11. South Africa 15   New Zealand 11
Newlands 16 July 1949
Crowd: 42 000
Referee: E W Hofmeyr (Transvaal)

NEW ZEALAND: R W H Scott, E G Boggs, R R Elvidge, F R Allen (c), P Henderson, J C Kearney, L T Savage, J G Simpson, E H Catley, K L Skinner, J R McNab, C Willocks, L R Harvey, L A Grant, N H Thornton

SOUTH AFRICA: J H van der Schyff, C Moss, F P Duvenage, M T Lategan, F Marais, J D Brewis, J J Wahl, C J van Jaarsveld, R P Jordaan, A O Geffin, L J Strydom, F du Plessis (c), H V Koch, B S van der Merwe, H S V Muller

For South Africa: 5 penalty goals by Geffin
For New Zealand: try by Henderson; dropped goal by Kearney; conversion, penalty goal by Scott.

12. **South Africa 12   New Zealand 6**
    Ellis Park, Johannesburg, 13 August 1949
    Crowd: 72 000
    Referee: R D Burmeister (Western Province)

NEW ZEALAND: R W H Scott, E G Boggs, R R Elvidge, F R Allen (c), P Henderson, J C Kearney, L T Savage, J G Simpson, E H Catley, K L Skinner, J R McNab, H F Frazer, L R Harvey, L A Grant, P Johnstone

SOUTH AFRICA: J H van der Schyff, C Moss, R A M van der Schoor, M T Lategan, F Marais, J D Brewis, P A du Toit, A C Koch, R P Jordaan, A O Geffin, L J Strydom, F du Plessis (c), H V Koch, J A du Rand, H S V Muller

For South Africa: tries by Brewis, Lategan; penalty goal by Geffin; dropped goal by Brewis
For New Zealand: penalty goal by Scott; dropped goal by Kearney

13. **South Africa 9   New Zealand 3**
    Kingsmead, Durban, 3 September 1949
    Crowd: 30 000
    Referee: E W Hofmeyr (Transvaal)

NEW ZEALAND: R W H Scott, W A Meates, R R Elvidge (c), M O Goddard, P Henderson, J C Kearney, N W Black, J G Simpson, E H Catley, K L Skinner, J R McNab, C Willocks, L R Harvey, P J Crowley, M J McHugh

SOUTH AFRICA: J H van der Schyff, C Moss, R A M van Schoor, M T Lategan, F P Duvenage, J D Brewis, P A du Toit, A C Koch, R P Jordaan, A O Geffin, J A du Rand, F du Plessis (c), P J Geel, H V Koch, H S V Muller

For South Africa: 3 penalty goals by Geffin
For New Zealand: try by Goddard

14. South Africa 11   New Zealand 8
Crusaders Ground, Port Elizabeth, 17 September 1949
Crowd: 28 500
Referee: R D Burmeister (Western Province)

NEW ZEALAND: R W H Scott, W A Meates, R R Elvidge (c), M P Goddard, P Henderson, G W Delamore, L T Savage, J G Simpson, E H Catley, K L Skinner, P J B Crowley, C Willocks, L R Harvey, P Johnstone, D L Christian

SOUTH AFRICA: J H van der Schyff, C Moss, R A M van Schoor, M T Lategan, E M Geraghty, J D Brewis, P A du Toit, A C Koch, R P Jordaan, A O Geffin, P Malan, W H M Barnard, H V Koch, B J Kenyon (c), H S V Muller

For South Africa: try by Du Toit; conversion, penalty goal by Geffin; dropped goal by Brewis
For New Zealand: tries by Johnstone, Elvidge; conversion by Scott

15. New Zealand 10   South Africa 6
Carisbrook, Dunedin, 14 July 1956
Crowd: 40 000
Referee: F G M Parkinson (Manawatu)

NEW ZEALAND: P T Walsh, R A Jarden, R H Brown, W N Gray, M Dixon, W R Archer, P B Vincent (c), M W Irwin, R C Hemi, I J Clarke, J B Buxton, R H Duff, R A White, D N McIntosh, S F Hill

SOUTH AFRICA: R G Dryburgh, J G H du Preez, B F Howe, J J Nel, P G A Johnstone, C A Ulyate, C F Strydom, H N Walker, A J van der Merwe, H P J Bekker, D S P Ackermann, J A du Rand (c), J T Claassen, D F Retief, G P Lochner

For South Africa: try by Howe; penalty by Dryburgh
For New Zealand: tries by Jarden, White; 2 conversions by Jarden

16. South Africa 8   New Zealand 3
Athletic Park, Wellington, 4 August 1956
Crowd: 48 000
Referee: F G M Parkinson (Manawatu)

NEW ZEALAND: P T Walsh, R A Jarden, R H Brown, W N Gray, M J Dixon, S G Bremner, P B Vincent (c), I J Clarke, R C Hemi, F S McAtamney, W H Clark, R H Duff, R A White, D N McIntosh, I N MacEwan

SOUTH AFRICA: S S Viviers (c), T P D Briers, A I Kirkpatrick, J J Nel, P G A Johnstone, C A Ulyate, T A Gentles, A C Koch, A J van der Merwe, H P J Bekker, G P Lochner, J A du Rand (c), J T Claassen, D F Retief, A J Pickard

For South Africa: tries by Du Rand, Retief; conversion by Viviers
For New Zealand: try by Brown

17. New Zealand 17   South Africa 10
   Lancaster Park, Christchurch, 18 August 1956
   Crowd: 51 000
   Referee: W H Fright (Canterbury)

NEW ZEALAND: D B Clarke, R A Jarden, R H Brown, W N Gray, M J Dixon, W R Archer, A R Reid, I J Clarke, R C Hemi, K L Skinner, W H Clark, R H Duff (c), R A White, S F Hill, P F Hilton-Jones

SOUTH AFRICA: S S Viviers (c), K T van Vollenhoven, W Rosenberg, J Nel, T P D Briers, C A Ulyate, T A Gentles, A C Koch, A J van der Merwe, H P J Bekker, D S P Ackermann, J A du Rand (c), J T Claassen, G P Lochner, D F Retief

For South Africa: tries by Rosenberg, Lochner; 2 conversions by Viviers
For New Zealand: tries by Jarden, Dixon, White; conversion, 2 penalties by Clarke

18. New Zealand 11   South Africa 5
   Eden Park, Auckland, 1 September 1956
   Crowd: 61 300
   Referee: W H Fright (Canterbury)

NEW ZEALAND: D B Clarke, R A Jarden, P T Walsh, W N Gray, M J Dixon, R H Brown, A R Reid, I J Clarke, R C Hemi, K L Skinner, W H Clark, R H Duff (c), R A White, S F Hill, P F Hilton-Jones

SOUTH AFRICA: S S Viviers (c), R G Dryburgh, P G A Johnstone, J J Nel, T P

226

D Briers, B F Howe, C F Strydom, H N Walker, A J van der Merwe, H P J Bekker, J J Starke, J A du Rand (c), J T Claassen, D F Retief, G P Lochner

For South Africa: try by Dryburgh; conversion by Viviers
For New Zealand: try by Jones; conversion, 2 penalties by Clarke

19. **South Africa 13   New Zealand 0**
    Ellis Park, Johannesburg, 25 June 1960
    Crowd: 75 000
    Referee: E A Strasheim (Northern Transvaal)

NEW ZEALAND: D B Clarke, R W Caulton, T R Lineen, T P A O'Sullivan, J R Watt, A H Clarke, K C Briscoe, W J Whineray (c), D Young, M W Irwin, K R Tremain, C E Meads, I N MacEwan, P F Hilton-Jones, R J Conway

SOUTH AFRICA: R G Dryburgh (c), H J van Zyl, A I Kirkpatrick, J L Gainsford, J G M Antelme, K Oxlee, R J Lockyear, A C Koch, G F Malan, P S du Toit, G H van Zyl, A S Malan, J T Claassen, H J M Pelser, J A Nel

For South Africa: 2 tries by Van Zyl; conversion by Dryburgh; conversion and penalty goal by Lockyear

20. **New Zealand 11   South Africa 3**
    Newlands, 23 July 1960
    Crowd: 46 000
    Referee: M J Slabber (Transvaal)

NEW ZEALAND: D B Clarke, R F McMullen, T R Lineen, K F Laidlaw, J R Watt, S R Nesbit, K C Briscoe, W J Whineray (c), D Young, I J Clarke, K R Tremain, I N MacEwan, R H Horsley, D J Graham, C E Meads

SOUTH AFRICA: R G Dryburgh (c), H J van Zyl, A I Kirkpatrick, J L Gainsford, J G M Antelme, K Oxlee, R J Lockyear, A C Koch, A J van der Merwe, P S du Toit, G H van Zyl, A S Malan, J T Claassen, H J M Pelser, J A Nel

For South Africa: try by Oxlee
For New Zealand: try by Meads; conversion, penalty goal, dropped goal by D B Clarke

21. South Africa 11   New Zealand 11
Free State Stadium, Bloemfontein, 13 August 1960
Crowd: 56 000
Referee: R D Burmeister (Western Province)

NEW ZEALAND: D B Clarke, R F McMullen, T R Lineen, K F Laidlaw, J R Watt, S R Nesbit, K C Briscoe, W J Whineray (c), D Young, I N Mac-Ewan, K R Tremain, C E Meads, R H Horsley, D J Graham, R J Conway

SOUTH AFRICA: L G Wilson, H J van Zyl, A I Kirkpatrick, J L Gainsford, J G M Antelme, K Oxlee, R J Lockyear, S P Kuhn, G F Malan, P S du Toit, G H van Zyl, A S Malan (c), J T Claassen, H J M Pelser, D J Hopwood

For South Africa: try by Oxlee; conversion, 2 penalty goals by Lockyear
For New Zealand: try by McMullen; conversion, 2 penalty goals by D B Clarke

22. South Africa 8   New Zealand 3
Boet Erasmus Stadium, Port Elizabeth, 27 August 1960
Crowd: 60 000
Referee: R D Burmeister (Western Province)

NEW ZEALAND: D B Clarke, R W Caulton, R F McMullen, K F Laidlaw, J R Watt, W A Davies, K C Briscoe, W J Whineray (c), D Young, I J Clarke, K R Tremain, R H Horsley, I N MacEwan, C E Meads, R J Conway

SOUTH AFRICA: L G Wilson, H J van Zyl, A I Kirkpatrick, J L Gainsford, J G M Antelme, K Oxlee, R J Lockyear, S P Kuhn, G F Malan, P S du Toit, G H van Zyl, A S Malan (c), H S van der Merwe, H J M Pelser, J A Nel

For South Africa: try by Pelser; conversion, penalty goal by Lockyear
For New Zealand: penalty by D B Clarke

23. New Zealand 6   South Africa 3
Athletic Park, Wellington, 31 July 1965
Crowd: 46 200
Referee: J P Murphy (North Auckland)

NEW ZEALAND: M Williment, M J Dick, R E Rangi, R C Moreton, W M Birtwistle, P H Murdoch, C R Laidlaw, W J Whineray (c), B E McLeod, K F Gray, K R Tremain, C E Meads, S T Meads, R J Conway, B J Lochore

SOUTH AFRICA: L G Wilson, G S Brynard, F du T Roux, J L Gainsford, J P Engelbrecht, K Oxlee, D J de Villiers (c), C G P van Zyl, G F Malan, A W MacDonald, J Schoeman, F C H du Preez, J P Naudé, J H Ellis, J A Nel

For South Africa: dropped goal by Oxlee
For New Zealand: tries by Birtwistle, Tremain

24.   New Zealand 13   South Africa 0
       Carisbrook, Dunedin, 21 August, 1965
       Crowd: 35 000
       Referee: J P Murphy (North Auckland)

NEW ZEALAND: M Williment, I S T Smith, R E Rangi, R C Moreton, W M Birtwistle, P H Murdoch, C R Laidlaw, W J Whineray (c), B E McLeod, K F Gray, K R Tremain, C E Meads, S T Meads, R J Conway, B J Lochore

SOUTH AFRICA: L G Wilson, G S Brynard, F du T Roux, J L Gainsford, J P Engelbrecht, K Oxlee, C M Smith (c), C G P van Zyl, G F Malan, A W MacDonald, J Schoeman, F C H du Preez, C P Goosen, J H Ellis, J A Nel

For New Zealand: tries by Tremain, McLeod, Rangi; 2 conversions by Williment

25.   South Africa 19   New Zealand 16
       Lancaster Park, Christchurch, 4 September 1965
       Crowd: 53 500
       Referee: J P Murphy (North Auckland), replaced by A R Taylor
       (Canterbury)

NEW ZEALAND: M Williment, M J Dick, R E Rangi, R C Moreton, W M Birtwistle, P H Murdoch, C R Laidlaw, W J Whineray (c), B E McLeod, K F Gray, K R Tremain, C E Meads, S T Meads, R J Conway, B J Lochore

SOUTH AFRICA: L G Wilson, G S Brynard, F du T Roux, J L Gainsford, J P Engelbrecht, J H Barnard, D J de Villiers (c), C G P van Zyl, D C Walton, A W MacDonald, J A Nel, F C H du Preez, J P Naudé, J H Ellis, D J Hopwood

For South Africa: tries by Brynard (2), tries by Gainsford (2); 2 conversions, 1 penalty goal by Naudé
For New Zealand: tries by Tremain, Moreton, Rangi; 2 conversions, 1 penalty goal by Williment

26. **New Zealand 20   South Africa 3**
    Eden Park, Auckland, 18 September 1965
    Crowd: 63 000
    Referee: D H Millar (Otago)

NEW ZEALAND: W F McCormick, I S T Smith, R E Rangi, J L Collins, W M Birtwistle, M A Herewini, C R Laidlaw, W J Whineray (c), B E McLeod, K F Gray, K R Tremain, C E Meads, S T Meads, R J Conway, B J Lochore

SOUTH AFRICA: L G Wilson, G S Brynard, F du T Roux, J L Gainsford, J P Engelbrecht, J H Barnard, D J de Villiers (c), C G P van Zyl, D C Walton, A W MacDonald, J A Nel, F C H du Preez, J P Naudé, J H Ellis, D J Hopwood

For South Africa: penalty goal by Naudé
For New Zealand: tries by Smith (2), Birtwistle, Conway; dropped goal by Herewini; conversion by McCormick

27. **South Africa 17   New Zealand 6**
    Loftus Versfeld, Pretoria, 25 July 1970
    Crowd: 55 000
    Referee: P Robbertse (Eastern Transvaal)

NEW ZEALAND: W F McCormick, B G Williams, G S Thorne, I R MacRae, M J Dick, W D Cottrell, C R Laidlaw (replaced by S M Going), A E Hopkinson, B E McLeod, B L Muller, I A Kirkpatrick, A E Smith, S C Strachan, T N Lister, B J Lochore (c)

SOUTH AFRICA: I D McCallum, G H Müller, J S Jansen, F du T Roux, S H Nomis, P J Visagie, D J de Villiers (c), J B Neethling, J F B van Wyk, J F K Marais, P J F Greyling, F C H du Preez, J J Spies, J H Ellis, A J Bates

For South Africa: tries by De Villiers, Nomis, a conversion, 2 penalties by McCallum
For New Zealand: try Williams, penalty by McCormick

28. New Zealand 9   South Africa 8
Newlands, 8 August 1970
Crowd: 52 000
Referee: W C Malan (Boland)

NEW ZEALAND: W F McCormick, G S Thorne, W L Davis, I R MacRae, B G Williams, E W Kirton, C R Laidlaw, A E Hopkinson, B E McLeod, B L Muller, I A Kirkpatrick, A R Sutherland, S C Strachan, A J Wyllie, B J Lochore (c)

SOUTH AFRICA: I D McCallum, G H Müller, J S Jansen, F du T Roux, S H Nomis, P J Visagie, D J de Villiers (c), J B Neethling, J F B van Wyk (replaced by R W Barnard), J F K Marais, P J F Greyling, F C H du Preez, J J Spies, J H Ellis, A J Bates

For South Africa: try by Jansen; conversion, penalty goal by McCallum
For New Zealand: tries by Laidlaw, Kirkpatrick; penalty by McCormick

29. South Africa 14   New Zealand 3
Boet Erasmus, Port Elizabeth, 29 August 1970
Crowd: 55 000
Referee: P Robbertse (Eastern Transvaal)

NEW ZEALAND: W F McCormick, H P Milner, I R MacRae, B G Williams, G S Thorne, E W Kirton, C R Laidlaw, A E Hopkinson, R A Urlich, N W Thimbleby, I A Kirkpatrick, C E Meads, S C Strachan, A J Wyllie, B J Lochore (c)

SOUTH AFRICA: I D McCallum, G H Müller, J S Jansen, F du T Roux, S H Nomis, P J Visagie, D J de Villiers (c), J L Myburgh, J F B van Wyk, J F K Marais, P J F Greyling, F C H du Preez, J J Spies, J H Ellis, J A Nel

For South Africa: tries by Müller (2); conversion, 2 penalty goals by McCallum
For New Zealand: penalty by Williams

30. **South Africa 20   New Zealand 17**
    Ellis Park, Johannesburg, 12 September 1970
    Crowd: 65 000
    Referee: T H Woolley (Eastern Transvaal)

NEW ZEALAND: G F Kember, B G Williams, I R MacRae, G S Thorne, M J Dick, B D M Furlong, S M Going, K Murdoch, R A Urlich, B L Muller, I A Kirkpatrick, C E Meads, A R Sutherland, T N Lister, B J Lochore (c)

SOUTH AFRICA: I D McCallum, G H Müller, J S Jansen, F du T Roux, S H Nomis, P J Visagie, D J de Villiers (c), J L Myburgh, J F B van Wyk, J F K Marais, P J F Greyling, F C H du Preez, J J Spies, J H Ellis, J A Nel

For South Africa: tries by Müller, Visagie; conversion, 4 penalty goals by McCallum
For New Zealand: try by Williams; conversion, 4 penalty goals by Kember

31. **South Africa 16   New Zealand 7**
    King's Park, Durban, 24 July 1976
    Crowd: 46 000
    Referee: I W Gourlay (Natal)

NEW ZEALAND: D J Robertson, G B Batty, B J Robertson, J L Jaffray, B G Williams, O D Bruce, S M Going, K J Tanner, R W Norton, K K Lambert, I A Kirkpatrick, H H Macdonald, P J Whiting, K W Stewart, A R Leslie (c)

SOUTH AFRICA: I W Robertson, J S Germishuys, P J M Whipp, J J Oosthuizen, E F W Krantz, G R Bosch (replaced by W J de W Ras), P C R Bayvel, J C J Stander, R J Cockrell, D S van den Berg, J H Ellis, J G Williams, J L van Heerden, J H H Coetzee, M du Plessis (c)

For South Africa: tries by Germishuys, Krantz; dropped goal by Robertson; penalty goal, conversion by Bosch
For New Zealand: try by Jaffray; penalty by Williams

32. New Zealand 15   South Africa 9
Free State Stadium, Bloemfontein, 14 August 1976
Crowd: 70 000
Referee: G P Bezuidenhout (Transvaal)

NEW ZEALAND: C L Fawcett, G B Batty (replaced by W M Osborne), B J Robertson, J E Morgan, B G Williams, O D Bruce, S M Going, B R Johnstone, R W Norton, W K T Bush, I A Kirkpatrick, H H Macdonald, P J Whiting, K A Eveleigh, A R Leslie (c)

SOUTH AFRICA: D S L Snyman, J S Germishuys, I W Robertson, J J Oosthuizen, C F Pope, G R Bosch, P C R Bayvel, J C J Stander, R J Cockrell, D S van den Berg, J H H Coetzee, J G Williams (replaced by K B H de Klerk), J L van Heerden, M T S Stofberg, M du Plessis (c)

For South Africa: 3 penalty goals by Bosch
For New Zealand: try by Morgan; conversion, 2 penalty goals by Going; dropped goal by Bruce.

33. South Africa 15   New Zealand 10
Newlands, 4 September 1976
Crowd: 38 000
Referee: G P Bezuidenhout (Transvaal)

NEW ZEALAND: C L Fawcett, G B Batty, B J Robertson, J E Morgan, B G Williams, D J Robertson, S M Going, P C Harris, R W Norton, K K Lambert, I A Kirkpatrick, H H Macdonald, P J Whiting, K W Stewart, A R Leslie (c)

SOUTH AFRICA: D S L Snyman, J S Germishuys, P J M Whipp, J J Oosthuizen, C F Pope, G R Bosch, P C R Bayvel, J C J Stander, J F B van Wyk, J H P Strauss, J H H Coetzee, K B H de Klerk, J L van Heerden, M T S Stofberg, M du Plessis (c)

For South Africa: try by Oosthuizen; two penalty goals, conversion by Bosch; dropped goal by Snyman
For New Zealand: try by Bruce Robertson; two penalty goals by Williams

34. **South Africa 15**   **New Zealand 14**
Ellis Park, Johannesburg, 18 September 1976
Crowd: 74 000
Referee: G P Bezuidenhout (Transvaal)

NEW ZEALAND: D J Robertson, G B Batty (replaced by T W Mitchell), B J Robertson, J E Morgan (replaced by W M Osborne), B G Williams, O D Bruce, S M Going, K K Lambert, R W Norton, W K T Bush, I A Kirkpatrick, F J Oliver, P J Whiting, K A Eveleigh, A R Leslie (c)

SOUTH AFRICA: W Robertson, J S Germishuys, P J M Whipp, J J Oosthuizen, C F Pope, G R Bosch, P C R Bayvel, J C J Stander, J F B van Wyk, J H P Strauss, J H H Coetzee, K B H de Klerk, J L van Heerden, J L Kritzinger, M du Plessis (c)

For South Africa: try by Kritzinger; two penalty goals, dropped goal, conversion by Bosch
For New Zealand: tries by Kirkpatrick, Going; dropped goal by Bruce; penalty goal by Williams

35. **New Zealand 14**   **South Africa 9**
Lancaster Park Oval, Christchurch 15 August 1981
Crowd: 40 000
Referee: L Prideaux (England)

NEW ZEALAND: A R Hewson (replaced by B J McKenzie), B G Fraser, S S Wilson (replaced by L M Cameron), A C R Jefferd, F A Woodman, D L Rollerson, D S Loveridge, J C Ashworth, A G Dalton (c), G A Knight, M W Shaw, G Higginson, A M Haden, K W Stewart, M G Mexted

SOUTH AFRICA: Z M J Pienaar, D S Botha, D M Gerber, W du Plessis, R H Mordt, H E Botha, D J Serfontein, H J van Aswegen, R J Cockrell, P G du Toit, E Jansen, H J Bekker, L C Moolman, M T S Stofberg (c), R J Louw

For South Africa: try by Bekker; dropped goal, conversion by H E Botha
For New Zealand: tries by Wilson, Rollerson, Shaw; conversion by Rollerson

36. South Africa 24   New Zealand 12
Athletic Park, Wellington 29 August 1981
Crowd: 31 000
Referee: C Norling (Wales)

NEW ZEALAND: A R Hewson, B G Fraser, S S Wilson, L M Cameron, F A Woodman, D L Rollerson, D S Loveridge, J C Ashworth, A G Dalton (c), G A J Burgess, M W Shaw, F J Oliver, A M Haden, K W Stewart, M G Mexted

SOUTH AFRICA: Z M J Pienaar, J S Germishuys, D M Gerber, W du Plessis (replaced by J J Beck), R H Mordt, H E Botha, D J Serfontein, O W Oosthuizen, W J H Kahts (replaced by R J Cockrell), P R van der Merwe, S B Geldenhuys. J de V Visser, L C Moolman, M T S Stofberg, W Claassen (c)

For South Africa: try by Germishuys; dropped goal, conversion, 5 penalty goals by Botha
For New Zealand: 4 penalty goals by Hewson

37. New Zealand 25   South Africa 22
Eden Park, Auckland, 12 September 1985
Crowd: 49 000
Referee: C Norling (Wales)

NEW ZEALAND: A R Hewson, B G Fraser, S T Pokere, L M Cameron, S S Wilson, D L Rollerson, D S Loveridge (replaced by M W Donaldson), J C Ashworth, A G Dalton (c), G A Knight, G H Old, G W Whetton, A M Haden, F N K Shelford, M G Mexted

SOUTH AFRICA: Z M J Pienaar (replaced by J W Heunis), J S Germishuys, D M Gerber, W du Plessis (replaced by J J Beck), R H Mordt, H E Botha, D J Serfontein, O W Oosthuizen, R J Cockrell, P R van der Merwe, R J Louw, H J Bekker, L C Moolman, S B Geldenhuys, W Claassen (c)

For South Africa: tries by Mordt (3); 2 conversions, 2 penalty goals by Botha
For New Zealand: tries by Wilson, Knight; 3 penalty goals by Hewson; penalty goal, dropped goal, conversion by Rollerson

235

38. South Africa 22   New Zealand 15
Newlands, 10 May 1986
Crowd: 38 000
Referee: K Rowlands (Wales)

NEW ZEALAND CAVALIERS: K J Crowley, C I Green, W T Taylor, V L J Simpson, M Clamp, G J Fox, A J Donald, J C Ashworth, H R Reid, G A Knight, M W Shaw, M J Pierce, A M Haden (c), F N K Shelford (replaced by M J B Hobbs), M G Mexted

SOUTH AFRICA: J W Heunis, C J du Plessis, D M Gerber, M J du Plessis, J Reinach, H E Botha (c), C Ferreira, A S Barnard, U L Schmidt, P R van der Merwe, W J Bartmann, L C Moolman, S W P Burger, G P Smal, J C Breedt

For South Africa: try by C J du Plessis; 2 dropped goals, conversion, 3 penalty goals by Botha
For New Zealand Cavaliers: penalty try; conversion, 3 penalty goals by Fox

39. New Zealand 19   South Africa 18
King's Park, Durban, 17 May 1986
Crowd: 42 000
Referee: K Rowlands (Wales)

NEW ZEALAND CAVALIERS: K J Crowley, C I Green, W T Taylor, V L J Simpson, M Clamp, G J Fox, D S Loveridge, J C Ashworth, H R Reid, G A Knight, M W Shaw, G W Whetton, A M Haden, M J B Hobbs (c), M G Mexted

SOUTH AFRICA: J W Heunis, C J du Plessis, D M Gerber, M J du Plessis, J Reinach, H E Botha (c), C Ferreira, A S Barnard, U L Schmidt, P R van der Merwe, W J Bartmann, L C Moolman, S W P Burger, G P Smal, J C Breedt

For South Africa: try by Reinach; conversion, 4 penalty goals by Botha
For New Zealand Cavaliers: tries by Taylor, Mexted; conversion, 3 penalty goals by Fox

40. South Africa 33   New Zealand 18
   Loftus Versfeld, Pretoria, 24 May 1986
   Crowd: 68 000
   Referee: K Rowlands (Wales)

NEW ZEALAND CAVALIERS: K J Crowley, C I Green, W T Taylor, V L J Simpson, M Clamp, G J Fox, D S Loveridge (replaced by A J Donald), J C Ashworth, H R Reid, G A Knight, M W Shaw, M J Pierce, A M Haden, M J B Hobbs (c), M G Mexted

SOUTH AFRICA: J W Heunis, C J du Plessis, D M Gerber, M J du Plessis, J Reinach, H E Botha (c), G D Wright, F S Erasmus, U L Schmidt, P E Kruger, W J Bartmann, L C Moolman, S W P Burger, G P Smal, J C Breedt

For South Africa: tries by Gerber, Reinach, Botha, Schmidt; 4 conversions, 3 penalty goals by Botha
For New Zealand Cavaliers: try by Crowley; conversion, dropped goal, 3 penalty goals by Fox

41. South Africa 24   New Zealand 10
   Ellis Park, Johannesburg, 31 May 1986
   Crowd: 72 000
   Referee: K Rowlands (Wales)

NEW ZEALAND CAVALIERS: R M Deans, C I Green, W T Taylor, V L J Simpson, M Clamp, W R Smith, A J Donald, S C McDowell, H R Reid, G A Knight, A J Whetton, G W Whetton, A M Haden, M J B Hobbs (c), M G Mexted

SOUTH AFRICA: J W Heunis, C J du Plessis, D M Gerber, M J du Plessis, J Reinach (replaced by H L Müller), H E Botha (c), G D Wright, F S Erasmus, U L Schmidt, P E Kruger, W J Bartmann, L C Moolman, S W P Burger, G P Smal, J C Breedt

For South Africa: try by Wright; conversion, 5 penalty goals by Botha; dropped goal by M J du Plessis
For New Zealand Cavaliers: try by Donald; 2 penalty goals by Deans

42. New Zealand 27   South Africa 24
Ellis Park, Johannesburg, 15 August 1992
Crowd: 70 000
Referee: A R MacNeill (Australia)

NEW ZEALAND: J K R Timu, V L Tuigamala (replaced by M J A Cooper), W K Little, F E Bunce, J J Kirwan, G J Fox, A D Strachan (replaced by J P Preston), R W Loe, S B T Fitzpatrick (c), O M Brown, M N Jones, R M Brooke, I D Jones, J W Joseph, Z V Brooke

SOUTH AFRICA: J T Janse van Rensburg, P Hendriks, D M Gerber, P G Müller, J T Small (replaced by H T Fuls), H E Botha (c), R J du Preez, P H Rodgers (replaced by J J Styger), U L Schmidt, L J J Müller, W J Bartmann, A Geldenhuys, A W Malan, I MacDonald, J C Breedt

For South Africa: tries by Gerber (2), Müller; 3 conversions, penalty goal by Botha
For New Zealand: tries by Timu, Kirwan, Z Brooke; 3 conversions, 2 penalty goals by Fox

43. New Zealand 22   South Africa 14
Carisbrook, Dunedin, 9 July 1994
Crowd: 41 000
Referee: B W Stirling (Ireland)

NEW ZEALAND: S P Howarth, J K R Timu, F E Bunce, A I Ieremia, J J Kirwan, S J Bachop, G T M Bachop, R W Loe, S B T Fitzpatrick (c), O M Brown, M R Brewer, M S B Cooksley, I D Jones (replaced by A R B Pene, replaced by C W Dowd), B P Larsen, Z V Brooke

SOUTH AFRICA: A J Joubert, C M Williams, P G Müller, B J Venter, J T Small, H P le Roux, J P Roux, I S Swart (replaced by G R Kebble), J Allan, J H S le Roux, C P Strauss (c), M G Andrews, S Atherton, R A W Straeuli, A H Richter

For South Africa: try by Straeuli; 3 penalty goals by Joubert
For New Zealand: try by Kirwan; conversion, 5 penalties by Howarth

238

44. New Zealand 13   South Africa 9
Athletic Park, Wellington, 23 July 1994
Crowd: 40 000
Referee: B W Stirling (Ireland)

NEW ZEALAND: S P Howarth, J K R Timu, F E Bunce (replaced by W K Little), A I Ieremia, J J Kirwan, S J Bachop, G T M Bachop, R W Loe, S B T Fitzpatrick (c), O M Brown, M R Brewer, R M Brooke, M Cooksley, B P Larsen, Z V Brooke (temporarily replaced by J W Joseph)

SOUTH AFRICA: T J Janse van Rensburg (replaced by A J Joubert), C M Williams, J C Mulder, B J Venter, J T Small, H P le Roux, J P Roux, G R Kebble, J Allan, J H S le Roux, C P Strauss, M G Andrews, S Atherton, J F Pienaar (c), A H Richter

For South Africa: 3 penalty goals by Van Rensburg
For New Zealand: tries by Timu, Z V Brooke; penalty by Howarth

45. New Zealand 18   South Africa 18
Eden Park, Auckland, 6 August 1994
Crowd: 50 000
Referee: R Yeman (Wales)

NEW ZEALAND: S P Howarth, J K R Timu, F E Bunce, A I Ieremia, J J Kirwan, S J Bachop, G T M Bachop, R W Loe, S B T Fitzpatrick (c), O M Brown, B P Larsen (replaced by M N Jones), R M Brooke, I D Jones, M R Brewer, Z V Brooke

SOUTH AFRICA: A J Joubert, C M Williams, J C Mulder, B J Venter, G K Johnson (temporarily replaced by J T Small), H P le Roux, J P Roux, I S Swart, J Allan, K S Andrews, J F Pienaar (c), M G Andrews, S Atherton, F J van Heerden, A H Richter

For South Africa: tries by Venter, Johnson; conversion, 2 penalty goals by Johnson
For New Zealand: 6 penalty goals by Howarth

46. South Africa 15   New Zealand 12
Ellis Park, Johannesburg, 24 June 1995
Crowd: 65 000
Referee: E F Morrison (England)

NEW ZEALAND: G M Osborne, J W Wilson (replaced by M C G Ellis), F E Bunce, W K Little, J T Lomu, A P Mehrtens, G T M Bachop (temporarily replaced by A D Strachan), C W Dowd (replaced by R W Loe), S B T Fitzpatrick (c), O M Brown, M R Brewer (replaced by J W Joseph), R M Brooke, I D Jones, J A Kronfeld, Z V Brooke

SOUTH AFRICA: A J Joubert, C M Williams, J C Mulder, H P le Roux, J T Small (replaced by B Venter), J T Stransky, J H van der Westhuizen, J P du Randt, C L C Rossouw, I S Swart (replaced by G L Pagel), J F Pienaar (c), J J Wiese, J J Strydom, R J Kruger, M G Andrews (replaced by R A W Straeuli)

For South Africa: 2 dropped goals, 3 penalty goals by Stransky
For New Zealand: dropped goal, 3 penalty goals by Mehrtens

SUMMARY OF RESULTS (EXCLUDING THE CAVALIERS)

Tests	Drawn	Won SA NZ	Points SA NZ	Tries SA NZ	Conversions SA NZ	Penalties SA NZ	Drops SA NZ
41	3	21 18	460 430	55 56	33 26	57 56	16 11

Summary of Results (with the Cavaliers), which, of course, will damage some susceptibilities, but then it will do so if it is omitted as well:

Tests	Drawn	Won SA NZ	Points SA NZ	Tries SA NZ	Conversions SA NZ	Penalties SA NZ	Drops SA NZ
45	3	24 19	556 492	62 61	40 29	72 67	19 12

The following refer to matches between South Africa and New Zealand only, omitting matches involving the New Zealand Cavaliers:

Highest score in a test:
South Africa: 24 (2nd test 1981, 1992)
New Zealand: 27 (1992)

Biggest winning margin in a test:
South Africa: 17-0 (1st test 1928)
New Zealand: 20-3 (4th test 1965)

Highest score on a tour:
South Africa: 83 (Nelson Bays, 1981)
New Zealand: 85 (North Eastern Cape, 1970)

Most tries on tour:
South Africa: 105 (1965)
New Zealand: 135 (1970)

Most tries in a match on tour:
South Africa: 14 (Nelson Bays, 1981)
New Zealand: 17 (North Eastern Cape, 1970)

Highest score against a touring team, other than in a test:
South Africa: 31 (Quagga-Barbarians, 1976)
New Zealand: 23 (Wellington, 1965)

Most victories on a tour:
South Africa: 18 (1965)
New Zealand: 20 (1970)

Most defeats on a tour:
South Africa: 6 (1956)
New Zealand: 7 (1949)

Most points on a tour:
South Africa: 485 (1965)
New Zealand: 687 (1970)

Most points on a tour by an individual:
South Africa: 129 (Naas Botha, 1981)
New Zealand: 175 (Don Clarke, 1960)

Most points in a match on tour by an individual:
South Africa: 31 (Naas Botha, Nelson Bays, 1981)
New Zealand: 34 (Gerald Kember, North Eastern Cape, 1970)

Most tries in a match on tour by an individual:
South Africa: 4 (Bill Zeller against Auckland-North Auckland, 1921 and Tom
van Vollenhoven against Nelson-Marlborough-Golden Bay-Motueka, 1956)
New Zealand: 4 (Grahame Thorne against North Eastern Cape, 1970)

Most tries on a tour by an individual:
South Africa: 15 (Jannie Engelbrecht, 1965)
New Zealand: 17 (Grahame Thorne, 1970)

Most test caps:
South Africa: 9 (Jan Ellis)
New Zealand: 10 (Colin Meads)

Most tries by a team in a test:
South Africa: 5 (1st test 1937)
New Zealand: 5 (2nd test 1965)

Most tries by an individual in a test:
South Africa: 3 (Ray Mordt, 3rd test 1981)
New Zealand: 2 (Jack Sullivan, 2nd test 1937 and Ian Smith, 4th test 1965)

Most points by an individual in a test:
South Africa: 20 (Naas Botha, 2nd test 1981)
New Zealand: 18 (Shane Howarth, 3rd test 1994)

Most points against a touring team by an individual other than in a test:
South Africa: 20 (Hugh Reece-Edwards for Natal, 1992)
New Zealand: 17 (Mick Williment for Wellington, 1965)

Most points by an individual in a series:
South Africa: 35 (Ian McCallum, 1970 and Naas Botha, 1981)
New Zealand: 38 (Shane Howarth, 1994)

Most tries by an individual in a series:
South Africa: 3 (Gert Muller, 1970 and Ray Mordt, 1981)
New Zealand: 3 (Kel Tremain, 1965)

Most tests refereed:
South Africa: 4 (Boet Neser, Ralph Burmeister)
New Zealander: 3 (Pat Murphy)

Most dropped goals in tests:
South Africa: 2 (Bennie Osler, Hansie Brewis, Naas Botha, Joel Stransky)
New Zealand: 2 (Jim Kearney)

Oldest test player:
South Africa: 35 years (Lofty Nel, 1970)
New Zealand: 41 years (Ned Hughes, 1921)

Youngest test player:
South Africa: 20 years (Mannetjies Michau, 1921)
New Zealand: 19 years (Bryan Williams)

Heaviest player:
South Africa: 132 kg (Flippie van der Merwe)
New Zealand: 118 kg (Craig Dowd, Jonah Lomu)

Lightest player:
South Africa: 60 kg (Billy Sendin)
New Zealand: 60,45 kg (Ginger Nicholls, Ponty Reid)

Tallest player:
South Africa: 2,04 m (Adolf Malan)
New Zealand: 2,02 m (Mark Cooksley)

Shortest player:
South Africa: 1,60 m (Tommy Gentles)
New Zealand: 1,60 m (Ponty Reid)

The Stars

THIS IS AN arbitrary selection and it excludes the captains, not because they were not stars, but because they appear as captains.

1921

1. **Pieter Gerhard Morkel**, the big South African fullback, played eight tests between 1912 and 1921. He was 33 when he went to New Zealand, but a man of clever positional play, carefully honed skills, powerful tackling and great durability. He was 43 when he last played first-league rugby.

The New Zealand opinion of the Springboks at the end of the tour said: "There were some outstanding individuals, amongst whom the veteran fullback Gerhard Morkel was exceptional."

His son Hannes was unlucky not to have played for South Africa. He did play against New Zealanders during the war and in 1949.

Born: Somerset West, 15 October 1888.

Died: Somerset West, 5 September 1963.

2. **John Steel**, called Jack, was a professional sprinter, a not uncommon form of sport in the Antipodes where betting is endemic.

For eight seasons he played for West Coast on the South Island of New Zealand, living proof that it is possible to scale the heights from obscurity.

He played wing in 6 tests for New Zealand between 1920 and 1925.

Born: Dillmanstown, 10 November 1898.

Died: in a motor accident at South Beach near Greymouth, 4 August 1941.

3. **Ernest Arthur Belliss**, called Moke, a loose forward who played in only three tests during his time as an All Black which stretched from 1920 to

245

1923. To the Springboks this marauding player was a scourge.
His son and his grandson played provincial rugby.
Born: Palmerston North, 1 April 1894.
Died: on his farm in the Taihape district, 22 April 1974.

4. **Gert Wilhelm van Rooyen**, called Tank, was Oubaas Markötter's discovery. Transvaal seldom chose him because they thought he was not intelligent enough but Markötter recognised his worth. Surprisingly he was not chosen for the first test, but there was no doubt in New Zealand minds that he was the best forward in the Springbok pack.
Born: Steynsburg, 9 December 1892.
Died: Cottage Hospital at Runcorn in Cheshire, 21 September 1942.
In England they called him George when he played rugby league there for Hull Kingston Rovers, Wigan and Widnes. He tried to get back to South Africa but could not afford it and instead worked as a lorry driver and then in the docks and died a poor man.

1928

1. **Benjamin Louwrens Osler** was the enigmatic player of his era. To some he was the ultimate hero – King Bennie, rugby's autocrat. To others he was, with his boot, the destroyer of South Africa's running game. To some he was an aloof genius, to others the most humble and gregarious of men.
Born: Aliwal North, 23 November 1901.
Died: Bellville, 10 April 1962.
When he retired Bennie Osler was the Springbok captain and had played a record of 17 tests at fly half. In all he scored two tries and a total of 46 points. That would look meagre in modern rugby. After all Simon Culhane scored 46 points in a single international during the 1995 World Cup. But in those days Osler's total was an enormous amount.
He was from a rugby family. His uncle Frank played for Scotland, his brother Stanley for South Africa and two cousins for Western Province.

2. **David Frederick Lindsay** played only in the 1928 series, but his defence, like Lionel Wilson's in New Zealand in 1965, was heroic, in the days when a fullback's only real task was defence. He was injured and missed the fourth test of the series.
Born: Studholm, 9 December 1906.
Died: Timaru, 7 March 1978.

246

He was a dentist, who studied in Dunedin, which was why he played his provincial rugby for Otago.

3. **Marcus Frederick Nicholls's** omission from the All Black side in the first three tests in 1928 is a mystery. There was talk of enmity between him and uncompromising Maurice Brownlie, and he was Brownlie's vice-captain. In fact he played only 11 of the 23 matches on the tour. There was also talk of loss of form. He had played well in 1921 and would end his test career after ten matches in 1930. That makes the three-test hiatus in 1928 all the odder. And then when he did come back into the side he turned in one of the most brilliant performances in the history of international rugby.

Bennie Osler said: "Mark Nicholls of New Zealand was the best fly half I ever played against. When he visited South Africa with the 1928 All Blacks, he was already a veteran and rather slow. But his tactical play was beyond reproach and in the last test at Newlands he played magnificently in the wet weather."

Born: Greytown, 13 July 1901.

Died: Tauranga, 10 June 1972.

He played for Wellington from 1920 to 1930. His brothers Doc and Ginger also played for New Zealand.

1937

The Springboks were the stars but to make a short list of them is difficult. Do you really leave out Lucas Strachan, Ebbo Bastard, Freddie Turner, or Mauritz van den Berg with one leg shorter than the other?

1. **Gerhard Hamilton Brand** was the star of the 1937 Springboks. They say he never missed a vital kick, never missed a tackle at all, and could run as well, though in his day a fullback was essentially a defender. His first cap for South Africa, when he was still 21, was on the left wing.

He was born in Sea Point on 8 October 1906. He went to Sea Point Boys' High and played his rugby for Hamiltons, a Sea Point club. His middle name was given him because Hamiltons won the Grand Challenge just before he was born.

His record for points on a tour of New Zealand – 119 – stood until Naas Botha went that way in 1981. But the 90 points he scored in Australia still stands. And in his day there were far fewer opportunities to score points by kicking than in the modern game. In his 16 tests he scored 55 points for South Africa. In all he scored 293 points in his 46 matches.

He died in Fish Hoek on 4 February 1996.

2. **Louis Babrow** had an astonishing tour of New Zealand and was one of the Springboks' creative geniuses on the tour. He was an exceptionally fast centre and had great footwork.

Born: Smithfield, 24 April 1915.

His rugby remained active during the war and afterwards he played in Britain and was elected a Barbarian.

In 1996 he was still working as a medical doctor.

3. **Matthys Michael Louw** was called Boy by all and sundry and The Master by those who revered him most, and there were many of those. Nobody in South Africa ever played for South Africa with a greater passion for rugby football and a greater passion for South Africa. Boy Louw was a man of intense loyalty. He was also a man of great charm and South Africa's greatest rugby humorist.

He played for South Africa in every position in the scrum, largely because he was willing to serve his team wherever needed. When his international rugby career came to an end in 1938 he had played 18 tests, a record at the time. He later went on to be a national selector, a provincial referee, and the coach of the successful 1960-61 Springboks in Europe.

He went to school in Wellington and then at Paarl Boys' High. After school he worked for the bank, which meant being transferred elsewhere, though his heart was in Paarl whither he returned till he went down to the Strand for his old age.

Born: Paarl, 21 February 1906.

Died: Stikland, 3 May 1988.

4. **Jan Willem Lotz** was a great hooker.

It is unusual for a hooker to be singled out, but Jan Lotz was an exceptional hooker, so much so that the Springboks chose only one on the tour to New Zealand. In New Zealand he played in all but two matches. And winning scrums was one of the most potent of Springbok weapons.

His last match for Transvaal was as captain against the 1949 All Blacks when, despite his age, he outhooked the legendary Has Catley.

Born: Krugersdorp, 26 August 1910.

Died: Krugersdorp, 13 August 1986.

5. **John Lorraine Sullivan** was the star All Black in 1937. He was the one player who had the verve and skill to make a real difference to a match. Unfortunately for New Zealand he had little support and was wasted on the wing.

He played for Taranaki from 1934 to 1940 and for New Zealand in six tests from 1936 to 1938. His rugby was a war casualty. First of all it stopped him playing in his prime and then permanently through a leg injury when playing rugby in Egypt. He became a great administrator and a close friend of Danie Craven. In 1960 he was the assistant manager of the All Blacks and was chairman of the NZRFU from 1969 to 1977, amongst many other achievements. He was awarded an OBE.

A carpenter by trade, he became managing director of Caltex Oil Company.

Born: Tahora, 30 March 1915.

6. **David Owen Williams** first played for South Africa at the age of 18. He was a noble and heroic wing, at a time when South Africa had great wings. After all, Dendy Lawton did not get a run in a test in New Zealand though he scored at least one try in every match he played in New Zealand.

He played in eight tests, and was certainly a first-choice player.

Born: Mowbray, Cape Town, 16 June 1913.

Died: Cape Town, Christmas Eve 1975.

1949

1. **Robert William Henry Scott**, MBE, was probably the star of the series, and also probably, certainly by his own admission, the most critical failure. Bob Scott was the liveliest of fullbacks, an attacking player long before his time.

His failure? Goal kicking. Bob Scott was a great kicker, but at vital stages in the series with South Africa he missed

Born: Wellington, 6 February 1921.

He did not have an easy childhood. He was raised in a Salvation Army Home and suffered a polio attack.

2. **Peter Henderson**, a wing, was the fastest player in the 1949 series, a New Zealand sprinter who got to the final of the 1950 Empire Games.

He would probably have played in more than seven tests had he not gone off to play rugby league.

Born: Gisborne, 18 April 1926.
A dental mechanic, he became a farmer.

3. **Evelyn Haswell Catley** was one of the greatest hookers of all time and one of the most controversial. He was a powerful man, claiming that Jan Lotz was the only hooker he played against who was stronger than he was. He played against the Springboks in 1937 and 1949, and was in the 1939 trials for the 1940 team which did not go to South Africa. He missed the first seven matches in South Africa after breaking his ribs at practice.

Has Catley played for Waikato between 1935 and 1955, and played against them for the Harlequins in 1956 when he was the co-coach of the Waikato side that beat the All Blacks. His son also played for Waikato.

Born: Hamilton, 23 September 1915.
Died: Hamilton, 23 March 1975.

4. **Lachlan Ashwell Grant** was the most dashing All Black forward of them all in 1949. He was the best line-out forward on both sides in 1949 and fiery about the field. Something happened after his visit to Kimberley with its diamonds and he made only one appearance in the last part of the tour.

Born: Temuka, 4 October 1923 and was there to watch the Springboks in Timaru in 1994.

5. **Hendrik Scholtz Vosloo Muller** changed the game. He was to the All Blacks the fearsome Marauder. He was as fast as any back, tackled ruthlessly, ran with skill and verve and could kick well. Add to that absolute concentration, dedication and determination, and you have one of the greatest rugby players the world has ever known. Bob Scott described him as "alert as a hungry hawk". Fred Allen said: "It is not too much to say that the 1949 All Blacks, who lost all four internationals with the Springboks in 1949, were beaten by the speed of one man, wing-forward Hennie Muller, known in Afrikaans as the 'greyhound of the veldt'." The New Zealanders hated his effectiveness.

He was captain of the Springboks nine times in his 13 tests between 1949 and 1953. After his playing days he stayed involved in rugby football and coached Western Province and, in 1965, South Africa.

Born: Witbank on 26 March 1922.
Died: while speaking to a primary school in Goodwood, Cape Town, 26 April 1977.

6. **Johannes Daniel Brewis** did not look the part. He was thin, delicate

looking, sallow and he was a chain smoker. But he could play. He had all the attributes of a great fly half – speed off the mark, sympathetic hands, breadth of vision, and a great boot on attack and defence.

Born: Oudtshoorn, 15 June 1920.

7. **Marthinus Theunis Lategan** almost was not picked. The selector who opposed his selection was Bill Schreiner, chairman of selectors. The selector who supported him was Danie Craven, then just a selector and the Springbok manager. Craven won, Lategan got in on a 3-2 vote and became one of South Africa's greatest centres. Schreiner had no qualms about his attacking ability but queried his defence, which, as it turned out, was never found wanting.

Born: Stellenbosch, 29 September 1925.

8. **Aaron Okey Geffin** was the biggest talking point of the 1949 series. Relatively unknown, he shot to stardom. He was photographed with his famous foot ringed. There were stories of his learning to kick in a prisoner of war camp and about the origin of his nickname which became his second name. And he perpetuated the South African superstition that a good Springbok team had to have a Jew in it. The fact that he was a really good prop forward, his scrumming technique honed by Bill Payn in the prisoner of war camp, is sometimes missed.

Born: Johannesburg, 28 May 1921, his parents immigrants from Russia.

1956

1. **Kevin Lawrence Skinner** was influential on the 1949 tour when he learnt to scrum so well that the All Black front row was more powerful than their Springbok counterparts. His performance in 1956, when he came in for the last two tests and used his boxing prowess in the service of his country, will forever be the most controversial aspect of the tour.

He was without a doubt a powerful prop forward, playing 60 matches for New Zealand, including 20 tests.

Born: Dunedin, 24 November 1927.

2. **Ronald Alexander Jarden** played 16 tests for New Zealand on the wing, surely none as effectively as the four he played in 1956. He was fast and strong and had many skills besides, one of them to be able to kick and chase with rare judgement.

Born: Lower Hutt, 14 December 1929.
Died: Wellington, 18 February 1977.
He sailed for New Zealand in the Americas Cup at Cowes in 1975.

3. **Patrick Timothy Walsh** first played for New Zealand at the age of 19 but missed the 1960 tour to South Africa because of the restriction on people with Maori blood. A versatile and talented back, he was also a forgiving man.
Born: Kaitaia, 6 May 1936.

4. **Richard Alexander White** was the tough, emotionless, relentless face of New Zealand rugby. He was big and strong but not tall for a lock. Despite this, like Frik du Preez, he could get up high in the line-out.
From an injury on his farm in the late Forties, he had a twisted spine. His left hand was partly paralysed and his back caused him great pain. He played with a special, reinforced harness, which was controversial.
Tiny White played 23 consecutive tests. His son played for Canterbury.
Born: Gisborne, 11 June 1925.

5. **Stanley Frank Hill**, called Tiny because he was so big, was a relentless forward in the best All Black tradition. He played lock or number 8.
He captained the New Zealand Maoris against the Springboks.
He was later a national selector and had a great influence on Colin Meads who called him "the hardest footballer I ever knew".
Born: New Plymouth, 9 April 1927.

6. **Peter Frederick Hilton-Jones**, known generally as Peter Jones, and nicknamed Tiger, he is famous for a great try in the fourth test, sealing South Africa's fate and for his famous statement afterwards: "I'm absolutely buggered." He was possibly the greatest loose forward of his time, big, remarkably fast, ruthless and hungry for the ball.
He had not played the first two tests because of a lack of fitness. But he worked and on the Sunday after the second test played in a specially arranged match at the Petone Recreation Ground. He was fit.
His slim autobiography, *It's me Tiger*, must surely be the most affecting rugby biography ever written.
Born: Kaitaia, 24 March 1932.
Died: Waipapakauri, 7 June 1994.

7. **Ronald Courtney Hemi** was an outstanding all-round sportsman. Has

Catley taught him to hook through rivalry rather than by tutelage, and he eventually took over from Catley.

He played against the 1956 Springboks but on the 1960 tour his rib cartilages were torn when Piet du Toit shoved Wilson Whineray up out of the scrum. He was replaced on the tour by Roger Boon and then later replaced Boon when the latter was himself injured.

Born: Whangarei, 15 May 1933.

8. **Alan Robin Reid**, called Ponty, was the inspiration behind Waikato's victory over the Springboks and was the New Zealand halfback in the series that year. He later captained the All Blacks – a small, clever halfback.

Born: Kuiti, 12 April 1929.

Died: Morrinsville, 16 November 1994.

9. **Ross Handley Brown** had good pedigree. His father and his uncle were both All Blacks. He was an inside centre who did well at fly half in the third test after Robin Archer went off injured. He stayed at fly half for the fourth test.

Born: New Plymouth, 8 September 1934.

10. **Daniel François Retief** played for Northern Transvaal as a wing before going into the forwards, a tough, fast loose forward. He had the difficult job of trying to fill Hennie Muller's shoes.

Born: Lichtenburg, 28 June 1925.

11. **Johannes Theodorus Claassen** was one of the great lock forwards of his time, tireless and determined. Surprisingly, he was also a goal kicker. He went on to captain South Africa and would later be a national selector, coach and manager and the vice-president of the SARB and SARFU.

Born: Prince Albert District, 23 September 1929.

12. **Hendrik Petrus Jordaan Bekke**r, a great Springbok of a family of Springboks, was the player who felt the wrath of Kevin Skinner above all. Jaap Bekker was an outstanding prop, astonishingly mobile.

Born: Dordrecht, 11 February 1925.

13. **Augustus Christoffel Koch** played for South Africa in three decades, starting against the All Blacks in 1949 and ending against them in 1960. In all he played in seven tests against the All Blacks. Even more than Jaap Bekker, he was mobile.

Born: Moorreesburg, 21 September 1927.
Died: Moorreesburg, 21 March 1986.

14. **Jan Albertus Pickard** was significant on the 1956 tour. He was the one forward willing to stand up to any form of intimidation, and he was dropped from the test team after the second test for that very reason. It was above all his leaping in the line-out, surging across from an angle, that annoyed the referees, which in turn incurred the wrath of the Springboks.

He was a fullback as a schoolboy and retained his kicking ability as a flamboyant forward in his playing career.

Later he was the President of the Western Province RFU, an executive member of the SARB, a member of the executive of the IRB, and on the World Cup committee.

Born: Paarl, Christmas Day 1927.

1960

1. **Colin Earl Meads**, MBE, of King Country, called Pinetree, has been for years one of rugby football's greatest characters, the impassive face of New Zealand rugby, the spirit that will not yield. In all he played 133 matches in an All Black jersey, 55 of them in tests. He played against the Springboks in 1956, 1960, 1965, and 1970. Nobody better epitomises the spirit of New Zealand rugby than Colin Earl Meads, MBE. He was the relentless forward, not big, but utterly committed and fearless. There was about him an aura of indestructible strength. Danie Craven chose him as one of the five greatest living players on the occasion of his 80th birthday.

Since playing Meads has been a selector, coach and a manager of New Zealand teams, including the All Blacks at the 1995 World Cup.

Born: Cambridge, New Zealand, 3 June 1936.

2. **Donald Barry Clarke** was the phenomenal kicker of his time. In 89 matches he scored 781 points for New Zealand. He played in 31 tests. Besides his boot, he was also big and strong on attack and defence. In 1960 his team relied heavily on him, almost to the exclusion of all else.

Clarke was only 17 when he first played fullback for Waikato for whom four of his brothers also played. The five Clarke brothers played together for Waikato in 1961.

He scored 1 851 points in first-class matches.

254

Born: Pihama, 10 November 1933.
He settled in Johannesburg.

3. **Raymond Frank McMullen**, a most skilful centre in eleven tests for New Zealand, scored the most exciting try of the tour in the third test and came close to scoring a try in the deciding fourth test. He was New Zealand's most exciting back on the tour.

Later Frank McMullen became an international referee.

Born: Auckland, 18 January 1933.

4. **Kevin Charles Briscoe** was, after Don Clarke, the player the All Blacks would have found hardest to replace in 1960 though he came on the tour as the second choice to Roger Urbahn but the tough, lively, little Taranaki halfback played in all four tests, not just because Urbahn was injured.

Born: New Plymouth, 20 August 1936.

5. **Hendrik Jacobus Martin Pelser** was the hard sort of forward that South Africa needed to take on the All Blacks. He had only one eye, but used it in ruthless pursuit of the ball and, in 1960, Kevin Briscoe, the All Black scrum half.

Born: Johannesburg, 23 March 1934.

6. There were people who thought that South Africa did not have a fly half and then along came **Keith Oxlee**. He did not have the biggest boot in the world, nor was he the fastest. But put all his attributes together and you have a very useful player, sharp on the break, courageous in the tackle.

Born: Johannesburg, 17 December 1934.

7. **Alexander Ian Kirkpatrick** played for South Africa with courageous passion, a great servant of the game in South Africa. He was an elegant centre who could run but, more so, could create opportunities for those around him. Players round him looked good. He began as a fly half but got a second wind as a centre, forming a great combination with John Gainsford.

Afterwards he coached and selected at national level and ended his working days as the national director of coaching.

Born: Bloemfontein, 25 July 1930.

8. **Lionel Geoffrey Wilson** changed in one match from a villain to a hero. The people of Bloemfontein did not want him at fullback for South

Africa in the third test in 1960. After the match they wanted him and kept wanting him as he became South Africa's most capped fullback of all time with 27 caps. He was Mr Dependable, the man who made the maximum use of his talents through dedication and concentration.

For a while he lived in Palmerston North, New Zealand.

Born: Cape Town, 25 May 1933.

9. **Hendrik Jacobus van Zyl** set the 1960 series alight with two great wing's tries at Ellis Park. In ten tests he scored six tries, three of them against the Wallabies in the first test in 1961.

Born: On the farm Bovenste Oog in the Ventersdorp district, 31 January 1936.

10. **Richard John Lockyear**, a scrum half with a long pass, took longer than he probably should have to get into the Springbok side but certainly made his mark there. His goal kicking, apart from anything else, played an important rôle in deciding the 1960 series.

He was a brother-in-law of Ian Kirkpatrick.

Born: Kimberley, 26 June 1931.

Died: 3 March 1988 as a result of his injuries in a car smash on the road between Postmasburg and Kuruman.

11. **Pieter Stephanus du Toit**, called Piet Spiere (Piet Muscles), was only nineteen when he was thrown into a frantic tour of New Zealand. He did not play a test then, but he played in all four in 1960, in 14 tests in all. In 1960 his scrumming power was significant and reduced the All Black front row to the ordinary, to the frustration of Wilson Whineray against whom he packed.

Born: Petrusville, 9 October 1935.

1965

1. **MacFarlane Alexander Herewini** first played for Auckland before he was eighteen and for New Zealand when he was 22. He was only 27 on the tour to the British Isles but his greatness had already passed. He was a great tactical kicker, an elusive runner with the ball and a sweet passer – the ideal first five-eighth.

Born: Mokai, 17 October 1940.

2. **Kelvin Robin Tremain**, called Bunny, was one of the greatest of New Zealand's rugby heroes – the strong, fearless, skilful, unemotional forward. He played in 38 tests for New Zealand, scoring nine tries. Whatever a loose forward had to do, he could do, and he was virtually unstoppable when close to the line.

In both his series against South Africa, in 1960 and 1965, he was one of the most important personalities.

His son Simon played for Eastern Province for a season.

Born: Auckland, 21 February 1938.

Died: Napier, 2 May 1992.

3. **Kenneth Francis Gray**, MBE, was one of New Zealand's greatest props, playing in 24 tests between 1963 and 1969, a big man.

He was a tower of strength in the All Black scrum and line-out in 1965 and good about the field as well. He took himself out of the 1970 tour to South Africa because of his distaste for apartheid, at a time when such an action was not fashionable. At the time of his death he was a Labour Party candidate for the 1993 election.

Born: Porirua, 24 June 1938.

Died: 18 November 1992.

4. **Gert Steenkamp Brynard** was a delicate wing of great speed and courage who scored magic tries in New Zealand in 1965. His dive in the third test at Lancaster Park is a part of rugby lore.

Born: Calvinia, 21 October 1938.

5. **John Leslie Gainsford** was a big player, a big presence on and off the field. New Zealanders felt his presence in 1960 and above all enjoyed it in 1965. He was the spark that started the revival in that dramatic third test at Lancaster Park. At his best he was universally regarded as the best centre in the world.

Born: Germiston, 3 August 1938.

6. Many of his contemporaries regard **Douglas John Hopwood** as the most skilled player of their era. He was a clever number 8 and a great leader, utterly devoted to his team. His bravest hour was against Wales in 1961, and for many years he battled with back pain which would have stopped people less determined.

Born: Cape Town, 3 June 1934.

7. William Murray Birtwistle's greatest year was 1965 when he did so well against South Africa. His speed and footwork were then at their best, but damaged afterwards by injury. He scored four tries on the wing in his seven tests.

Born: Auckland, 4 July 1939.

8. Ronald Edward Rangi, short, tough and rugged. He was a great tackler and also scored two tries in the 1965 series. He played ten tests for New Zealand.

When John Gainsford picked the best opponents he had had in his career he chose as centres Jacques Bouquet of France and Ron Rangi.

Born: Auckland, 4 February 1941.

1970

1. Bryan George Williams burst onto the South African and world rugby scene an instant hero in 1970. He had all the impact of Jonah Lomu in 1995. He was young, good-looking, part Samoan, a fast and skilful wing. He was without a doubt the success of the 1970 tour when he was not yet 20. He was back again in 1976. He regarded his second try scored against Eastern Province in 1970 as the best of his career.

Later he turned his attention to Samoan rugby and was part of its rise to great fame in the world.

Born: Auckland, 3 October 1950.

2. Grahame Stuart Thorne was a man of astonishing versatility. On the field he had every skill to make a great three-quarter, which he was. His greatest achievements were probably in South Africa in 1970.

After the tour he stayed on in South Africa for three years and was once considered a possible Springbok.

Off the field this charming man did many things – studied law, owned a bottle store, sold insurance, commentated on television and became a member of parliament.

Born: Auckland, 25 February 1946.

3. Ian Andrew Kirkpatrick, MBE, played in 39 tests for New Zealand, 38 of them consecutively. He played in two series against South Africa, and eventually captained the All Blacks. He was a fast, strong flank forward. He was also a scrupulously clean player.

In 1986 he was the manager of the New Zealand Cavaliers to South Africa.

Born: Gisborne, 24 May 1946.

1976

1. **Peter John Whiting** was the great line-out forward of his time, and also a player of immense courage. Not even a succession of injuries in 1976 could stop him from being one of the most influential players in the series.

Born: Auckland, 6 August 1946.

2. Just the perky cheek, the fearless cockiness, the speed and daring of little **Grant Bernard Batty** made him one of the great personalities of the 1976 tour. He was the sort of player every crowd loved. And he did not like losing. He was a great wing.

He first played for Wellington when he was eighteen.

Born: Greytown, 31 August 1951.

3. **Sidney Milton Going**, MBE, arrived in South Africa in 1970 as one of the first Maoris to visit the country, a fact which raised no eyebrows and evoked little interest. When he came back in 1976, he was a better player and his Maori origins were of no interest.

He was a halfback who always needed watching and had a variety of skills, strength and determination amongst them. Tall loose forwards found him a handful. Gareth Edwards said of him: "Very few teams in the world can claim to have got the better of this outstanding scrum half."

His brother Ken played for New Zealand and another brother Brian came close to doing so.

A Mormon, he refused to play on Sundays.

After his playing career he became the coach of Northlands.

Born: Kawakawa, 19 August 1943.

4. **Sydney Harold Nomis** was really fast, but he was a lot more than that. He was also skilled and utterly devoted. He holds the record for most consecutive matches for South Africa – 22. And yet probably he is best known for the injury inflicted on him by Fergie McCormick, the cramp that nearly stopped him from scoring in France and for that intercept try

against New Zealand in 1970. He started his international career as a centre and then moved to the wing, a wonderful team man.
Born: Johannesburg, 14 November 1941.

5. **François du Toit le Roux** flew fighter aircraft at one stage of his life. He was the spitfire of South African rugby as well – the cheeky, rapid fighter who took you by surprise. Mannetjies had moments of genius, was always highly competitive and fearless.
Born: Victoria West, 12 April 1939.

6. **Gert Hendrik Müller** was in magnificent form against the 1970 All Blacks, this burly, upright, flying wing with the high knee action and the big swerve. He scored four tries in 14 tests, but his debut series in 1970 was the best of his rugby.
Born: Vryheid, 10 May 1948.

7. **Ian Duncan McCallum** was the precise boot of the 1970 series. In series with the All Blacks, the presence or absence of a kicker has often been decisive. McCallum's left boot certainly was effective for South Africa. In all he played eleven tests and scored 62 points, 37 of them against New Zealand in 1970. He was a fullback who started his provincial career on the wing for Western Province.
Born: Kitwe, Northern Rhodesia, 30 July 1944.

8. **Joachim Scholtz Jansen** was one of the great tacklers of South Africa's rugby history. His tackling was so great that it is often overlooked that Joggie was a great runner with the ball in the centre, possessing clever feet for a big man.
Born: Griquatown, 5 February 1948.

9. **Petrus Jacobus Visagie** was a vastly underestimated fly half. He had marvellous hands, which made scrum halves look better than they were, a boot which was both powerful and clever, and a great break.
He played 25 tests for South Africa, scoring 130 points. He scored six tries in tests.
Born: Kimberley, 16 April 1943.

10. **Pieter Johannes Frederik Greyling** formed a great partnership with Jan Ellis – a tall elegant flanker of great destructive capability.
He played for Rhodesia, where he spent childhood years, Transvaal,

260

Northern Transvaal and Orange Free State. He captained South Africa in one test – against England in 1972.

Born: Zastron, 16 May 1942.

11. Was there ever a rugby player to equal **Frederick Christoffel Hendrik du Preez** whom the world called Frik? He was a great line-out forward without being tall. He could run with the best of backs and kick with the best of kickers, and everything that he did he could do in a joyous, happy spirit that made it all seem carefree and spontaneous.

He became the most capped Springbok of all time.

Born: Rustenburg District, 28 November 1935.

12. There was a special quality about **Jan Hendrik Ellis**, the loner in the team game, the player who set himself goals of fitness that were far ahead of his time, the man who would play and struggle for his team with courage and yet find mixing with them afterwards a chore. One of the great loose forwards of all time, he came from remote Windhoek and played all over the world to great admiration as he loped with those deceptive strides, ball in one hand.

Born: Brakpan, 5 January 1942.

1976

1. **Gerald Raymond Bosch** was the educated boot of the Seventies, amongst other feats scoring 22 points against France in a test in 1975. In nine tests the Transvaal fly half scored 89 points.

Born: Vereeniging, 12 May 1949.

2. **Johannes Lodewikus van Heerden** was generally known as Moaner, a big, aggressive, competitive lock in 17 tests for South Africa. Nelie Smith regarded him as a first-choice player for the New Zealand tour in 1981 but Moaner was injured.

Born: Pretoria, 18 July 1951.

3. **Johannes Gerhardus Williams** was called the Jolly Jumper by the 1974 Lions who could not understand why South Africa dropped its best line-out forward during the series. He was also effective in this department against the 1976 All Blacks till a damaged nose removed him from the series.

Born: Johannesburg, 29 October 1946.

4. **Rangitane Will Norton** was one of the greatest hookers New Zealand ever produced. He was a hooker who could play outside of the scrum. He played his first test at the age of 29 and then 27 consecutive tests for New Zealand.

He was over 35 years of age when he was appointed captain of the All Blacks for the first time, against the Lions in 1977.

Born: Waikiri, 30 March 1942.

5. **Johannes Servaas Germishuys**, known as Gerrie, was a great wing. He was fast, had a great stride and a good swerve, and could concentrate. His hands improved greatly. In 1976 he scored a magnificent try against the All Blacks, was full of energy and daring against the 1980 Lions and got a great try in the second test in 1981. In all he scored twelve tries in twenty tests.

Born: Port Shepstone, 19 October 1949.

6. **Bruce John Robertson** played centre for New Zealand in 34 tests between 1972 and 1980, an especially fast and elusive player. He was a player who maintained a high standard from match to match throughout his career.

In 1981, like Graham Mourie, he refused to play against the Springboks.

Born: Hastings, 9 April 1952.

1981

1. **David Jacobus Serfontein** was one of the Players if the Year in New Zealand in 1981. Certainly he was one of South Africa's best-ever scrum halves. He had a sharp break, a pass that was quick and accurate and useful boot. Divan Serfontein captained South Africa in two of his 19 tests.

Born: Krugersdorp, 3 August 1954.

2. **Louis Christiaan Moolman** was without equal as a line-out forward in his day and in addition scrummed well and was strong and mobile about the field. In his test career from 1977 to 1986 he played 24 tests. But then only 26 were played in that time. This gregarious lock was a first-choice player.

Born: Pretoria, 21 January 1951.

3. **Raymond Herman Mordt** was big, fast wing and a fitness fanatic. He

scored hat tricks of tries in successive tests in 1981 – against the All Blacks in the third test and against the USA in the only test. In 18 tests he scored 12 tries.

Born: Ceres, 15 December 1952.

He grew up in Rhodesia and played for them before moving to South Africa. In 1985 he went to Wigan to play rugby league. He later coached Transvaal and became an assistant coach of the Springboks.

4. **Daniel Mattheüs Gerber** was without a doubt the greatest centre in the world at his time, big, fast off the mark and over a long distance, great of hand and foot, the best player in any position from broken play, aggressive and competitive. New Zealanders saw the best of him when he played against the Cavaliers in 1986.

Born: Port Elizabeth, 14 April 1958.

5. **Alan Roy Hewson** will be remembered forever if only for the last kick at goal of the 1981 series when he showed remarkable calm. He played 16 consecutive tests for New Zealand at fullback, broke the individual's record for a test with 26 points against the Wallabies in Auckland in 1982 and scored 46 points in the 1983 series against the British Lions in 1983. In all he scored 167 points in tests for New Zealand.

Born: Lower Hutt, 6 June 1954.

6. **Mark William Shaw**, called Cowboy, was an impressive forward. In every game he played this tall, strong, energetic, physical flank would have an effect on the game, a player in the mould of Peter Jones. No opponents could ignore him. He was especially effective in combination with Murray Mexted and Graham Mourie.

Born: Palmerston North, 23 May 1956.

7. **Douglas Leslie Rollerson** and Naas Botha did not get on well in 1981 but both of them were crucial at fly half in the 1981 series. Rollerson, perky and confident, had twinkling feet and a clever boot, unafraid of having a go with a dropped goal. He was not the All Blacks' first-choice kicker but he scored a try, two conversions, a dropped goal and a penalty goal in the series.

Born: Papakura, 14 May 1953.

8. **Murray Graham Mexted**, the son of an All Black, was one of the great personalties of the rugby world with his skilled, athletic, aggressive play at

number 8. After playing all over the world, including a stint with Natal in 1982, he retired as New Zealand's most capped number 8 with 34 caps.
Born: Wellington, 5 September 1953.

9. **David Steven Loveridge**, a lively halfback with a great pass, was possibly past his best in 1986 but he was still very, very good. In 1981 he was great against the Springboks with his snappy pass and ability to dictate the game. In all he played 23 tests, including stints as captain.
Born: Stratford, New Zealand, 22 April 1952.

10. **Gary Albert Knight** was one of the great props of rugby football's history – a big strong scrummager who got about the field. He played in 37 tests for New Zealand.
He won a bronze medal for wrestling at the Commonwealth Games.
Born: Wellington, 26 August 1951.

11. **Stuart Sinclair Wilson** had the explosive speed and instinctive skill to cut any back line to ribbons. With his hands, feet and willowy body he could play in any position in the back line. He played in 34 tests for New Zealand.
He captained New Zealand in 1983.
Born: Gore, 22 July 1955.

1986

1. **Johan Wilhelm Heunis** was badly hit by isolation. Had that not been the case, he would certainly have been regarded as the best of fullbacks in his time – strong, fearless, skilled, and fast. He could attack and defend and had a better-than-average boot. He went to New Zealand in 1981 in the shadow of Gysie Pienaar who had performed miraculously against the 1980 Lions but found New Zealand fields cloying a year later. Heunis was a star against the Cavaliers in 1986. Sadly, isolation did not give him the world recognition his dedicated skill and judgement deserved.
Born: George, 26 January 1958.

2. **Ulrich Louis Schmidt** was a Blue Bull of a line of Blue Bulls. His grandfather had been president of the Northern Transvaal RFU. His father played for Northern Transvaal and South Africa, the first to be called a Blue Bull. Son Uli was a hooker of exceptional fitness, strength, skill,

courage and aggression. There were few things on a rugby field that he could not do, and the crowds loved him for it.
  Born: Pretoria, 19 July 1961.

3. **Grant James Fox**, MBE, made a name for himself on the Cavaliers tour and blazoned that name in lights at the World Cup the next year. He retired in 1993 as New Zealand's most capped first five-eighth with 46 tests in which he scored 645 points. His kicking was characterised by his meticulously slow routine when kicking at goal and his up-and-unders of pin-point accuracy.
  Born: New Plymouth, 16 June 1962.

4. **Kieran James Crowley** was courageous, skilled, adventurous and durable. He was still playing fullback for Taranaki when they made him a life member of the union.
  Born: Kaponga, 31 August 1961.

5. **Craig Ivan Green** was a wing much in the Syd Nomis mould – fast, elusive and dedicated. He got a great hat trick of tries against Orange Free State in 1986 and altogether played in twenty tests for New Zealand.
  Born: Christchurch, 23 March 1961.

6. **Hikatarewa Rockcliffe Reid** was one of the great hookers during an era of great New Zealand hookers. He was strong in the scrum, accurate in the line-outs and a fourth loose forward about the field. In his time other All Black hookers were Tane Norton, Andy Dalton and, at the end, Sean Fitzpatrick.
  Born: 8 April 1958.

7. **Gary William Whetton** was New Zealand's most capped lock forward when he retired in 1991 after making his debut in the third test a decade before. He had then played 58 tests – a strong line-out forward who got about the field athletically. He went on to captain New Zealand.
  His twin brother, Alan, also played for New Zealand.
  Born: Auckland, 15 December 1959.

8. **Jacobus Reinach** broke the South African record for the 400 m. He certainly was athletic but he was also certainly a rugby player – aggressive, determined and able to swerve at speed. He scored crucial and thrilling tries on the wing in 1986.

Jaco Reinach was born in Ceres on 1 January 1962. He was educated at Grey College in Bloemfontein, made his name in the Orange Free State, and then rather lost his rugby way.

9. They called **Carl Johan du Plessis** the prince of wings, for he was so majestic, so elegant. He seemed able to sweep past defences, upright and gliding, the lordly falcon of the rugby field. Again the world had too little opportunity to savour his greatness. The best New Zealanders saw of him was in 1986.
Born: Somerset East, 24 June 1960.

10. **Gert Petrus Smal** may just have been the best flank forward in the world in 1986 – tall, skilled, fast, ruthless. He was good in the line-outs, could run strongly, and tackled really hard. Some people called him the Sheriff, because of his ability to sort out the bad men amongst the opposition.
Born: Kimberley, 27 December 1961.

11. **Robert James Louw** had the charisma of a star. On the field he was fast and athletic, the ideal flank who could create and destroy. He had a marvellous season in 1980, but New Zealand probably did not see him at his best as management rather curtailed his opportunity to play, presumably because the gregarious man was too friendly.
Born: Wynberg, 26 March 1955.
He played his provincial rugby for Western Province before going off to play rugby league for Wigan, a venture devoid of success.

1992-94 (SOUTH AFRICA)

1. **Joost Heystek van der Westhuizen** was so soon such a star in the firmament of the rugby world and is so much in demand as a scrum half that it is astonishing that he was not selected sooner, forced as he was to play second fiddle to Robert du Preez and Johan Roux. He rejected huge offers from rugby league.
He is big, agile, fast and has a competitive eye.
Born: Pretoria, 20 February 1971.

2. **Jacobus Cornelius Mulder** was chosen as a replacement centre on the tour to New Zealand in 1994 and walked into the test side, from which he was not dropped in 1995, for he is fast and skilled,

passes well and is solid on defence.
   Born: Springs, 18 October 1969.

3. **Jacobus Petrus du Randt** rose from youthful obscurity to being rated as the best loose-head prop at the 1995 World Cup. His strength and bulk belie his mobility about the field which enables him to tackle powerfully and run skilfully with the ball.
   Born: Elliot, 8 September 1972.

4. **Mark Gregory Andrews**, despite his youth, was the only classy tight forward South Africa had till Os du Randt arrived. Both were born in the same tiny town in the same year. He was for some time South Africa's best line-out forward and his mobility meant that he also played at number 8 at the World Cup.
   Born: Elliot, 21 February 1972.

5. **Ruben Jacobus Kruger** was at one stage considered too short, especially because of South Africa's poor showing in line-outs, but his dedicated, determined strength and skill as a flank brought him into the side and at the end of 1995 he was voted South Africa's Rugby Player of the Year. His tackling alone was a match winner.
   Born: Vrede, 30 March 1970.

6. **André Johan Joubert** was voted international player of the year in 1994. He is a player who has got better with age, partly because of his athleticism, partly because of his eye for a chance to attack from the fullback position, and partly because of his uncanny, unerring positional play.
   Born: Ladysmith, 15 April 1964.

7. Nobody who was alive and in South Africa in 1995 will forget a drop kick by **Joel Theodore Stransky** at Ellis Park, for it won the Rugby World Cup for South Africa.
   He was, inexplicably, not chosen for the 1994 tour to New Zealand, but was soon South Africa's first-choice fly half, for he has an excellent boot, handles well, is willing to take on defences and is a committed tackler.
   He was South Africa's main scorer at the World Cup with 61 points from four matches. In 15 tests he scored 176 points for South Africa.
   Born: Pietermaritzburg, 16 July 1967.

8. First Newlands and then the whole of South Africa and then all the

world fell in love with **Chester Mornay Williams**, the bright young wing from Paarl who made it onto the world stage without blistering pace or awesome strength. He made it with consummate skill honed by hours of practice and he did it his way – with a cheerful smile.

In 16 tests he has scored 13 tries. In that bag of tries he has included a South African record by becoming the first Springbok to score four tries in a test match.

Born: Paarl, 8 August 1970.

1992-94 (NEW ZEALAND)

1. **Zinzan Valentine Brooke** was actually christened Murray Zinzan Brooke, but opted for Zinzan because there were so many Murrays in his class. His name was changed by deed poll. Valentine was chosen because he was born on St Valentine's Day.

He is a great Number 8 with a great repertoire of skills. Nobody who saw it, will forget his dropped goal from 40 m out against England in the 1995 semifinal of the World Cup.

Born: Waiuku, 14 February 1965.

2. **John James Patrick Kirwan** was a great wing three-quarter in 1985 when the All Black tour was cancelled and against the Springboks scythed through for a try at the posts at Ellis Park in 1992. Strong and fast, he was also intuitively clever in his ability to run himself into advantageous positions. When he retired he was New Zealand's most capped international with 63 caps and he had scored the most tries, 35, in tests.

Born: Auckland, 16 December 1964.

3. **Michael Niko Jones** was perhaps the best of the All Blacks in the 1992 test at Ellis Park, a remarkably fast loose forward who was also strong and skilled. He was not tall but outstandingly deep in the line-out. His test career suffered because of his principle of not playing on Sunday, something the NZRFU accommodated with respect. That, and injuries to his knee, his elbow, his jaw and his back meant that he played fewer tests than he would otherwise certainly have done.

In 1994 he came on as a replacement in the third test at Eden Park in what may have been a tactical switch with Blair Larsen. Jones was the best forward on the field for the 35 minutes after he came on.

He played for Western Samoa in 1986 and then burst on the scene at

the 1987 World Cup and was almost instantly dubbed the best rugby player in the world.
   Born: Auckland, 8 April 1965.

4. **Va'aiga Lealuga Tuigamala**, called Inga, played against South Africa only once – at Ellis Park in 1992, for he later went off to Wigan to play rugby league. He was the forerunner of Jonah Lomu – big, fast and skilled – an even more potent weapon for the All Blacks than John Kirwan. He rated the test at Ellis Park as the pinnacle of his playing career, even greater than playing in the 1991 World Cup. Like Lomu, he did not score a try against the Springboks, but, like Lomu, he took a lot of watching and caused the Springboks many problems with his powerful running.
   He was born in Western Samoa but the family migrated to Invercargill when he was a young boy. From there they made their way to Auckland where Inga made his name as a rugby player.
   Born: Apia, 4 September 1969.

5. **Jonah Tali Lomu** took the rugby world by storm at the 1995 World Cup in South Africa. He was, even more than Campese had been in 1991, the star of the tournament with his size, speed and elusiveness. There was no need for him to be flamboyant to attract attention. Everything he did was awesome. In five World Cup matches he scored seven tries and set up several others. He destroyed England in the first four minutes of the semifinal at Newlands, and South Africans spent a nervous week before the final, wondering how their team was to handle the great Tongan wing.
   When he played against France at Lancaster Park in 1994, he became the youngest All Black ever.
   Born: Auckland, 12 May 1975.

6. **Glen Matthew Osborne**, a young, long-striding fullback from North Harbour, appeared suddenly on the rugby scene with stupendous displays of energy, skill and a sense of adventure. Even amongst several great fullbacks at the tournament – André Joubert, Jean-Luc Sardourny, Gavin Hastings and brave Matthew Burke – he was regarded as a great player, up there with the best.
   BORN: Wanganui, 27 August 1971.

7. When **Frank Eneri Bunce** tackled, his opponents knew they had been hit. But he developed far more than that in his great centre partnership with Walter Little. He came more and more into his own as elusive run-

269

ner with the ball, fit as ever even though he could be considered a veteran. In the 1992 test at Ellis Park he had an especially great game.

He played for Western Samoa at the 1991 World Cup.

Born: Auckland, 4 February 1962.

8. **Walter Little** contrives to look shy and retiring, mildly worried in fact, but the truth is that he is one of the world's very best centres and one of the most elusive.

Born: 14 October 1969.

9. **Stephen John Bachop** tortured South Africa from first five-eighth in 1994. He was clever on the break, kicked with great tactical skill and was a courageous defender himself.

He played for Western Samoa in the 1991 World Cup.

Born: Christchurch, 2 April 1966.

10. **Graeme Thomas Miro Bachop** was a lively halfback in the 1994 tests in New Zealand and then went off to play his rugby in Japan, rather than in the 1995 World Cup. He and Stephen are brothers.

Born: Christchurch, 11 June 1967.

11. **Robin Matthew Brooke** was the engine room of the New Zealand pack in 1991 and 1994, perhaps less recognised by the public than by his opponents who would have noticed his uncompromising presence. He and Zinzan are brothers.

Born: Warworth, 10 December 1966.

12. **Ian Donald Jones** was an immense force for New Zealand in the line-outs and also managed to get about the field with great skill and determination. His greatest performance against South Africa was in the second half of the World Cup Final when he simply took over the line-outs.

Born: Whangarei, 17 April 1969.

13. **Joshua Adrian Kronfeld** was the action man of the 1995 Rugby World Cup, always there, always in support, a determined and skilled flanker.

Born: Hastings, 20 June 1971.

14. **Craig William Dowd** was taller than most props, which gave him extra value as a line-out forward. He was probably better against South Africa in New Zealand in 1994 than at the World Cup in 1995.

Born: Auckland, 26 October 1969.

The Referees

1921

1. Edward McKenzie
Born: Greytown, 26 May 1878;
Died: Carterton, 7 September 1946.
He played for Wairarapa from 1898 to 1907.
This is the only test match he refereed.

2,3. Albert Ernest Neilson
Born: c. 1878;
Died: Palmerston North, 17 August 1965.
These are the only two test matches he refereed.

1928

1-4. Vivian Herbert Neser
Born: Klerksdorp, 16 June 1894;
Died: Pretoria, 22 December 1956.
Altogether he refereed 9 tests between 1924 and 1933.
He captained South Africa at cricket.
He was later a judge.

1937

1. Lyndon Ewing Macassey
Born: Dunedin, 16 May 1909;
Died: Dunedin, 6 November 1992.
This was his only test.

2,3. Joseph Stewart King, MBE
Born: c. 1897;
Died: Auckland, 20 October 1970.
These are the only two tests he refereed.
He was the president of the New Zealand Rugby Referees' Association.

1949

1,3. Edwin William Neilsen Hofmeyr
Born: Glasgow, 13 March 1920;
Died: Johannesburg, 6 June 1995.
He refereed four tests between 1949 and 1963.

2,4. Ralph Douglas Burmeister
Born: Cape Town, 6 April 1919;
Died: Cape Town, 27 September 1990.
He refereed 8 tests between 1949 and 1961.
He was a nephew of Arthur Burmeister, the 1906 Springbok.

1956

1,2. Francis Graham Milne Parkinson
Born: Marton, 1919.
He refereed three tests in 1955 and 1956.

3,4. William Henry Fright
Born: Christchurch, 1913.
These were the only tests he refereed.
He had played for Canterbury.

1960

1. Erdam Albert Strasheim
Born: Ermelo, 17 November 1916.
He refereed eight tests between 1958 and 1968.
His father was also a test referee.

2. Michael John Slabber
Born: Darling District, 7 December 1913;
Died: Johannesburg, 2 January 1983.
He refereed two tests, one in 1955 and the other in 1960.

3,4. Ralph Douglas Burmeister

1965

1-3. John Patrick Murphy
Born: Dargaville, 16 March 1923.
He refereed 13 tests between 1959 and 1969.
He had played rugby for Wellington and North Auckland.

4. David Howard Millar
Born: Dunedin, 25 March 1932.
He refereed seven tests between 1965 and 1978.

1970

1,3. Pieter Robbertse
Born: Brits, 19 September 1930.
He refereed four tests between 1967 and 1970.
He was the chairman of the SA Referees' Society from 1979 to 1995.

2. Wynand Charl Malan
Born: Arushia in Tanzania, 23 August 1927.
In 1970 and 1971 he refereed three tests.

4. Thomas Herbert Woolley
Born: Krugersdorp, 21 November 1919.
This was the only test he refereed. He is the oldest South African to have
refereed a test.

1976

1. Ian Watson Gourlay
Born: Glasgow, 27 August 1932. This was the only test he refereed.

2-4. Gert Peter Bezuidenhout
Born: Pretoria, 5 July 1934.
These were the only tests he refereed.

1981

1. Lawrence Prideaux (England)
Born: Cambourne, 8 October 1945.
He refereed seven tests between 1980 and 1985.

2,3. Clive Norling (Wales)
Born: Neath, 5 April 1950.
He refereed 25 tests between 1979 and 1991.

1986

1-4. Kenneth Rowlands (Wales)
Born: Ynysbwyl, 7 June 1936.
Including these, he refereed eight tests.

1992

Alexander Robb MacNeill (Australia)
Born: Tamworth, New South Wales, 7 July 1947.
He refereed 12 tests between 1988 and 1993.

1994

1,2. Brian William Stirling (Ireland)
Born: Belfast, 13 January 1951.
He refereed eight tests between 1989 and 1995.

3. Robert Yeman (Wales)
BORN: Port Talbot, 17 May 1955.
He refereed a test in 1993 and another in 1994.

1995

Edward Francis Morrison (England)
BORN: Bristol, 6 September 1951.
   He refereed 12 tests between 1991 and 1994 and then another three tests at the 1995 World Cup, including the Final.

In addition to these men who refereed matches between South Africa and New Zealand, the following referees, from either South Africa or New Zealand, refereed matches involving either South Africa or New Zealand in the days of unattached referees:
   Freek Burger (South Africa), Dave Bishop (New Zealand), Colin Hawke (New Zealand), Glenn Wahlstrom (New Zealand).

The Presidents and Chairmen

THE SOUTH AFRICAN Rugby Football Board, the South African Rugby Board and the South African Rugby Football Union have had presidents, the New Zealand Rugby Football Union chairmen.

1921

NZRFU: George William Slade was chairman from 1919 to 1922.

He was born in 1883 and died in Wellington on 10 June 1940.

He owned a printing company.

SARFB: John Godlieb Brink Heyneman was president from 1915 to 1927.

He was born in Cape Town on 7 December 1861 and died there on 28 May 1927.

He was a lawyer and Master of the Supreme Court.

1928

SARFB: Andries Jacobus Pienaar was president from 1927 till his death in 1953.

Sport Pienaar was born in Aliwal North on 8 May 1884 and died in Sea Point, Cape Town on 12 October 1953.

He was a lawyer.

At one stage he was the president of the South African Cricket Association as well as the SARFB.

NZRFU: Stanley Sydney McPherson Dean, OBE, actually played rugby in the Transvaal before returning to New Zealand. He was chairman from 1922 to 1947.

He twice managed the All Blacks, in 1922 and 1924-25.

He was in insurance. He was born in Auckland on 8 August 1887 and died in Wellington on 17 March 1971.

1937

NZRFU: Stanley Sydney McPherson Dean
SARFB: Andries Jacobus Pienaar

1949

SARFB: Andries Jacobus Pienaar
NZRFU: Alan StClair Belcher was chairman from 1948 to 1952.

He was born in Auckland on 10 November 1893 and died in Wellington on 15 April 1972.

He was in insurance.

1956

NZRFU: Cuthbert Stuart Hogg, CMG, was chairman from 1953 to 1961.

Cuth Hogg was born in Auckland on 1 April 1911 and died in Wellington on 21 April 1973.

He was an accountant.

He lost a leg in a rugby accident as a schoolboy.

SARFB: Edgar Dryden Tudhope was president from 1954 to April 1956 when he retired and was succeeded by Danie Craven.

Edgar Tudhope was born in Queenstown on 3 November 1894 and died in Kenilworth, Cape Town, on 17 December 1984.

He was a lawyer.

Daniel Hartman Craven was president of the SARB and SARFB from 1956 to 1992 when SARFU was established. He was executive president of SARFU from 1992 till his death.

Danie Craven was born in Lindley on 11 October 1910 and died in Stellenbosch on 4 January 1993.

He played for South Africa. He was a university professor.

1960

SARFB: Daniel Hartman Craven
NZRFU: Cuthbert Stuart Hogg

1965

NZRFU: Thomas Clarence Morrison, CBE, was chairman from 1962 to 1968.

He was born in Gisborne on 28 July 1913. He died in Wellington on 31 August 1985.

He played rugby for New Zealand in 1938 and was elected an honorary vice-president of the SARFB.

He was an outfitter.
SARFB: Daniel Hartman Craven

1970

SARFB: Daniel Hartman Craven
NZRFU: John Lorraine Sullivan, OBE, was chairman from 1969 to 1977.

He played rugby for New Zealand.

He was a director of Caltex Oil Company.

1976

SARFB: Daniel Hartman Craven
NZRFU: John Lorraine Sullivan

1981

NZRFU: Cecil Alfred Blazey, OBE, was chairman from 1977 to 1985. He actually served on the Council of the NZRFU from 1957 to 1985.

Ces Blazey was born in Hastings on 31 July 1909.

He was in insurance.
SARB: Daniel Hartman Craven

1986

SARB: Daniel Hartman Craven
NZRFU: Russell William Thomas, OBE, was chairman from 1986 to 1989.
He was three times the manager of the All Blacks.
He was born in Christchurch on 17 February 1926.
A grocer.

1992

SARB: Daniel Hartman Craven
NZRFU: Edward James Tonks was chairman of the NZRFU from 1990 to 1995 after being deputy chairman for three years. He was deputy chairman of the Wellington RFU for 17 years.

Eddie Tonks played rugby for the same club, Onslow, for 25 years, ten of them in the first team. He was born in Wellington, 30 December 1934.

The chairman of Independent Casing.

1994

NZRFU: Edward James Tonks
SARFU: Louis Luyt was the first elected president of the South African Rugby Football Union which was formed in 1992. He remained president of the Transvaal Rugby Union.

He played many matches for Orange Free State and once for Northern Transvaal as a lock forward.

In 1960 he played for Orange Free State when they beat the All Blacks.
Louis Luyt was born at Britstown on 18 June 1932.
A business man.

1995

SARFU: Louis Luyt
NZRFU: Richard Alan Guy took over the chairmanship when Eddie Tonks surprisingly retired.

In his playing days he represented North Auckland from 1966 to 1974 and was an All Black in 1971-72, playing four tests. After his playing days he became an administrator and the president of North Auckland (Northlands). In 1984 he became a NZRFU councillor.

He was the manager of the All Blacks in 1986 and again for the World Cup in 1987.

He was born in Lower Hutt on 6 April 1942.

A beef farmer.

1996

SARFU: Louis Luyt
NZRFU: Richard Alan Guy

The Selectors

1921

SOUTH AFRICA: W F R Schreiner, S A Townsend, A F Markötter, C V Becker, J Leck
NEW ZEALAND: A J Griffiths, G W Nicholson, D M Stuart

1928

NEW ZEALAND: A A Adams, A J Geddes, W A Guy
SOUTH AFRICA: W F R Schreiner, S A Townsend, A F Markötter, G St L Devenish, T B Pienaar

1937

SOUTH AFRICA: W F R Schreiner, S A Townsend, A F Markötter, G St L Devenish, H R Barlow
NEW ZEALAND: A A Adams, J T Burrows, E McKenzie, M F Nicholls, G W Nicholson, W J Pearson, F H Masters

1949

NEW ZEALAND: R R Masters, N A McKenzie, H S Strang
SOUTH AFRICA: W F R Schreiner, W C Zeller, F W Mellish, D H Craven, J J Kipling

1956

SOUTH AFRICA: F W Mellish, W C Zeller, D H Craven, B J Kenyon, J W Lotz
NEW ZEALAND: A E Marslin, T C Morrison, J L Sullivan

1960

NEW ZEALAND: R A Everest, R R King, J L Sullivan
SOUTH AFRICA: F W Mellish, G L van Reenen, M Zimerman, B J Kenyon, J W Lotz

1965

SOUTH AFRICA: F W Mellish, M M Louw, G H Brand, M Zimerman, J W Lotz
NEW ZEALAND: F R Allen, D L Christian, F L George

1970

NEW ZEALAND: I M H Vodanovich, R H Duff, P T Walsh
SOUTH AFRICA: G P Lochner, A S Malan, A I Kirkpatrick, J T Claassen, D J Swiegers

1976

NEW ZEALAND: J J Stewart, E A Watson, J Gleeson
SOUTH AFRICA: J T Claassen, A I Kirkpatrick, D J Swiegers, C M Smith, G P Lochner

1981

SOUTH AFRICA: G P Lochner, C M Smith, D M Dyers, D J Swiegers, B Irvine, A I Kirkpatrick, E M Mboya
NEW ZEALAND: P S Burke, S F Hill, D B Rope

1986

SOUTH AFRICA: D J Swiegers, D M Dyers, G F Malan, J F K Marais, C Moss, J B September, B J Wolmarans

1992

NEW ZEALAND: L M Mains, P Thorburn, E W Kirton
SOUTH AFRICA: D J Swiegers, J Abrahams, W Jardine, G F Malan, J G Williams, V J Zwelibanzi

1994

SOUTH AFRICA: J F K Marais, J Abrahams, D M Dyers, W J H Kahts, I B McIntosh, Z M J Pienaar, D S L Snyman
NEW ZEALAND: L M Mains, G L Colling, E W Kirton

1995

SOUTH AFRICA: G M Christie, J F K Marais, Z M J Pienaar
NEW ZEALAND: L M Mains, G L Colling, E W Kirton

1996

SOUTH AFRICA: A T Markgraaff, G M Christie, P Jooste
NEW ZEALAND: J B Hart, R Cooper, G Hunter

The Managers

ORIGINALLY PLAYERS WERE important. A manager went with the team to make some of the speeches, answer the mail and see to things like hotels, itinerary, laundry, togs and any negotiations necessary with the local unions. He did the old-man side of the tour. There was no coach. Such a position comes late in the history of international rugby.

Then the manager became less important than the coach. It is difficult to give this a date. In 1956 Craven was both manager and coach, but Hennie Muller was largely overlooked as coach in 1956 and Kobus Louw was the big man. Vodanovich was important but J J Stewart certainly forced his way to a higher profile than Noel Stanley had had. In 1981 Johan Claassen was more in the limelight than Nelie Smith. In 1994 there was no doubt, despite Jannie Engelbrecht's prominence, that Ian McIntosh was the coach. But by then Laurie Mains of New Zealand was certainly of higher profile than any manager, even the great and glorious Colin Meads.

To provide a bit of consistency, we have stuck to managers only and only those of touring teams, except for the World Cup when in a sense all teams were touring teams.

1921

SOUTH AFRICA: Harold Collier Bennett was born in Queenstown in 1880. He died in Kimberley on 23 January 1923 as a result of injuries received in a car smash.

He played rugby for the Pirates RFC in Kimberley and for Griqualand West. He was later the president of the Griqualand West RFU.

A lawyer.

1928

NEW ZEALAND: William Francis Hornig was born in Havelock on 5 June 1879 and died in Wellington on 30 September 1963. He played club rugby and soon entered club and provincial administration. He was a Wellington selector in 1917 and a member of the NZRFU management committee from 1923 to 1928.

An outfitter.

1937

SOUTH AFRICA: Percy Ware Day was born in Exeter on 14 March 1871. He was keen on horseracing and died on 11 August 1953 on board the *Edinburgh Castle* as it entered Table Bay on his return from racing in Durban.

He refereed an international match in 1903 and was a national selector. Secretary of the South African Turf Club for 34 years.

1949

NEW ZEALAND: James Hislop Parker, CBE, was born at Lyttleton on 1 February 1897 and died in Auckland on 11 September 1980. He played for Canterbury and then for New Zealand, retiring in 1925 after the All Black tour to the UK and Ireland. He was on the executive of the NZRFU from 1939 to 1956 and became a life member of the NZRFU in 1959.

A fruit grower.

1956

SOUTH AFRICA: Daniel Hartman Craven
Strangely for the man who seems to have done everything over and over again, this was the only tour on which he managed the Springbok team. After he had been appointed manager, he was elected president of the SARB. He nonetheless went to New Zealand as manager and coach, and his presidency survived the tour's disasters.

A university professor.

1960

NEW ZEALAND: Thomas Henry Pearce was born in Auckland on 4 June 1913 and died there on 10 November 1976. He was a prop for Auckland between 1934 and 1946. He was president of Auckland RFU and the NZRFU, became a life member of the NZRFU and a life vice-president of the SARB.

A haulage contractor.

1965

SOUTH AFRICA: Jacobus François Louw came close to playing for South Africa in 1937. An ex-Matie, he played for Western Province, Orange Free State, Eastern Province and Northern Transvaal. He was vice-president of the SA Rugby Football Board.

An educationist, he was part of the Department of Coloured Affairs.

1970

NEW ZEALAND: Ronald Leslie Burk, DSM, was born in Auckland on 5 June 1916 and died there on 21 March 1981. He was a top referee and served on the NZRFU from 1963 to 1970.

A brewery executive.

1976

NEW ZEALAND: Noel Henry Stanley was born in New Plymouth on 28 July 1919. He was chairman of the Taranaki RFU and on the council of the NZRFU from 1966 to 1980.

A dairy farmer.

He died at Opunake on 11 August 1994.

1981

SOUTH AFRICA: Johannes Theodorus Claassen played 105 times for Western Transvaal. He played 28 tests between 1955 and 1962, scoring two tries. He

286

was captain in nine tests. In all he played 57 times for the Springboks.

After his playing days were over he was a national selector, coach and manager and was the vice-president of the SA Rugby Board and SARFU. He has been one of the great servants of rugby in South Africa.

A university professor.

1992

NEW ZEALAND: Neil James Gray became a NZRFU councillor in 1988 and was the manager of the All Blacks in 1992-93.

His long association with Waikato, whom he helped to coach, caused him to be elected a life member of the Waikato RFU in December 1995.

He was born in Morrinsville on 13 June 1943.

1994

SOUTH AFRICA: Jan Pieter Engelbrecht was one of South Africa's great wings and, as the manager of the Springboks, one of its greatest ambassadors. He played for Western Province from 1959 to 1971. He played 67 times for the Springboks, 33 times in tests. In tests he scored eight tries, 44 for South Africa altogether.

A wine farmer.

1995

NEW ZEALAND: Colin Earl Meads, MBE, was born in Cambridge, New Zealand, on 3 June 1936. He played for King Country from 1955 to 1972 and in 133 matches for the All Blacks, including 55 test matches.

A farmer.

SOUTH AFRICA: Morné du Plessis, one of the most charismatic Springboks of all time, was born in Vereeniging on 21 October 1949. Both his parents were Springbok captains – his father at rugby, his mother at hockey. Morné himself captained South Africa in 15 of the 22 tests in which he played.

He is involved in the sports goods trade and in sports management.

1996

NEW ZEALAND: Michael Conrad Francis Banks played 17 matches for Manawatu between 1976 and 1979. He was born in Hamilton on 30 January 1948.

A hotelier.

SOUTH AFRICA: Morné du Plessis

The All Blacks and the Springboks

IN 1905 DAVE GALLAHER'S New Zealanders went to the UK, and they wore black, except for the silver fern on the breast and two thin silver bars on the tops of their stocking.

They were called the All Blacks.

Some think it was an unimaginative description of their uniform. But there is an amiable story.

A reporter, J A Buttery of the *Daily Mail*, was taken with their ability to combine forwards and backs in passing movements and especially the skill of the forwards in these movements when they beat Hartlepool Clubs 63-0 at West Hartlepool on 11 October 1905. He wrote that they were like all backs. A wandering l got into the text and they have remained All Blacks ever since. It may be just a story.

They had not always worn black. In 1884 they had a blue jersey with a golden fern. Since the turn of the century they have worn black with the silver fern.

Sometimes the All Blacks have worn white, in 1930 against Great Britain who wore dark blue that year and against Scotland for example when they come to visit.

South Africa used to play in local jerseys, of clubs or provinces, as their captain chose. In 1896 their captain was Barry Heatlie Heatlie of the Old Diocesan RFC who played in green. South Africa played in green, and won their first test match ever. In 1903 they had played and drawn two tests when they came to play the third at Newlands, and again Heatlie produced green jerseys and again they won. The jersey was settled as green.

In 1906 they toured the UK, Ireland and France and added the Springbok, a badge which had first been proposed for the 1903 team by Gerald Orpen, who had played for Western Province and Transvaal, with support from Fairy Heatlie and Biddy Anderson.

In analogy with the All Blacks a reporter asked them if they wanted to be known as the All Myrtles because that was the particular shade of green of their jerseys. Paul Roos objected, as one might have expected, and insisted that they be called the Springbokken, the Dutch form of the plural though the early minutes of the SA Rugby Football Board referred to them as Springbucks. Sometimes the Springboks have worn white – against Australia at home in the days when the Wallabies wore green and against Ireland, away in 1906 and at home in 1961 and 1981.

Sometimes the springbok has changed its shape. The jersey got gold trim and the shorts changed from black to white. In 1986 the Toyota badge was used on the right breast and after 1992 the Lion Lager logo. Also with unity the badge gained a string of four proteas, divided by a rugby ball, below the springbok to signify the new unity in South African rugby with the birth of the South African Rugby Football Union. The new badge was designed by Lindy de Waal of the advertising firm Ogilvy and Mather. Her father, Louis, is a well-known rugby personality in the Cape.

The Grounds

1. **Carisbrook**, near the cold sea in Dunedin, the home of rugby in Otago, known to its visitors as the House of Pain, was first used for international matches in 1908 when New Zealand thrashed the Anglo-Welsh 32-6. The All Blacks lost there first in 1930. They lost there for the second time in 1971. The Springboks have never won there.

   Capacity in 1995: 41 000

2. **Eden Park** in Auckland has traditionally become the ground where the last test of a series is played and "Now is the Hour", the Maori farewell, is sung.

   Originally it was a lake. The land was reclaimed and the Springboks had the honour of playing the first test match ever played on the ground, and they won it in 1921. The Springboks played before the biggest-ever crowd at the ground – in 1956 when the All Blacks won the rubber for the first time. The Springboks also played there when Marx Jones dropped flour bombs in 1981.

   The first-ever Rugby World Cup Final was played there in 1987.

   Capacity in 1995: 50 000

3. **Athletic Park**, the windy ground in windy Wellington, has become a ramshackle place as decisions are made about its future, hampered partially by Maori claims to the land on which it is built. Its most remarkable, and scary, building is the Millard Stand, built in 1961 and opened on a day when even Wellington thought the weather was wild.

   It was first used for a test match in 1904.

   Capacity in 1995: 40 000. (In 1959 it held 57 000 when the Lions played there.)

4. **Kingsmead** in Durban is now solely a cricket ground. In 1928, when it

was used for a rugby test for only the second time, it was primarily a cricket ground. Altogether five rugby tests were played there. The French were the last touring team to play there, in 1958. After that rugby moved to King's Park.

Its biggest crowd was 32 000.

5. **Ellis Park** is now one of the greatest of grounds. Named after J Dowell Ellis, the Mayor of Johannesburg in 1911 and 1912, whose name was given to the suburb in which the ground stands, it was first used for a test match when the All Blacks played there in 1928. As the Springboks won the first test at Eden Park, so the All Blacks won the first test at Ellis Park.

The 1995 World Cup Final was played there. As with the 1987 final at Eden Park, the home team won.

Capacity in 1995: 63 000. (In 1955 more than 95 000 spectators watched the Lions play there.)

6. **Crusader Park**, named for the famous Eastern Province club, is now solely a cricket ground. It is situated in leafy St George's Park, close to the centre of Port Elizabeth.

In 1960 international rugby in Port Elizabeth moved to Boet Erasmus Stadium.

In 1935 37 000 people watched the Lions play at Crusaders.

7. **Newlands**, the home of South African rugby, was first used for a test match in 1891 when the touring British beat the South Africans. In 1896 it was the scene of South Africa's first victory in a test match when the home team first wore green. In 1903 it was the scene of South Africa's first victory in a series.

Capacity in 1995: 50 000

8. **Lancaster Park** in Christchurch was first used as a rugby ground in 1882. The first test played there was in 1913 when Australia beat the All Blacks. It was the scene in 1965 of a famous Springbok victory.

Capacity in 1995: 35 000

9. **Free State Stadium** in Bloemfontein first came into use on 14 September 1955. The first test played there was the 1960 match. The biggest crowd it ever had was 73 000 for the 1976 test.

In 1995 the new Free State Stadium was opened, on the same site but dedicated for rugby use.

Capacity: 40 000

10. **Boet Erasmus Stadium** was first used in 1960 when the Scots played South Africa there. It is named after J C K "Boet" Erasmus, who was greatly involved in rugby in the Eastern Cape and who was mayor of Port Elizabeth.
Capacity: 39 000

11. **Loftus Versfeld** was laid out as the Eastern Sports Ground, largely thanks to the initiative of Robert Owen Loftus Versfeld, a remarkable man who was at the birth of the rugby unions in the Western Province, the Eastern Province and Transvaal. He died watching rugby at Ellis Park in 1932 and the Pretoria ground was named after him in 1933.
Capacity: 50 000

12. **King's Park** was originally intended for club rugby while the big stuff would continue at Kingsmead nearby. But rugby realised the value of its own headquarters and a ground dedicated to the game. It was opened in 1957 and first used for a test when the Lions toured in 1962. It was refurbished in 1985 and again in 1990. It is an intimate ground. The king in the name was George VI, for whose train the station was built which gave its name to the park.
Capacity: 51 000

Jargon

ALL ACTIVITIES HAVE their jargon, and rugby is not different. Various countries have various terms which they use and these terms may well differ from country to country. A fly half, a first five-eighth, a stand-off half or simply stand-off, and an outside half or an out-half are all the same person.

The idea of the five-eighth originated in Dunedin. Originally there were three backs who played in the quarters, three quarter-backs. They were referred to as three-quarters, two wings and the fellow in the middle was called the centre, as happens with the stumps at cricket with equal mathematical inexactitude. Then Cardiff used a fourth three-quarter. In all but New Zealand this produced even greater mathematical inexactitude by having two centres.

In New Zealand a cobbler in Dunedin, James Duncan, an international player between 1897 and 1903 and an All Black captain who later refereed a test, liked the idea of four three-quarters, but being a man used to working with exact measurements, decided that there had to be a fraction between a half and a three-quarter and that was a five-eighth. Then New Zealanders did not play their non-wing three-quarters left and right but inside and outside. The outer one was called a centre and the inner one a five-eighth – the man between the half and the three-quarter. When the halfbacks separated into one who stood close to the scrum and one further away, the one further away was also between the half and the three-quarter and was called the first five-eighth while the one that the rest of the world called the inside centre was called the second five-eighth.

The following are some bits of rugby jargon that may differ in the two countries:

294

NEW ZEALAND	SOUTH AFRICA
first five-eighths	fly half
second five-eighths	inside centre
halfback	scrum half
loosies	loose forwards
centre	outside centre
number eight, no. 8	eighthman
force, force down	ground the ball behind the goal line
a speculator	fly-kick (noun)
speculate	fly kick (verb)
dab	run on attack
pot	drop at goal
rep match, representative match	provincial match
Ranfurly Shield, the Log: New Zealand's challenge trophy	South Africa's provincial trophy: Currie Cup
Willie Away	peeling off at the line-out
up-and-under, Garryowen	skop-'n-charge, skop-skiet-'n-donder
zambuck	first aider
first spell, second spell	first half, second half
to ruck	to trample
donnybrook	fight
joker	ou, oke, chap, fellow
the aftermatch function	the cocktail party
the aftermatch	the cocktail
barbecue, barbie	braaivleis, braai
to front up	to pitch up
to sink/put the boot in	to kick (somebody)
footie	rugby
barrack	shout (in support or against)
shout	buy a round (of drinks)
shed	dressing room, changing room, change room
short side	blind side
park, pitch, patch, paddock	rugby field

Acronyms

NZRFU: The New Zealand Rugby Football Union, founded in 1892.

SARFB: The South African Rugby Football Board, founded in 1889 in Kimberley. It was the body affiliated to the International Rugby Football Board.

IRB or IRFB: International Rugby Board or International Rugby Football Board, founded in 1886. It is the body responsible, primarily, for establishing the laws by which the game is played.

SACRB: The South African Coloured Rugby Board, founded in Kimberley in 1896, to look after "nonwhite" rugby in South Africa.

SABRB: The South African Bantu Rugby Board, founded in Port Elizabeth in 1936, to look after black/African rugby.

SARFF: The South African Rugby Football Federation, founded in 1959 as a breakaway from the SACRB.

SAARB: The South African African Rugby Board, a name changed from the SABRB.

SARU: The South African Rugby Union, the lineal descendant of the SACRB which took the new name in 1966.

SARA: The South African Rugby Association, which took the place of the SAARB.

SARB: The South African Rugby Board, which was formed as an amalgamation of the SARFB, SARFF and SARB in 1978.

SARFU: The South African Rugby Football Union, formed in 1992 as the unification of the SARB and SARU.

Sources

Allen, Fred. *On Rugby*. Cassell, 1970.

Badenhorst, Capri. *SWA Rugby*. 1978.

Barrow, Graeme. *All Blacks versus Springboks*. Heinemann, 1981.

Booyens, Bun. *Danie Craven*. SARB, 1975.

Boshier, F W. *All Blacks in South Africa*. 1960.

Bryden, Colin and Colley, Mark. *Springboks under Siege*. Now Publications, 1981.

Cairns, Ray and Taylor, Alan. *One for the Ref!*. 1994.

Chapple, Geoff. *1981: The Tour*. Reed.

Chester, R H and McMillan, N A C. *Centenary – 100 Years of New Zealand Rugby*. Moa, 1984.

–. *The Encyclopedia of New Zealand Rugby*. Moa, 1981.

Visitors. Moa, 1990.

Claassen, Wynand. *More than Just Rugby*. Hans Strydom, 1985.

Clarke, Don & Booth, Pat. *The Boot*. A H & A W Reed, 1966.

Craven, D H. *Springbok Annals*. Mimosa, 1965.

–. *Legends of Springbok Rugby*. Keith Clayton, 1989.

–. *Springbok Story*. R Beerman, 1974.

–. *Springboks down the Years*. Howard Timmins, 1956.

David, G R. *Rugby and Be Damned*. Hicks, Smith & Sons, 1970.

Difford, Ivor. *History of South African Rugby*. Speciality Press, 1933.

Dobson, Paul. *Rugby in South Africa*. SARB, 1989.

–. *A Century of Tests*. Richard Whittingdale, 1989.

–. *Doc – the Life of Danie Craven*. Human & Rousseau, 1994.

–. *Great Moments in South African Sport*. Don Nelson, 1988.

–. *Rugby World Cup Review*. Sable, 1995.

–. *Chester*. Sable, 1995.

–. *30 Super Springboks*, Human & Rousseau, 1995.

Edwards, Gareth. *100 Great Rugby Players*. Macdonald, 1987.

Ferreira, J T; Blignaut, J P; Landman, P J; Du Toit, J F. *100 Years.* TRFU, 1989.

Fox, G J. *The Grant Fox Story.* Rugby Press, 1992.

Friedlander, C K and Tebbutt, Patrick. *A Short Cut to Rugby.* CNA, 1949.

Gainsford, John and Leck, Neville. *Nice Guys Come Second.* Don Nelson, 1974.

Gallaher, D and Stead, W J. *The Complete Rugby Footballer.* Methuen, 1906.

Gault, Ian. *For the Record.* Rugby Press, 1984.

Gerber, Hennie. *Craven.* Tafelberg, 1982.

–. *Danie Craven se Top-Springbokke.* Tafelberg, 1977.

Godwin, Terry. *The Complete Who's Who of International Rugby.* Blanford Press, 1987.

Greyvenstein, Chris, *The Bennie Osler Story.* Howard Timmins, 1970.

–. *20 Great Springboks.* Don Nelson, 1972.

–. *Springbok Rugby.* Sable, 1995.

Greyvenstein, Chris and Clayton, Keith. *The Craven Tapes.* Human & Rousseau, 1995.

Grundlingh, Albert; Odendaal, André; Spies, Burrdige. *Beyond the Tryline.* Ravan Press, 1995.

Haden, Andy. *Boots 'n All.* Rugby Press, 1983.

–. *Lock, Stock 'n Barrel.* Rugby Press, 1988.

Holmes, Noel. *Trek out of Trouble.* Whitcombe & Tombs, 1960.

Howitt, Bob. *Super Sid.* Rugby Press, 1979.

–. *New Zealand Rugby Greats.* Moa, 1975.

–. *21 Years of Rugby News.* Rugby Press, 1991.

–. *Inga the Winger.* Rugby Press, 1993.

Irvine, Andy. *Andy Irvine.* Stanley Paul, 1985.

Jenkins, Vivian. *Lions Down Under.* Cassell, 1960.

Jones, Peter; Harris, Norman. *It's Me, TIGER.* A H & A W Reed, 1965.

Kirwan, John. *John Kirwan's Rugby World.* Rugby Press, 1987.

Knight, Lindsay. *They Led the All Blacks.* Rugby Press, 1991.

Labuschagne, Fred. *Goodbye Newlands, Farewell Eden Park.* Howard Timmins, 1974.

–. *All Blacked Out.* Howard Timmins, 1970.

Le Roux, Johan. *Biting Back.* 1995.

Luckmann, Joan; Sorensen, K C. *Medical-Surgical Nursing.* W B Saunders Company, 1980.

Macfarlane, Neil. *Sport and Politics.* Collins, 1986.

McLean, T P. *The Battle for the Crown.* Howard Timmins, 1956.

–. *Beaten by the Boks.* Howard Timmins, 1960.

–. *The Bok Busters.* A H & A W Reed, 1965.

–. *Goodbye to Glory.* A H & A W Reed, 1976.

–. *Great Days in New Zealand Rugby*. Fontana, 1979.
McCarthy, Winston. *The All Blacks on Trek Again*. Sporting Publications, 1950.
–. *HAKA!*. Pelham, 1968.
McCarthy, Winston and Howitt, Bob. *Haka – the Maori Rugby Story*. Rugby Press, 1983.
Medworth, C O. *Battle of the Giants*. A H & A W Reed, 1960.
Meurant, Ross. *The Red Squad Story*. Don Nelson, 1982.
Muller, Hennie. *Totsiens to Test Rugby*. Howard Timmins, 1953.
Muller, Willie. *A Century of E.P. Rugby*. EPRU, 1988.
Nicholls, M F. *With the All Blacks in Springbokland*. L T Watkins, 1928.
Nicholls, Syd. *The Mighty Springboks*. Truth (N Z), 1956.
Palenski, Ron. *Our National Game*. Moa, 1992.
Parker, A C. *Giants of South African Rugby*. Howard Timmins, 1955.
–. *The All Blacks Juggernaut in South Africa*. Tafelberg, 1960.
–. *Now Is the Hour*. Howard Timmins, 1965.
–. *Western Province Rugby Centenary*. WPRFU, 1983.
Price, Maxwell. *Springboks at Bay*. Longmans, 1956.
–. *The Springboks Talk*. Howard Timmins, 1955.
Roger, Warwick. *Old Heroes*. Hodder & Stoughton, 1991.
Sacks, John E. *South Africa's Greatest Springboks*. Sporting Publications, 1938.
Shnaps, Teddy. *A Statistical History of Springbok Rugby*. Don Nelson, 1989.
Steyn, Neil. *Weer Wêreldkampioene*. J P van der Walt en Seun, 1970.
Swan, A C; Chester; R H & McMillan, N A C. *The History of New Zealand Rugby*, Volumes 1-4. Moa, 1948, 1958, 1992.
Sweet, Reg. *Springbok and Silver Fern*. Howard Timmins, 1960.
–. *The Kiwis Conquer*. Howard Timmins, 1956.
Theron, Paul. *Boland Rugby*. Boland RFU, 1989.
Urbahn, R J; Clarke, D B. *The Fourth Springbok Tour of New Zealand*. Hicks, Smith & Sons, 1965.
Van Rensburg, F. *G W Rugby*. Noordkaaplandse Drukkers, 1986.
Van Rooyen, Quintus. *Rugby in Kettings*. J P van der Walt en Seun, 1976.
Van Zyl, M C (ed.). *Noord-Transvaal Rugby 50*. NTRU, 1988.
Veysey, Alex. *Fergie*. Whitcoulls, 1976.
–. *Ebony and Ivory*. Moa, 1984.
Winch, Jonty. *Zimbabwe Rugby Centenary*. Zimbabwe RFU.
Zavos, Spiro. *After the Final Whistle*. Fourth Estate Books, 1979.

The following Newspapers and Magazines:
The Argus
Die Burger
Cape Times
Sunday Times
Rugby News
SA Rugby
Rugby XV
The Star
EP Herald
Rapport